More Praise for *The Last Pick*

"Dave McGillivray has shown that he knows what it takes to motivate and inspire people to accomplish goals beyond their expectations. I am proud to say he has inspired the people of Boston and especially our children to reach farther and achieve more. With *The Last Pick*, Dave's wisdom will be available to everyone seeking guidance as they reach for the stars."

Thomas M. Menino
Mayor of Boston

"Dave McGillivray is the type of person that fits my definition of an off-the-field hero. He may not have been picked by others long ago to be on their team, but he'd be the first I'd pick to be on my team now."

Alberto Salazar
Boston Marathon and
NYC Marathon Champion

"Every amateur and professional athlete, every coach, fan, parent of a child in sports, referee, sports organizer, sports agent, team owner, announcer, and sports bar proprietor needs to read this book to understand why humans were given the ability to run, jump, throw, kick, tumble, and catch in the first place. Answer: to advance the cause of humanity. This is what Dave is all about, and everyone . . . needs to read about this one guy who lives that ideal."

Dave Cowens
Boston Celtics All-Star, NBA Hall of Fame,
NBA MVP, NBA Rookie of the Year

"McGillivray truly understands that success is about overcoming the obstacles that life brings—whether they be physical, mental, or emotional challenges—and then using these experiences as motivation to prove the critics wrong."

Doug Flutie
NFL Quarterback, 1984 Heisman
Trophy Winner, Pro Bowl Selection

"Dave shows that, through perseverance, self-confidence, and a willingness to accept any sacrifices involved, no road is too long and no challenge is too great."

Dennis Eckersley
Hall of Fame Pitcher, Cy Young
Award Winner, 6-time All-Star

"I've known Dave since his first run across the US and know well his story. Dave is well respected in the running community in the US and beyond. No one deserves that respect more."

Bill Rodgers
4-time Boston and NYC Marathon Champion

"His energy in his work and in helping others inspired me to attain the goals I set in my athletic dreams. His enthusiasm for everything he does is from his heart, and he is so determined in such an athletic-competitive way. It's a privilege to know and respect him."

Rod Dixon
1972 Bronze Medalist, 1500m, New Zealand;
1983 NYC Marathon Champion

"Dave McGillivray knows firsthand how participation in athletics can inspire individuals to reach personal heights greater than ever imagined. His book might not make you win an Olympic gold medal (or maybe it will), but it will help you reach your dreams of 'gold-medal living.'"

John Naber
1976 Olympic Games—4 gold, 1 silver (swimming);
Network Commentator; Author; Speaker

"Dave McGillivray is an amazing man. He is proof that the impossible is possible, and this book will inspire readers to follow their wildest dreams. His words will ring in my head the next time I hear 'you can't.' . . . Dave shows that I can."

Alexandra Paul
Hollywood Actress (Baywatch);
Ironman Triathlon and Boston Marathon finisher

"I have stood on the sidelines for the past three decades watching Dave McGillivray, through sheer determination and grit, accomplish amazing feats while raising funds for many worthwhile charities. Read his story in *The Last Pick* and I am more than confident that you will come away with something that will help you in life."

Mike Andrews
Chairman, The Jimmy Fund;
Former Major League Baseball Player

"Dave McGillivray has shown that it is not always the biggest, toughest, or most intimidating that are successful. Many, like Dave, succeed because they have the biggest heart, are the toughest mentally, are better prepared, and have more determination to succeed than the so-called 'most talented.' His story is an inspiring one for all of us."

Steve Grogan
New England Patriots Quarterback,
Patriots All-Time Career Passing Leader

The
Last
Pick

*The Boston Marathon Race
Director's Road to Success*

David J. McGillivray with Linda Glass Fechter

Foreword by Joan Benoit Samuelson, Olympic gold medalist
and 2-time Boston Marathon champion

RODALE

Notice

This book is intended as a reference volume only, not as a medical manual. The information given here is designed to help you make informed decisions about your health. It is not intended as a substitute for any treatment that may have been prescribed by your doctor. If you suspect that you have a medical problem, we urge you to seek competent medical help. Mention of specific companies, organizations, or authorities in this book does not imply endorsement by the publisher, nor does mention of specific companies, organizations, or authorities imply that they endorse this book. Internet addresses and telephone numbers given in this book were accurate at the time it went to press.

Interior design by Gavin Robinson
Cover design by Susan Eugster

Library of Congress Cataloging-in-Publication Data

McGillivray, David J.
    The last pick : the Boston Marathon race director's road to success / David J. McGillivray with Linda Glass Fechter.
        p.   cm.
    Includes index.
    ISBN-13 978-1-59486-422-3 paperback
    ISBN-10 1-59486-422-5 paperback
    1. McGillivray, David J.   2. Runners (Sports)—United States—Biography.   3. Success   4. Motivation (Psychology)   I. Fechter, Linda Glass.   II. Title.
GV1061.15.M36A3   2006
796.42'52092—dc22   2006000400

Distributed to the trade by Holtzbrinck Publishers

2 4 6 8 10 9 7 5 3 1 paperback

We inspire and enable people to improve their lives and the world around them

For more of our products visit **rodalestore.com** or call 800-848-4735

Contents

Foreword

I am honored and humbled to write this foreword for *The Last Pick*. Personally, I think a more appropriate name for this section of the book would be "Fast Forward," as there aren't many people in this world who can keep Dave's pace on or off the roads.

Harry Truman is credited with saying, "It is amazing what you can accomplish if you do not care who gets the credit." Dave McGillivray should be credited for living it. With a heart the size of Boston, I can't think of anyone who does more things for more people, without expecting anything in return, than Dave McGillivray. His work ethic, his energy, his athletic feats, and his generosity are legendary; and he's earned my vote for the greatest organizational and management genius of our lifetime. Yet few people outside the running world even know his name. I hope this book will change that!

I feel sorry for the bookstore owner trying to find the proper shelf for Dave's book. Like Dave, this book seems to belong everywhere. It's a management book, a self-help book, a sports book, a biography, and even a history book. Most important, this book reveals stories that describe the making of a motivational and organizational mastermind. It *will* get you off the couch!

Among Dave's many responsibilities and titles is race director for the TD Banknorth Beach to Beacon Race in Cape Elizabeth, Maine. Although the Bank and I are cited as "founders," I credit Dave for the success and popularity of this event. At the heart of this race are thousands of volunteers, and Dave keeps the Beach to Beacon heart revved and pumping—with power and pleasure. Like electricity, Dave's presence is critical and powerful yet virtually unseen. With Dave, there's no grandstanding, no schmoozing or self-promoting—just a burning desire to present the best race possible. Every year he succeeds, earning the respect, admiration, and gratitude of runners of every level.

I picture Dave on his 100th birthday, running his age, as has been his tradition for many years. And at mile 100, I will greet him with a memento inscribed as follows: "You Are What You Run! Thank You!"

Joan Benoit Samuelson, 1984 Olympic Gold Medalist, Marathon;
1979 and 1983 Champion, Boston Marathon

Acknowledgments

At age 25, I started to write a book about my run across the country, but I never finished it. This is *not* that book. The finish of that run led to the start of a new one and countless other runs and journeys after that. Ironically, it was actually a struggle to motivate myself enough to set aside the time to write a book whose main purpose was to motivate others. What started as a depiction of an 80-day run across the United States led to a story not about running but about what's possible if you have a few guts and don't underestimate your own ability.

Well, at the age of 51—26 years and literally thousands and thousands of miles later—I have finally completed my book. Speaking of the number 26, this was a marathon in and of itself—no, an *ultra*marathon! We paced ourselves and, yes, even did the survivor's shuffle on occasion, but we have finally crossed the finish line.

My thanks and appreciation go out to the following people, who have always made me feel like the *first* pick, not the *last,* and who were instrumental in helping to make this dream, among many others, come true.

To Linda Fechter—you truly are the person who courageously and patiently kept in the race, stayed the course, and brought this epic journey across the finish line. My heartfelt thanks and appreciation go out to you for not only keeping a promise but being the finest example of what this book is truly about.

To the staff at Rodale Inc., in particular Heidi Rodale and Hope Clarke, and with special appreciation for the incredible editing skills of Rachelle Laliberte—I am so fortunate to be published by a company whose mission of inspiring and enabling people to improve their lives matches my own.

To my wife, Katie—because of your caring, understanding, and wonderful attitude, you inspired me and allowed me to finally complete this chapter of my life.

To my son Ryan—because of your determination and passion, I know you, too, will "run" around Fenway Park someday, not as a runner but as the preeminent professional sports groundskeeper that you aspire to be.

To my son Max—because of the same determination and passion as your brother, I know you will be standing on the mound in Fenway Park someday as a leading pitcher in the major leagues.

To my 2-year-old daughter, Elle—just wait until you get a little older and truly realize what a kook you have for a father. Ignorance is bliss.

To my mom and dad, my true heroes—you trusted me, believed in me, and allowed me to be me. A son couldn't ask for more.

To my brothers and sisters, Bob, Susan, Denise, and Alan—thanks for helping your baby brother take not only his very first steps but the hundreds of thousands of steps since then.

To my wonderful friends and Team DMSE colleagues mentioned within these pages and all those too numerous to mention—friends are family you choose for yourself. You are all worthy of having your own stories told.

To Grandpa Eaton—you taught me that I needed to earn the right to set a goal. I hope I earned the right to write this book, a book I hope will effectively impart and convey your important message to countless others.

To Ken Coleman—not only were you the voice of the Red Sox, you were the voice that gave me the *chance* I needed in life. Because of the chance you gave me, I hope a lot of goodwill and kindness were realized.

To all the kids being treated at the Jimmy Fund Clinic and children everywhere in need—I dedicate this book to all of you.

Those of us who have been dealt a fair hand have an obligation and responsibility to help those who have not been as fortunate. Know that you will never be alone. We are all in this trek through life together.

—*Dave McGillivray*

To my husband, Michael, my best friend for nearly 20 years. I am constantly astounded by your unwavering patience, nurturing, and love.

To our children, Morgan and Jack, for their understanding of all the nights, weekends, and vacations that Mommy spent at the computer. Your hugs and kisses sustained me.

To my mom and pop, Cooky and Larry, who have seemingly broken the land-speed record from Bondville, Vermont, to Cohasset, Massachusetts, whenever I called to say, "I need you" . . . which I always do.

To all the rest, including family and friends . . . for all those times you listened, entertained the children, provided words of encouragement, and, most important, delivered a cup of hot coffee to my door at precisely the right moment. You know who you are, and I thank you from the bottom of my heart for being there from the beginning to "the end."

To Mrs. Stein, my third-grade teacher at Forest Park Elementary School, who passed away before I had the chance to thank her for instilling in me a love of writing that has not wavered since that first meeting of "Author's Club."

Finally, to Dave, for believing in me, inspiring me, and doing what his own mentor did for him . . . thank you for giving me a chance.

—*Linda Fechter*

CHAPTER 1

The Home Run

Ladies and gentlemen, a Fenway Park greeting for Dave McGillivray . . .

*Ken Coleman, executive director
of the Jimmy Fund, August 29, 1978*

The man standing at the microphone just behind home plate at Fenway Park was Ken Coleman, a legendary sports announcer whose voice was known for reporting at bats, strikes, and home runs for the Red Sox. But on that night, he stood in his role as executive director of the Jimmy Fund—the official charity of the Boston Red Sox.

It was 7:40 p.m., August 29, 1978.

I couldn't see the 32,000 baseball fans from my vantage point just outside the gate entrance near the left-field wall, but I could hear Ken's booming voice echoing throughout the stands. It was Jimmy Fund Night at Fenway Park, a night when a portion of ticket sales went to support cancer research and patient care. The crowd was on hand to watch the Red Sox face the Seattle Mariners and also to welcome home a 24-year-old runner who had just completed a solo transcontinental run of 3,452 miles across the United States: *me*.

It wasn't until my support team and I had crossed the

Mississippi River that I allowed myself the luxury of thinking about the actual finish ceremony and how it would feel to be reunited with the family and friends I'd left behind. Prior to that point on the route, there was too much doubt looming in my psyche as to whether or not I would make it—and make it on time. But after passing that milestone, I felt that I was heading out of the woods. Fenway became a magnet pulling me home.

I had begun in June at the Seattle Kingdome, also during a pregame ceremony. But being well over 3,000 miles from home, as well as running out into a rather empty stadium, rattled my confidence a bit. I hadn't accomplished anything yet, and as Tom Kinder—my support-crew member—and I stood there on the field, I had briefly wondered if what I was about to embark upon made any sense at all and if I would succeed.

In fact, it was not my reputation as an athlete that led me from the former Seattle Kingdome to Fenway; it was just the opposite. As a youth, I reached a height of 5 feet 4 inches—and then stopped, while others my age grew taller and taller. It was my small stature and people's incorrect perceptions that got me cut from both baseball and basketball in high school. I was chosen *last* for most teams in gym class and at recess. I was also the boy who often got into fights while defending my brother or myself about our somewhat vertically challenged bodies.

Somehow, I always held on to my desire to be an athlete. I believed I had ability, and for most of my boyhood years, I shared the dream of so many: to be a baseball player. I practiced throwing, catching, and hitting for hours on end. At age 15, on the Babe Ruth All-Star team, I got the closest I'd come to the majors—until now. I believe that I was the first person, other than the ballplayers themselves, to ever run around inside the park, a place steeped in history and superstition.

On that summer of '78 night, I wondered what the reaction of the sold-out Fenway crowd would be: Would they heckle me or, worse, make no noise at all as they scratched their heads in bafflement at the kid in running shorts who was delaying the start of their favorite pastime? The answer came as the doors I waited behind opened to the thunder of 64,000 hands clapping together and I began a victory lap around the warning track.

Prior to going out on the field, I had asked Ken if I should do one lap or two. "It's up to you," he said. Toward the end of the first lap, I felt that the crowd was as full of adrenaline as I was, so I decided to go around once more; after the thousands of miles I'd already run, what did it matter? As I passed the Red Sox dugout, Bill Campbell, a relief pitcher, threw his cap to me. I put it on my head, and the applause of the fans grew even louder. I glanced up into the stands and saw that even Mrs. Yawkey, the owner of the Red Sox, was applauding.

Running onto the field felt like my own little Olympics, as if I'd just completed the marathon and was running into the Olympic stadium. I was a good runner, a solid runner; but I would never make such an elite team, so I savored every moment in that ballpark. It was the first time I ever felt like a legitimate athlete.

As I ran, I turned a bit to get a good look at the billboard hanging in right field: "Help Make a Dream Come True," read the sign that had led me to call Coleman just 8 months before. It was an advertisement to encourage people to donate to the Jimmy Fund. For 3 months, my support team and I did all we could to educate people beyond New England about the Jimmy Fund's mission. Knowing that the organization was counting on me helped me stay the course. Quitting was never an option.

The standing ovation lasted for what seemed like 10 minutes. I wondered if there were any former cynics or playground bullies from my childhood in the stands—those who knew me in high school and had low expectations of my success in any sport at all. On that night, I knew I had made believers out of doubters. One's genetic makeup is not as important as the will to succeed. I, Dave McGillivray, of Medford, Massachusetts—always the last pick—had done something I was proud of, and that night, I was 10 feet tall. "I knew I could do this," I thought to myself as I decided to go that second time around.

The guy who stands 5-foot-4 dares to stand apart. He challenges others to do the same in their lives, whatever their dreams may be.

*Barry Scanlon, the **Lowell Sun**, March 29, 2000*

It began because I wanted and needed a challenge . . . a big one. My desire was to do something unique that very few people had done before. As I told David Hartman during a *Good Morning America* interview the day after I ran into Fenway, the reason I ran was twofold. First, I wanted to dedicate a good portion of my time to running something that I didn't have to qualify for; there were no real parameters other than what I set for myself. Second, as I told people across the country, "Strong legs are running so weak legs can walk."

I've always had a deep concern for those who weren't given a fair chance in life, especially children. Even so, there are always skeptics who question the motives of those doing positive things. Was I really running for charity—or for myself? No one in my family was ill with any particular ailment, though my mother has since been diagnosed with cancer.

The bottom line is that I felt a responsibility to help, and I still do. I didn't have the financial wherewithal to give away thousands of dollars to charity, but I thought I could persuade those who did to step up to the plate.

The Red Sox connection went deeper than the use of the stadium for my official finish. My idea to run across the country had been years in development, yet it wasn't until I called the Jimmy Fund and met Ken Coleman that I truly believed it was possible. This man—the "voice" of the Boston Red Sox for many years—truly gave me a chance. He brought the Red Sox into the fold of the run plans and instantly turned my personal goal into something of greater magnitude and very much in the public eye.

The moments of the two victory laps were not for me alone to celebrate. I had a sponsor, Pro Specs. Without their financial help, the outcome might have been different. I also had a support crew of guys who only 80 days before had been strangers to each other and over the course of the run became people I counted on: Dan Carey, Jeff Donahoe, Tom Kinder, Kent Hawley, and my brother Alan. Last, and maybe most important, I had the people in New England who supported me. I thanked them all when I was allowed to say a few words.

I wanted nothing more than to convey my exhilaration as I ran around the park. I did everything I could to show the crowd how excited and appreciative I was to be home and among all those who had followed my progress and stuck with me the whole summer.

When you give to someone else, the feeling you get back is worth significantly more. The Jimmy Fund received 1,500 donations from people who had been at Fenway or were listening to the radio. The gifts for that night added up to more than $19,000, including a check for $1.26 from an 8-year-old boy who'd been at the game. That total, in addition to the money we'd raised before and during the run, helped the Jimmy Fund. Knowing that perhaps we'd introduced a new audience to the groundbreaking research being done at the Sidney Farber Cancer Center (now the Dana-Farber Cancer Institute), however, was all the incentive we needed to keep putting one foot in front of the other.

> Excuse me if I cry a little. I want you to know this: David . . . called me on the phone, and I thought, "Well, I can't imagine anyone wanting to do something like this." And when he came in, he was with me and my assistant, Charles Kilty, for some 3 hours because I wouldn't let him go. And believe me when I tell you that this trip was no ego trip. This trip was done for the children and the adults we see at the Sidney Farber Cancer Center and the inpatients at Children's Hospital.
>
> *Ken Coleman*

One might assume that running across the country was the culmination of my little-known athletic career, yet it was only the beginning, a catalyst for a lifetime of journeys. I calculate that my feet have logged approximately 130,000 miles thus far. If there's a challenge that few have done or many believe cannot be done, then that is what I strive for, including a 24-hour run, a 24-hour swim, competing in eight Ironman triathlons, and even my annual tradition of running my age in miles on my birthday. These activities may sound off the wall, but they're simply ways I've found to challenge myself. When I started my birthday run, I was 12 years old, so I ran 12 miles. The challenge is much different now that I'm 51, but pushing myself and keeping my body and mind in working order are a big part of who I am.

Running across the country was a life-altering experience. I learned about logistics, planning, discipline, and overcoming odds. I realized that doing something that seems impossible is a lot easier when you break it down into attainable pieces. It wasn't a run for 80 days; it was 1 day of running, 80 days in a row. The same with fund-raising: I didn't need to help thousands. If I made a difference in one life, that was good enough for me.

I lost more weight organizing the trek across the country than the 9 pounds I shed during the 2½ months running it. I put everything I had into preparation and planning, the two elements that are key to every success I've had. At the time, as I checked and rechecked, I didn't realize that I was also preparing myself for the future. I now plan and execute events for a living. I used to joke that my job as a race director is very secure because no one else would want it. The truth is, even with all the challenges that present themselves with each project, I don't see it as work. I'm passionate about it—I took the hobby I loved and made it into my career.

We all have the capacity to make great things happen in our lives. I believe in all that self-fulfilling-prophecy thinking. I'm not saying there won't be hardships; I've literally been to rock bottom and back again. If you think back to what brought you to where you are today or imagine where you see yourself in the future, you'll likely find that your life direction has been shaped by a handful of well-made decisions. When the high school basketball coach cut me, self-pity could've prevented me from pursuing anything requiring physical ability. Instead, I saw it as a challenge. It was a choice.

I go with my gut, even when an idea defies logic or practicality. Unfortunately, it can take a long time to find out if I've chosen the right path. If I truly believe in something, though, then it's worth giving it a try. I have no regrets. I learn from each experience, even when the results aren't as planned. Running helps me maintain positive self-esteem and confidence and provides some direction to my life. It has lifted me up when I thought I couldn't get any lower, and it has been a significant part of my overall happiness due to the friends and experiences I've encountered along the way. Some other sport or vocation might have served as well, but running is what I know and enjoy. Yes, the cross-country run was an athletic challenge, but for me, it was not as much about athleticism as it was about accomplishing a goal.

> Maybe for once, the game will not be the story tonight, but David McGillivray's amazing trek across the country for the Jimmy Fund—no matter what happens in the next few hours—will be the story.

> *Dick Stockton to Ken Harrelson, Red Sox announcers*

On that one Fenway night, I shared common ground with heroes whom I had admired since I was old enough to count to Ted's number 9. It was 15 minutes of fame that will last a lifetime. The Red Sox won the game that night, 10–5. A number of players, including Carl Yastrzemski, George Scott, and Carlton Fisk, hit home runs. In a sense, after 4 years of planning and 80 days on the road, I had done the same.

CHAPTER 2

Please God, Make Me Grow

I truly believe that every person on this planet has ability. It just takes guts to find out what that ability is and to draw it out.

Dave McGillivray

I heard a commotion in the school hallway. I was in the seventh or eighth grade, and I followed the crowd down the stairway to see what was happening. What we all saw was this *big* bully who had this *little* guy by the shirt, using it as a handle to hold the smaller boy up against the wall and dangle him a few inches off the ground. My first thought was of how awful the situation was and how badly that kid must have felt. My second thought was: "Oh, my gosh—that 'kid' is my brother Alan!"

Of course, I went crazy and started punching the instigator. I'm not sure if I actually hurt him—he towered over me—but at least I was meddling where he didn't want me. After a few minutes of my Chuck Connors/*Rifleman*–type moves (based on one of my all-time favorite TV shows), the bigger guy got frustrated and eventually released Alan from his grip—but not before beating me up a little, too.

Alan got picked on because he was small, just like me. This smallness, according to our oldest sister, Susan, is our "biological inheritance"—a nice way of saying that all of the McGillivrays share *short* genes. My sister Denise actually enjoys being the littlest in our family. She measures in at 4 feet 10 inches, and that's with thick socks on. She always got attention for being little. Sometimes being short got me attention too, but not the kind anyone would want.

Around age 11, human nature took over, and I began to compare myself to other kids my age. I checked them out and sized them up according to my own personal spec sheet. There was a trend: Most boys in my hometown were starting to surpass me in height. The greater the distance grew between me and the tallest kids in the neighborhood, the more emotional distance I put between us.

> athlete: a person possessing the natural or acquired traits, such as strength, agility, and endurance, that are necessary for physical exercise or sports, especially those performed in competitive contexts

> *The American Heritage Dictionary*
> *of the English Language*

Boston is a fanatical sports town. Whether in the city or the suburbs, it's nearly impossible to find someone who does not possess a favorite sports-team T-shirt or cap that's faded or tattered from years of twisting and clenching during that team's difficult times. Growing up in this environment only fueled my desire to be an athlete. At a young age, my notion of an athlete was quite simple: I wanted to play on a school team.

I did play Little League. Both of my coaches, Mr. Matta and Mr. Henry, were very encouraging. Baseball at that level was all about the game. Any boy with a pulse and a desire to play got the chance. The top players made the all-star team, as I did after putting in a lot of practice. During Little League's off-season, Alan and I could be found playing with the Medford Park League. Each day was devoted to a different sport. Mondays were baseball and Tuesdays were basketball, the two sports I most enjoyed.

Back then, the "park" consisted of a rundown basketball court, the Little League field, and the "piles"—enormous piles of broken concrete and debris that had been dumped along the woods and forgotten. The big kids used to "hide" within its makeshift walls to drink and smoke cigarettes. During the summer of '67—a memorable time because the "Impossible Dream" Red Sox team was vying for the pennant, which until recently was not a usual occurrence—the "piles kids" were extra active. One morning, Alan and I went up to shoot hoops but were taken aback by Carr Park's striking resemblance to Fenway Park. Some of the kids had snuck into Fenway and stolen the American League play-off banners, which now hung from the basketball poles. I admit, they were cool to see up close, but the Boston police and the Yawkeys, longtime owners of the Red Sox, were understandably hot under the collar when they got to *their* park that day.

You can observe a lot by watching.

Yogi Berra, Baseball Hall of Famer

I loved baseball but was obsessed with basketball. I went to the park nearly every day and waited for the court to free up. It was time well spent. I studied the techniques of some of the juniors and seniors like "Oscar," nicknamed for the legendary player, 6-foot-5 Oscar Robertson, a National Basketball Association Most Valuable Player; and Mucka Morse, another neighborhood phenom. Both were excellent shooters who would play with their friends late into the day. When it got too dark to see, someone would take the cinder block that always seemed to be nearby and toss it at the utility pole a few times. There was a short in the wiring, and just the right hit would illuminate the court so play could continue.

I kept to my foul shots and stayed well under the radar of some of the kids with too much time on their hands. After a while, they seemed to develop a quiet respect for what I was doing and left me to the process of shooting free throw after free throw (after free throw). Another reason I loved the game: I could practice alone. Eventually my efforts paid off. I was making 80-some baskets in a row from the foul line, and I held the unofficial Carr Park record for 2½ years. It was Mucka Morse who finally broke my streak.

All those foul shots were just the tip of the iceberg regarding activities of a repetitive nature. Patterns in my life may at times seem a bit out of the ordinary. I want to do the best I can at all things; to improve; to surpass expectations. Foul shots began with a few simple shots, but after those went in, I couldn't help but do more, then more. What begins as a thought of "What if . . . ?" or "I wonder if I can do that . . . " becomes a commitment; the commitment becomes a promise to myself to keep going; and voilà, I have started a streak.

I wasn't going for the *Guinness Book of World Records* when I was shooting foul shots every day for hours on end. However, I did try to break the record for situps, which at that time was well into the thousands. As a teenager, I would do 200 to 300 situps at a time every day for weeks on end. Then one day, I got home from school and got down on the living-room floor to do my situps. I did 100, then 200 . . . 300 . . . 400 . . . and kept on going: 500 . . . 600 . . . 700 . . . 800 . . . 900 . . . 1,000. . . . I got up to about 1,600. I was really on my way, but then my mom called me for supper, a request I could not ignore, so I stopped. That was it. I had done 1,600 situps! I quickly moved on to the chicken and mashed potatoes awaiting me at the dinner table. I'm sure my abs appreciated the rest, though I was a bit disappointed that I had to stop my effort. The self-important title of Situp Champion would have to wait another day.

> I guess I never thought about how the McGillivray "streak" is in us all. We are all loyal; we take our responsibility seriously and don't give up.
>
> *Susan McGillivray West, Dave's sister*

Goal setting is a common thread in my family. My sister Susan never missed a day of school from the fourth grade on. The only reason her elementary-school record wasn't completely clean was due to a bout of measles. She had perfect attendance in junior high, senior high, and nursing school! She has never missed church on Sunday and has never uttered a swear word in her life, much to the amusement of her kids, who have tried hard to get her to slip up. My dad worked for 30 years without missing a single day, and my mother went to her hospital volunteer job even when emphysema made her breathing so labored that she needed to rest after taking only a few steps. Though this full-throttle approach to life yields positive results, I sometimes think it's based on stubbornness that none of us can deny—well, I can, but I won't.

> We were furnishing our house on Belle Avenue. I noticed a new furniture store had just opened around the corner from where I worked. In the display window, I saw two blue swivel chairs that I thought would fit nicely on either side of our fireplace. I told my wife about them, and we decided to buy them. When I brought them home, Dave looked at them and said, "I'm never going to sit in those chairs." Why? I do not know. At one time Dave's brothers tried to force him to sit in one of the chairs, but he escaped. As far as I know, he kept his promise and never sat in either of those chairs.
>
> *Francis "Macadoo" McGillivray, Dave's dad*

When I start certain habits, like not sitting in the blue chairs, I don't think too much about it. I don't talk about the "commitment," because I don't know at the time that I'll continue it. It just happens. The idea becomes a patterned behavior, part of my personal fabric, whether it makes sense or not.

It used to be necessary to request a pass to leave a classroom to, say, go to the bathroom. Most kids asked for one all the time. For some strange reason, I decided to see if I could get through a day without asking for a pass. I succeeded, and a day grew into a week, then a month—and suddenly, I decided to try to get through all of junior high and high school without ever raising my hand and disrupting class to request a pass. Why did this become a "thing" for me? I have no idea, but I did persevere, and my bladder hasn't been the same since!

In junior high, a perfect attendance record was denied me but only because of an emergency appendectomy in the eighth grade. After that, my record held throughout high school and all 4 years of college. You might say I got my money's worth.

The best example of my tendency toward repetitiveness is that each year on my birthday, since turning 12, I have run my age in miles. This past year, I ran 51 miles to celebrate my 51st year. I use the word *run* loosely. By the 51st mile, it was more like a crawl . . . but I did it.

Whatever you want to call this habit of repetition, it seems to work for me. By going to the extreme, I may be overcompensating for the awful frustration of not being as tall as I'd wanted to be. I have a hunch, though, that even if I were 6-foot-7 instead of 5-foot-4, I'd be the same way. I've run 34 consecutive Boston Marathons and will continue to run until I'm no longer physically able. There is a club called the Streakers that consists of runners just like me, who have run Boston for most of their lives. Can all of us be wrong?

Since the McGillivray apples don't fall far from the tree, I imagine it will be only a few years before my sons, Ryan and Max, attempt their own personal challenges. My daughter, Elle, lovingly nicknamed Yell-ee, has already made her place in the history books for having the best set of lungs for a 2-year-old.

"McGillivray Leader in Fitness Tests"

Medford Daily Mercury headline

Foul shots, situps, birthday runs . . . I didn't realize it at the time, but they were preparing me for the important moment when my life changed forever, a moment when I discovered a "purpose." Most people don't know what they want out of life until well after the age of acne and first dates. I was in my mid-teens when all those small physical accomplishments lit the athletic fire in my belly. It was sparked by a bit of politics.

The leader of the free world—in fact, several leaders—had a huge impact on my 16-year-old self. Dwight D. Eisenhower established the President's Council on Youth Fitness, with the objective of raising public awareness regarding the lack of exercise among the American public. Subsequent presidents added their own marks to the program over the years.

In 1970, the newly established President's Council on Physical Fitness and Sports took it a step further to encourage lasting fitness gains through sports and games. My entire freshman class was required to take part in the first-ever athletic "testing," which took place in schools nationwide. The results were to yield the recipients of the Presidential Physical Fitness Award for exceptional achievement by boys and girls ages 10 to 17.

The gym teacher administered the test. None of us knew what to expect, right up to the moment we were asked to do as many situps as possible in 2 minutes, followed by the same time limit for squat thrusts, pushups, and chinups. There was also a 300-yard dash.

We went one at a time. I gave every task my all, because I was up against my toughest critic and competitor: *me*. I push myself hardest when I try to live up to my own standards of achievement rather than competing against others. Taken individually, all that we were asked to do may not have added up to much, but as a whole, it was a measure of our overall physical fitness, which was precisely what the US government was trying to determine. The effort was initiated after a survey concluded that American youth were not as healthy as their European counterparts.

I didn't think much about it until the following afternoon. I knew I had done my best and done well, but I didn't realize how well until I began my paper route after school. There, on the front page of the sports section of the *Medford Daily Mercury*, was a story about how I was the leader of the overall test. I didn't even realize we were being scored or compared to each other. I hadn't known there was an award to be won, but I had won it! I was in a bit of shock as I rode my bike around my neighborhood, throwing papers with "McGillivray" in a bold headline onto everyone's front porches and driveways.

I was proud to be recognized for an athletic endeavor. To put it in perspective, my high school had the second-largest student body in the state of Massachusetts at that time—and I had finished *first*. It confirmed to me that there was truly something "there," that I possessed some ability I could hone in on. I have the president of the United States to thank for that boost to my self-esteem.

> On the basketball court, he taught himself how to shoot. Dave would just stand there and hit free throw after free throw after free throw. He was just a naturally gifted athlete.
>
> *Alan McGillivray, Dave's brother*

As a sophomore, I faced a few unanticipated obstacles to my aspirations to play team sports—specifically, basketball. These barriers were actually *people*, and at least one of them was 6-foot-5. I envied how easy it was for other kids my age, like Allie McCormick, Danny Denufrio, and John Mancuso to play the game. Filling their shoes would be a challenge, especially since they were probably at least a size 13.

When it came time for basketball tryouts, I went in with confidence. What I lacked in height, I made up for in skill. But this was not grade school anymore; I was in the big leagues now, and Coach Don Tremblay saw my role on his team differently than I did. Though I hung in until the end, eventually I was the last one cut. In a misconstrued effort to help ease the inevitable, the coach said, "Dave, if you were 5 inches taller, you'd be my starting guard." But the point was, I wasn't 5 inches taller.

Before I left the court, I challenged one of the centers on the team to a one-on-one game to 21. I needed to prove something to myself and, perhaps, to anyone watching. I *beat* him. Then I walked off the court and decided never to let anyone tell me that I couldn't do what I truly believed I could do.

I went straight home that night, not sure if I was more disappointed or more angry about the circumstances. I went up to my room and with a thick, black, permanent marker, I wrote on a piece of cardboard: "Please, God, make me grow!"

It's good to go to the most influential person you can think of when you need a response to an important issue. So, with a bit of masking tape and a lot of faith, I hung the sign up over my headboard, where it remained for months.

I had a lot of trouble working through the feelings of being left out of something that meant so much, something I believed I was good at. Anger was a lonely emotion, but it won over the sadness. A switch went on in my brain, and I began to work out like a kid possessed. I was determined to one day be recognized as an athlete. Team or not, I continued the foul shots I had practiced for years at the park, only now they took on greater importance. I wanted to be the best basketball player I could be, even if I was a team of only one.

> You have to have confidence in your ability, and then be tough enough to follow through.
>
> *Rosalynn Carter, former first lady*

Months went by. I could still taste the disappointment, but time brought a new sport season and a new chance. I had confidence enough to try out for varsity baseball. I survived cut after cut, but on the final day, it was déjà vu all over again (ironically, a phrase coined by a baseball great, Yogi Berra). I didn't make the cut. My baseball career was over.

I had no interest in going out for hockey or football, so one of the only sports left was soccer. Height didn't seem to be a requirement for that. I tried out and made the team. Running, especially during warmups, is a big part of the sport. Most of the other players held back lazily in practice because it was just that—*practice*. I did the opposite, focusing and pushing hard to get the most out of each workout. I wasn't the best or the fastest, but I was always up front because I put more into it. I even made varsity.

One day, someone took notice of the fact that I was always in front. Joe Orpin, the cross-country coach, happened to be watching the soccer field during practice. Afterward, he came over and introduced himself. He reminded me of the older coach from the movie *Chariots of Fire*. He asked me if I wanted to run cross-country. Without hesitation, I said, "No. I don't want to run. I want to play sports."

Ouch. It's hard to imagine now that there was a time I didn't consider running an official sport. But the more the coach talked, the more intrigued I became.

Cross-country and soccer were on the same fall-season practice schedule. Participating in both would be my first foray into multitasking. As always, my mom and dad left the decision to me, and since I rarely turn down the opportunity to do something unconventional, I decided to try it: The greater the challenge, the sweeter the reward.

On the days soccer and cross-country overlapped, I found myself needing to be in two places at once. I went to the meet first, crossed the finish line, and kept running. En route to the soccer field, I changed from my running shoes into my cleats. It was like the transition aspect of a triathlon. I had everything ready to go so I could make the switch from one sport to the other as quickly and efficiently as possible. As with all else in my life, success was in the preparation.

Running cross-country and continuing on the soccer field was very similar to my experience of both directing and running the Boston Marathon. By the time I took the job as race director, my love of running was already established. I was asked to organize the race, but I didn't want to give up running it. With a little vision on both sides, the Boston Athletic Association and I came up with a formula for me to do both. That was more than 18 years ago; who knows where my life would've gone had Coach Orpin not taken the time to explain to me that running is a legitimate sport!

I loved running cross-country. Eventually, I became cocaptain of the team, along with a kid named Tony Cirella. We ran 5 miles a day together, every day, always starting and finishing at the high school. I'll never forget one particular afternoon during our senior year. Tony and I started out at the same pace, but I wanted to go a bit faster. We agreed I would run ahead. I got back, showered, and waited in the locker room for him. A long time passed, but I didn't think anything of it; maybe he'd met some friends and decided to put in more miles.

The next time I saw Tony was at his funeral. He'd collapsed of a massive heart attack out on the course. He was 16 years old. That spring, the school created an award in Tony's memory, and I was honored to be one of two recipients of the $100 scholarship.

> Dave struggled in grammar school, and I can remember coming home in tears because I had gotten a B. He said, "I got a couple of Ds—what are you crying about?" Again, in junior high school, he studied hard to do well; good grades came easier to me.
>
> *Denise Potts, Dave's sister*

I applied the same intense behavior I used to improve my athletic skills to the academic side of high school. I was not last in this arena as I had been in some sports. In fact, I was first, but it was not as much due to my brainpower as to my work ethic. I didn't care if I was number one; studying hard was about the individual goal of wanting all As.

I didn't go through grade school or most of middle school with the same stellar record I did in later years. It wasn't until the eighth grade that I started to put a lot of effort into my studies. My brother points out that my first set of high marks coincided with my appendectomy. I attribute the positive results to my effort and do not recommend surgery as a means of entry to an Ivy League school.

Once I decided I wanted top grades, I decided to immerse

myself in the world of others who had the same work ethic, just as I had done on the basketball court. Whenever I could, I studied with good students, such as the Carpenito twins. They were hardworking and intelligent, and working with them enhanced my study habits. It was another streak of sorts, but this one actually led me somewhere. I was valedictorian of my high school and college classes.

Learning has always been paramount in my life, be it studying American history or figuring out the perfect stance and position to make foul shots. Being the top in my class was an honor, but notoriety in team sports had eluded me. (Sports was a constant battle of wills for me: *Will* I make the team or *will* I not?) The prize I truly coveted, as did any kid who played Medford High sports, was the Phelan Award, presented each year after graduation at a banquet hosted by the Mustang Club of Medford.

> Dedicated to honor student-athletes who have exhibited the selflessness, the desire, and the regard for school and community, which was the embodiment of the character of the person for whom this affair is perpetuated.

> *Phelan award banquet program, 1976*

I was nominated for the award the year I graduated. I had run indoor and outdoor track my sophomore and junior years, along with playing soccer and running cross-country through my senior year. Though I had worked tirelessly to prove myself as an athlete, the possibility of winning the award never seriously entered my mind. There were about 5,000 students in my high school that year, so there was some serious competition. I even debated whether or not to attend the ceremony, but I decided to go. I wanted to get my varsity letters, as well as support everyone else's efforts.

The days between graduation and the banquet were spent with friends or at my part-time job, pushing a lawn mower a few hours a day at Oak Grove Cemetery. One afternoon, I was doing some edging at the cemetery. It was a really hot day, so I took a break when my boss left to go on an errand. It was quiet, for obvious reasons. I soon fell asleep, leaning against one of the tombstones. As I got up to get back to work, I noticed that I had been leaning against the marker of Richard J. Phelan, an esteemed Medford athlete, scholar, and educator. Among hundreds, perhaps thousands of people buried in that cemetery, there he was. It was almost like *he* found *me*.

Four days later, I was at the Phelan Award banquet at Carroll's Restaurant, which was filled with local politicians, local celebrities, and media. I tried to anticipate which larger-than-life athlete would go home with the coveted prize. I will never forget the words spoken that night by the headmaster, William McCormack: "Ladies and gentlemen, the winner of the Richard J. Phelan Award is . . . David John McGillivray."

I nearly choked on my dinner: "Did he just say 'Dave McGillivray'?"

I, David John Phillip McGillivray, the last pick, had won my school's most prestigious sports award, whose namesake I had literally stumbled upon a few days before. To put my feelings in perspective: It felt like I had won the Cy Young Award, the MVP Award, and the Nobel Prize all in one moment. My self-esteem rocketed to an all-time high. It was an honor and an evening that I will never forget.

It had been less than a week since I had delivered the valedictorian address, but when I got up to the podium, I was speechless. That same night, I also took home the Medford Moose Award as the school's Most Improved Athlete and the MVP Award for track. I floated home, telling myself that I had to keep pursuing sports.

As we learn more, we are struck by the realization of how little we really know. However, this frustration is the catalyst that spurs us deeper into the learning process, enriching our lives with the experience by which we may periodically reevalute our position in the world by the standards of intellect and rationality. Thus, my final words to you are words of encouragement. Learning will evolve regardless of specific intentions. Since it is there, reach greedily into it, whether through books or through manual and physical work. Some will seek higher forms of education, others won't—both can capitalize on the learning experience. It is there—reach for it, and it is yours!

Dave, Medford High valedictory speech, 1972

With graduation behind me and the Phelan Award on my shelf, I headed to Merrimack College that fall. Academic success followed me there, but getting good grades doesn't necessarily mean you know what to do with your knowledge. I recall exploring potential future occupations from as early as middle school. With the exception of my paper route, my ultimate goal was not so much financial reward as it was to gain insight into different vocations. I had as many different jobs as there are flavors of ice cream; I just wanted a little taste of each one to see if I liked it or not—and why. It was research for the life ahead of me.

One summer, I worked for my dad, who was a master electrician at Sexton Can Company in Everett, Massachusetts, which made all types of cans, from aerosol cans to garbage pails. Dad helped build the machines used for manufacturing. I did mechanical drawings, including all his electrical drawings for the wiring of machinery he built. He described to me what he wanted, and I took the ruler and drew the plan, using the symbols and templates he gave me. I was pretty good at it; it was very meticulous work, and I enjoyed the details. I sat at the drawing board for hours, making lines and symbols. I signed all my drawings with my initials and the Olympic circles (which Dad thought looked like a bunch of grapes). Playing sports was always at the forefront of my mind.

People from all walks of life worked downstairs on the assembly line. They got paid to take a can, or "barrel," put it on the conveyor belt, flip it, take another one, put it on the belt, flip it . . . 8 hours a day. They went home and returned at 7 a.m. the next day and did it again. This intrigued me, so I asked my dad if I could work downstairs the following summer. I wanted to know what it was like on the assembly line.

My brother Alan joined me, and we alternated working on different lines all summer, each day gaining a greater appreciation for what it took to do the various jobs. When we worked the aerosol line, we had to put a cork on the top of each can in an endless line. We sat on a bar stool all day, doing nothing but that. (The cans continued on the conveyor belt to be painted white, and the cork prevented the paint from getting inside the can.)

Working a line requires a certain pace. There were incentives for the entire assembly-line team, called Bs for "bonuses." The older guys on the line would yell, "Let's go, McGillivray—we got to get our Bs!" and they meant *get going!* Sometimes I'd just knock a can off on purpose because I couldn't keep up. Sexton would've gone broke if I'd stayed there on the line.

It's also a very dangerous job. Just as curiosity killed the cat, my curiosity about the assembly line nearly took my brother's head off when Alan and I worked on a machine called a double-seamer. One person gets a piece of steel and holds it while it goes through a welder, producing a drum. The drum needs two covers—one on the top, one on the bottom. Then it all has to be sealed. My job was to take the drum from the belt, take a top cover and a bottom cover, put the drum between the grips of the machine, then step on a lever that spun it on the top and bottom and sealed it. Then I lifted my foot off the lever and placed the drum on another belt that carried it to someone else with an entirely different job.

Someone not paying attention could easily get a hand chopped off, or the cover of an improperly placed drum could fly off and become a lethal weapon. That's what happened to me—the cover flew in Alan's direction, but he ducked just in time.

My father knew the dangers of the machines and wasn't thrilled that we were doing that job. I took the work even though I suspected I wouldn't like it, but I had to satisfy my curiosity. Walking out of the factory on the last day of the summer, I knew that I had paid my dues on the assembly line, and it was time to move on.

On other jobs, I absorbed other knowledge. I worked at night in the toy department of the Turnstyle (our local version of Kmart), where I oversaw "facing"—making sure the toys on the shelves faced outward. My sole responsibility was to keep the aisles neat and rotate older toys to the front. In retail, you don't want people taking only new packages. The job suited me because it really honed my organizational skills. I meticulously arranged each shelf and kept everything in order.

By the time I'd graduated from college, my search for the perfect job had, of course, intensified. My expectations were sky-high. I wanted to see the world, meet new people, and gain worldly knowledge—and being a flight attendant would meet all of my requirements. However, I didn't meet all of the airline's; it was basketball tryouts all over again. Only this time, I thought I could triumph.

I knew there was a minimum height requirement, but I went to the interview anyway. I wore platform shoes stuffed with tissues. I must have been well over 5-foot-6 that day—a virtual giant in the McGillivray family. I suppose I was only kidding myself, because of course the interviewer knew, and I knew she knew.

She asked me questions, to which I thought I gave all the right answers. Next, she got up from behind her desk and walked past me. As she made her way to the door, she told me to take my shoes off, and she wasn't that pleasant about it. As I got up, I saw it for the first time: There on the back of the door was a height chart. The door had remained open throughout the interview. It was almost as though she'd been concealing it from me until the end.

She shut the door and asked me to stand with my back against the chart. I was busted.

When it came time to declare a major in college, I chose math, a subject I'd excelled at in high school and a choice my guidance counselor had encouraged. A math major was logical, based on my strengths, but I wasn't convinced it was the best choice. In fact, I might have preferred business, marketing, accounting, or even acting—anything but math. As it turns out, however, the discipline and organization required for all those college math courses provided an excellent background for producing athletic events. Math can be applied to course layout, event logistics, and the general planning that goes into putting on a race with several thousand participants.

> God has chosen each person to be the person that they are. None of us needs to be like the next person. Each of us is unique, due entirely to the 46 chromosomes that in different combinations create our individuality.
>
> *Susan*

My drive and my own measure of success are in large part due to the overwhelming desire I had to prove myself in the face of those who doubted me. If there's one thing I truly believe in, it's my ability to succeed, but it did not come without a price. Teasing, bullying, and a few "altercations" in grade school taught me to look out for myself and also for those I care about. People not only picked on me but wrongly assumed that being small meant I wasn't good at sports—virtually any sport. Until I was given a chance to prove otherwise, I just sat on a bench. Sometimes it was worse than being the last pick—it was not being picked *at all*. It was even more painful when my own peers didn't choose me when we bucked up for sides to play ball after school.

As an adult, it's easy to understand that someone who makes fun of you and your dreams is putting you down in a misguided attempt to elevate his or her own self-worth. But as a child, you just feel the uneasiness when you're at basketball tryouts or walking by a group of big guys at the neighborhood ball field.

My oldest sister, Susan, teaches a sixth-grade church-education program. Each student is encouraged to find something unique about himself or herself, something that makes each one feel special and provides a source of self-confidence. Each semester, she tells a new crop of students about her brother Dave, the "little" kid who wanted only to play basketball. The kids learn how I looked to God for help when I made the sign that hung over my bed. I'm glad my story may help prevent another adolescent from feeling as low as I did. I believe my prayers to grow worked. I was driven to overcome my pain. I could blame myself or encourage myself, and I chose the latter. People such as my mom, my dad, Susan, and others have served as my teachers.

A few years ago, I saw Coach Tremblay, the basketball coach, at a function at which I was asked to speak. Ironically, it was a sports award banquet to promote athletic excellence among high school students. I publicly thanked the coach for giving me my start. He spoke after I did and told the crowd that he hadn't seen me since he cut me from the team. "I may have a page in that book," he joked. Not being selected for the basketball team was one of the most painful and also greatest things that ever happened to me. Not only was he right that he does have a page, but perhaps I should've dedicated this entire book to him.

I had no vendetta against anyone when I was younger; I was simply mad at the world and perhaps a bit frustrated with God. Why did he choose for me to be so small? What possible reason could there have been? Perhaps it's this: I chose a life of producing athletic events that impact others' self-esteem and personal goals. In some small way, I effect change for the better. Perhaps that was all part of the grand scheme.

A successful man is one who can lay a firm foundation with the bricks that others throw at him.

David Brinkley (1920–2003), television journalist

In the final analysis, my prayer was answered. Though my height never changed, I did eventually discover the true meaning of what I had written. I grew, but in a different way. I've made a conscious effort to help others whenever possible and make the most of the life I've been given. Being short had been a "handi-cap" and caused me a lot of heartache. I feel fortunate that I had the strength to turn it around and prove my ability in the face of those who doubted me. Never let those who say it can't be done get in the way of those who are doing it. Though not everything is possible, there's only one way to find out what is.

CHAPTER 3

Breaking the Tape

I knew that Dave ran track, and I remember him talking about wanting to run the marathon. He talked about it with the cross-country coach, who, I remember, tried to dissuade him because he thought it was too long and stressful a race for a kid whose body was still developing. Yeah, right—as if anyone can talk Dave out of anything he wants to do.

Ron Black, Dave's high school friend

Prior to the morning of April 17, 1972, the longest distance I had ever run nonstop was 11 miles. One of the great things about being 17 years old is that in your own mind, you can do anything. You're invincible. It's a shame that for most of us, this belief does not continue throughout our lives.

I had little idea of the difference between 2.6 miles and 26.2 miles. I thought I could excel at the longer distance. After all, a marathon is really only a little more than 26 one-mile runs. I could do that. So, after reading about the Boston Marathon—which I had heard about all my young life—I put down that day's issue of the *Boston Globe* and decided that I wanted to be part of it. I would run among the best in the world. It was

Patriots' Day, a Massachusetts holiday, which non–New Englanders sometimes confuse with a celebration for the marathon itself. I had the day off from school and no other plans. Hopkinton, here I come.

I asked my brother Alan for a ride to the start of the race. Alan, who is 1 year and 1 day older (and wiser) than I, never questioned my ability to run the distance; he wanted to know only if I would be allowed to participate without an official bib number. Good point! If I could solve this small but significant problem, then running the course would be easy. So I called Allie McCormick, another of my cross-country cocaptains. Allie had run some races and probably had a generic bib number I could borrow. It didn't matter to me that it wasn't a BAA (Boston Athletic Association) bib. However, as I now know, it certainly did matter to the BAA. Allie's mom answered the phone that morning. Her son wasn't home, but she was kind enough to give me number 942 from a race Allie had recently run. So 942 became my first official number for the Boston Marathon—official according to me, anyway.

Then I considered other details, such as whether or not I should wear socks. For most marathon runners, it's no question. Socks are a necessary part of the sport; they support you and keep your feet dry. They can also make the postevent experience more pleasant for you and everyone nearby when you remove your running sneakers at day's end. However, I opted against them. I didn't wear socks for cross-country or track, so I figured I didn't need them for Heartbreak Hill—logical. Everything seemed logical that morning, at least prior to my admittance to Newton-Wellesley Hospital.

Running the marathon was a selfish act. My family and friends didn't know I was doing it. I was cocaptain of the spring track team, and the season was just beginning. What if I had injured myself? How would that have affected the team's performance? No matter; it was something that I had to do.

Often in life, we make choices for ourselves while also seeking support from and approval of those who are important to us. For that reason, my last act before Alan and I got in the car was to phone my grandfather, who lived in Brighton, Massachusetts, not far from the marathon route. He walked everywhere, except for long distances, when he would take the "T" (Boston lingo for "train").

My grandfather was very interested in each of his grandchildren. My parents did not have a lot of money, so rather than going out for dinner on Saturday nights, they would get together with friends and family, make costumes, and do skits, and my grandfather was always a part of it all. Late in the evening, knowing that my siblings and I were still awake, he would sneak snacks up to our bedrooms and tell us what was going on at the party. He used to call my mom every day at 12:30 p.m., just to check in. Now it was my turn to call him.

"Grandpa," I began, "I'm going to run that big race today that goes right through Brighton."

He, like my brother, did not question my desire to run. He said he would walk out to the course and wait to see me run by at Coolidge Corner, not far from his house.

Even at age 17, I was thinking of logistics. I had established my transportation: Alan. My bib number was pinned to my shirt: 942. Socks: I knew that my initial decision to not wear any could change, so I gave Alan a pair to bring along. He dropped me off at Hopkinton Town Green among the other 1,081 runners. Today there are 20,000 runners, and the roads around Hopkinton are closed to traffic. These days, dropping someone off at the start actually means taking them to a location where the runners then board shuttle buses to the Athletes' Village, and from there they walk to the start. It's all very organized—I should know—but it's not like the old days, as they say.

Alan and I arranged for him to drive 5 miles down the course, then park and wait for me. He was going to be ready with some fluids for me—my own personal water stop. He also supplied me with encouragement throughout those few hours (more to the point, he's helped sustain me throughout my entire life). I was technical director of myself; Alan was my support crew. Fifteen years later, I would become technical director and then race director of this very race.

Spectators of the marathon line the streets from Hopkinton to Boston. One reason for the turnout is that the race takes place on a state holiday. The other reason may be that for thousands of people in the western suburbs and in Boston itself, a section of the course is always within walking distance.

Simply watching can be an endurance event. Spectators are out there from sunup to sundown, screaming, cheering, and offering sustenance to the thousands. The fans are a lifeline for 26.2 miles of road. The *Boston Herald* (in those days, the *Herald American*) used to print the list of runners in the Patriots' Day edition. The list was in bib order so that as the runners went by with their race numbers pinned to their shirts, the crowd could encourage them on a more personal level. It is this crowd of collective voices, made up of family members, friends, and total strangers, that to this day can carry even the most exhausted athlete toward that Boylston Street finish line.

Throughout that day, I was met with cries of "Go, Gus, go!" "You can do it, Gus!"

"Who exactly is Gus?" I wondered. "Could it be that this guy is running at my same pace and has been right behind me the whole time?" It turned out that Gus was the person listed in the newspaper as number 942. I later learned his full name, Gus Wagonhoffer. (I never met him, but I hope he finished the race.) The entire Wagonhoffer family must have been as confused as I was that afternoon. All these years later, computer chips and the athlete tracking system set up at several checkpoints along the route make cases of mistaken identity a rarity.

So the gun went off at noon, as it has since 1897. True to his word, Alan was at the 5-mile mark. I had no problems, so I sent him up to meet me at the 10-mile mark. From there, I continued to 15. I was in good shape. Alan, however, was another story. He was at the mercy of Boston traffic and going nowhere fast. Again, technology today is vastly different from the way it was then. There was no cell phone tucked away in my running shorts (my 100 percent cotton gym shorts—no moisture wicking going on). Alan and I had no way of contacting each other.

Alan was pounding the dashboard of my 1967 Datsun, spewing expletives at people in the cars in front of him, about the same time that I decided I could really use those socks. I had run 18 miles—the farthest I'd ever run! However, my own two feet were not impressed with what I deemed an exceptional feat.

But then some select body parts stopped functioning. They simply lost the spirit of cooperation that they normally shared with my brain. In a nutshell, I collapsed with muscle spasms, not to mention some fairly significant blisters. A police officer noticed I wasn't doing very well, immediately helped me into his car, and, with flashing lights and all, sped me to Newton-Wellesley Hospital.

> When we got to the hospital to take him home, we almost had to tie Dave into the car.
>
> *Francis "Macadoo" McGillivray, Dave's dad*

I had no idea as to Alan's whereabouts, but by the time my parents arrived to pick me up, I felt okay. As usual, my mom and dad were extremely supportive of me. I had only one thought, however, and it was not about the soreness of my muscles—it was of the image of my grandfather, who most likely was still standing at Coolidge Corner, waiting for me. I tried calling his house. There was no answer.

I asked my parents to drive me to the point on the course where I had dropped out. I wanted to finish what I'd started. Though my parents understood how determined I could be—when I was very young, I once bit a toothbrush in half because I simply did not want to brush my teeth—they didn't give in. Because I was in a moving vehicle, I had no choice but to go along with their decision. Besides, on big issues, I did not question my parents. I did what I was told. I sat quietly as we drove directly home. I was frustrated and angry with myself.

It was 5 p.m. when we finally reached our house. Alan was there waiting for us. He knew he'd missed me and decided it was futile to keep looking for me among the runners and spectators, so he went home. He knew I'd show up eventually.

The marathon had officially ended several hours earlier. I called my grandfather again. Still no answer. I called again at 6 p.m. Finally, at 7, he picked up the phone. Good to his word, he had waited. And waited some more. He not only saw the last runner go by, he also saw the cleanup crew. He believed in me, and I felt I had somehow let him down. My dropping out at mile 18 was the first "failure" I'd ever had. Running 18 miles without training may have been an incredible accomplishment, but it wasn't the result I had hoped for. Today I can chalk this one up to being naive about the distance, but at the time, I was really disappointed in myself.

My grandfather tried to comfort me. "Experience is a good thing. We'll make a pact," he said. "You train for next year, and I'll be there, too." Deal; no handshake required.

Two months after he had waited for me on that Brookline street, my grandfather went out to the grocery store late in the day and never came back. My grandmother called to say she was worried about him. We all thought perhaps he had stopped at a bar on the way home. He had lots of friends in the neighborhood, so it wouldn't be out of the ordinary for him to stop to share a few stories and a drink. Bob, my older brother, went out to look for him.

On his way home from the store, my grandfather had had a heart attack on a train. Because of the time it took to get him to the hospital, then the difficulty of reaching a relative in the days before answering machines and cell phones, it took police several hours to track down one of us. Eventually, it was Bob, just 24 at the time, who bore the burden of going to the morgue to identify the body. That was an unimaginably difficult thing for a grandson to do and likely was a moment in time he will never forget.

My grandfather was 75 years old and loved by all of us. We were devastated by his sudden death. It was a major turning point of my life. As I look back, I realize that one particular race and my interaction with my grandfather that day literally helped put me on a road that led to my career producing events as well as to an appreciation for lasting friendships. I knew I needed to run the Boston Marathon and finish it the next year at age 18— and for years beyond that.

I would not let either one of us down ever again.

"Grandad's Memory Pushing Dave"

Medford Daily Mercury headline, April 1973

I trained for the next marathon as though possessed. I ran an unheard-of 100 miles per week. The Medford paper published an article describing my determination to run for my grandfather, initiating one of my personal strategies for meeting a goal: Make it public. My world knew about my plans. I had to finish.

The day before the race, Mr. Murphy and his infamous law paid me a visit—I came down with a stomach virus. My parents said, "Why don't you take a pass?" I knew that was not an option, and I think they did, too. Now, as a parent myself, I have utmost admiration for my mom and dad, who could easily have said, "Don't run." But they didn't; they left the decision to me, no matter how painful it was for them to allow me to run a road race when I clearly would have been better off in bed. I had received my official bib from the BAA. I was 18. Nothing was going to stop me.

On race day, my parents drove me to Hopkinton. The starter's gun went off, and I began to run—and then vomit. My parents went to the 5-mile mark and saw me not looking any better. At the half in Wellesley, my dad was snapping photos, but my mom had tears streaming down her face. She knew I was in bad shape. Despite my overwhelming aches and fever, my mom was in worse pain as she looked on, helplessly worried about her youngest child.

The virus caused me to run, walk, run, and walk, with other assorted bodily functions occurring in between. Every few miles, I left a little of the previous night's carbo-loading dinner along the pavement. It served as incentive for every runner behind me to pass me *and do it quickly*. It's amazing that I decided to ever set foot in Hopkinton again. Pushing yourself to your utmost limit to achieve success comes with a price. However, the end result is truly a gift.

To this day, that second marathon holds the esteemed title of Most Difficult Marathon I've Ever "Run." It was head-to-toe agony every step of the way. With every stride, I swore never to do it again.

The 18-mile point was the same spot where I had dropped out the year before. When I reached that mark, I was in tremendous pain, but I kept going until about mile 21. By then I was down to a walk. "That's it for me," I thought. I stepped out of the race and onto the sidewalk.

I slouched down on the curb, my head between my legs, mentally and physically defeated. I thought, "Here I go again; it's just like last time." I wasn't sure where I was along the course, and it didn't really matter; it was the end of the road for me. I was quitting—at least that was my intent, until I looked up and saw the sign for Evergreen Cemetery.

I was leaning against the wrought-iron fence that surrounded the very place where my grandfather had been buried only 9 months before—he had told me 1 year ago to the day that he would wait for me. And here he was, serving as my inspiration to get back in it and finish what I'd started. His silent voice was the loudest encouragement I heard that day. I got back in the race.

I crossed the finish line in 4½ hours—the slowest time I've ever run for any marathon. The pain was excruciating, but even so, I felt immediate gratification as I stepped across the finish line. Grandpa, we did it.

> Ambition: to do what my parents have done for me; also, to run the Boston Marathon.
>
> *Dave, Medford High yearbook, 1972*

What started all those years ago as a whim can only be referred to today as a "commitment." Accomplishing an unconventional or seemingly unattainable goal is a challenge, one we can all meet if we so choose. If you undertake a project, physical or otherwise, you must first make the decision to reach the goal, then put all your energy into it and not doubt yourself in the process.

A few years ago, I was addressing hundreds of runners who were participating in our marathon charity program that year.

A show of hands indicated that most had decided to run Boston as their first marathon-distance event. At first I was shocked: Why would they choose this race as their first? Certainly there are flatter, faster courses. . . . But then I stopped and thought again: "Oh yeah—I do understand." Funny how the mind forgets.

I started to run more and more marathons, and a local newspaper made reference to my "saintly concentration" while jogging. I don't know if I agree with the "saintly" aspect. I think the reporter was just trying to illustrate that I'm focused. Staying focused deters anything from clouding my view of the finish line.

I didn't finish the first marathon, because I hadn't trained for it. I wasn't totally committed to it. How could I be, when my decision to run was made on a whim? My failure was not so much in execution as in preparation. I had not earned the right to run, and, therefore, I don't think I deserved to succeed. However, in the years since, I've done the work necessary to make it to the finish. I made that commitment to run the race 34 consecutive Boston Marathons ago. By the time I ran my 13th Boston, I was training by running 100 to 200 miles per week. All those miles, the time I spent training with Bill Rodgers and other top runners, and giving myself more than a few hours of lead time before deciding to run a marathon helped me put my best foot forward for the future. My best time now stands at 2:29:58. Johnny Kelley, the Elder, who was my friend and mentor, won the 1935 Boston Marathon with nearly that same time of 2:32:07.

Preparation became my middle name; it led me to success in most areas of my life. In fact, the times I most enjoy myself are those when I have been diligent in planning and preparation, and this applies to just about any activity, not just sports and business. Observe a parent who has not brought along extra clothes, food, or diapers to a family outing, and see how a situation can quickly go from great to stressful! Of course, nobody's perfect. In fact, my most valuable lessons have come from mistakes, be they my own or those of others. However, I like to think they're only "mistakes" if I make them twice; the first time is a learning experience.

To date, I have started 118 marathons and completed all but that impulsive one in 1972. My close friends suggest that I ran that first marathon because it was the year that women received official sanctioning to run Boston. However, I emphatically deny that meeting the opposite sex was the reason I began running—there were much less painful ways to get a date.

Even so, I did somewhat combine romance and running. I had a girlfriend, Susan, who happened to be the roommate of a young woman whose mom lived practically on top of the start of the marathon, on a street called Hayden Rowe (now the street that hosts some of the runner corrals). This woman, Mrs. Dryden, was so generous to my family and me. She even invited my mom and dad to come to her house before the race. Thanks to her, I could use a real bathroom instead of a portable toilet before the start, which made the whole race experience more pleasant. That lasted about 5 years, until Susan and I broke up. Then Dr. Bob Johnson, who lived in the first house after the starting line, invited us into his home on race day. The kindness of these people made every subsequent Boston better and better for me. I was going to be a lifelong participant of this great race.

The 1987 Boston Marathon was better known for pandemonium than for the winner's podium. As the gun sounded to signal the start, it was discovered that a restraining rope designed to hold back the 5,315 runners had not been properly removed. A police officer and two BAA officials were still standing in front of the rope as the onslaught of racers began to move forward. The defending champion and course record holder, Rob de Castella, caught his leg in the rope, tripped, and fell. He suffered minor scrapes and finished sixth. The bigger bruise, perhaps, was to the public face of the marathon itself.

That wasn't the only disaster that year. It was a rainy day, and roads were slick. Just moments after the wheelchair start (prior to the noontime gun), those participants took off down that hill, and a few of the athletes caught their wheels in grooves in the road and bumped into each other. Several went down, and it was a terrible scene.

The wheelchair accident and the rope incident both got a lot of public attention and were the impetus that led to my job. That 1987 experience was a wake-up call for the BAA, much to their merit, and I was honored that they answered it by calling me. The field of runners was growing, as was the BAA's determination to ensure the well-being of every participant.

I was known locally for putting on races through my company, DMSE (Dave McGillivray Sports Enterprises), which organized and produced triathlons and road races throughout New England and in other parts of the country. I wouldn't say there were many candidates to choose from at the time; road races certainly weren't in the mainstream as they are today. Only a few of us actually organized them—lucky for me.

Then race director Guy Morse (now the executive director) asked me if I'd be interested in coming on board as technical coordinator. The BAA wanted to take a fresh look at how the course was organized; that is, they needed someone to solve the start problems and oversee the road cones, Porta-Johns, buses, and so on, but mainly they wanted me to ensure that runners got from point A to point B safely and efficiently, with, yes, a little bit of fun thrown in.

The start problems were easily fixed the next year: For the wheelchairs, we instituted a controlled start, using four-wheeled vehicles and motorcycles to pace the runners, like in the Indy 500. We maintained a 15-mile-per-hour speed for the first half mile, and then the race participants took off when it was safe to do so. We also got rid of the rope and put control back in the hands—literally—of the people. About 30 minutes before the noontime start, we had 20 volunteers line up and form a human chain to keep the runners behind the starting line until right before the gun fired. No high-tech solution needed; just a little volunteer elbow grease.

It was a great time to get involved with the event. The Boston Marathon was about to embark on a renaissance of sorts. I joined an already great ensemble, and we began to revamp and refine the race from nearly every angle. Even today, we are constantly putting specific pieces of the race under a microscope, dissecting them carefully and methodically, and searching for improvements.

On paper, the decision to accept the offer seemed an easy one. However, I'd been running the Boston Marathon consecutively since 1972, and taking the job would mean the end of my streak (although I prefer to think of it as a "commitment"). I faced a dilemma yet felt a sense of urgency to take the job. I put the concept of continuing as a race participant aside for the moment, knowing I'd come up with a solution. Sometimes you have to decide that you're doing the right thing and trust you'll work out the details later. Once I got my feet wet with the BAA and had a clear understanding of the job, I realized that maybe I could continue my tradition after all. However, I could never consider it a true *race* anymore from a personal standpoint; I would always know from the outset that I was destined to be the last finisher.

I checked with the BAA to see if being both a consultant and a participant was all right. I also contacted Chris Lane of the Massachusetts Track and Field Officials Association. He and his colleagues oversee the officiating of the race, and I asked him if I could still receive a finishing time if I ran the race after hours. "Sure," he said, "as long as one of us hangs around long enough to continue timing the race and give you your actual time." He wanted to be clear that the time would be an overall time from the official noontime gun. Even if I ran the race in 3½ hours, my official time would show an 8- or 9-hour time.

I'm fortunate that the organization made the seemingly impossible a reality for me. The BAA could so easily have said no. In fact, it was Chris Lane himself who stayed late into the evening that first year that I worked and ran. He stood in the elements after his own hard day's work, just to time my run. And on any given year since then, he's always been waiting for me at the finish line to give me my "official" time, which he scribbles on an index card. Each of these cards is pinned to a wall in my office—the only proof that I'm not as slow as people might think when they look back at the history records of the world's oldest marathon.

Since 1987, the Boston Marathon has grown to what I consider the benchmark for marathons worldwide. A great team has been assembled to organize and execute the event. The Boston Marathon comprises not only a world-class staff, led by Guy Morse, and an extremely active Board of Governors, but also dedicated volunteers, who are truly the backbone of the race.

One would never consider world-renowned orchestra conductors the likes of Arthur Fiedler or Keith Lockhart to be race directors. However, I would argue that all good race directors could be considered conductors of their own special orchestras. A conductor has the uncanny skill of tying together all the parts to make up the whole. One word truly sums up what he or she does best: communicate. Communication is perhaps the single most important ingredient that separates a good event from a great event.

Like a conductor, an event director must communicate well to create a harmonious event. Directors communicate their thoughts with regard to their objectives and goals, as well as communicate effectively with the media, sponsors, participants, and, especially, volunteers.

Volunteers make up a race's organizing committee. They donate their time—a lot of it. I could write an entire book about each volunteer, but it all comes down to that theme of surrounding oneself with good people. It works. It is this collective experience that I truly believe is Boston's greatest asset. It separates us from every other race in the world.

During my first year as technical coordinator, I was riding in one of the lead vehicles, and as we entered Wellesley, a rotund fellow holding an alcoholic beverage yelled, "Hey, you lazy bum, why don't you get out and run like everyone else?" Little did he know I would be doing that very thing later in the day, when as daylight gave way to darkness, I went from race director to participant. Many years after signing on the dotted line with the Boston Marathon, I described in an essay for *Runner's World* magazine what it's like to run at night.

Of course, no matter how you run it, 26 miles is a long way. And it's even longer when you lead up to it by spending 12 hours on your feet under stressful conditions, during which you're getting very little to eat.

Most of the house parties are going full tilt when I run by. "Hey, you slug, the race is over!" is a typical greeting. "The 80-year-old guy went by hours ago. Pick it up." Ouch. I try to ignore the insults and continue shuffling on my way. To be fair, there are also many good-natured honks of the horn and friendly waves (at least I interpret them to be friendly.)

I always think back to earlier in the day, when the course was lined with hundreds of thousands of cheering spectators. Almost all of them are gone when I run, though a smattering remain to clap for the last runner (me) and to offer refreshments. The kindness of these few strangers always helps get me to the finish.

It's dark when I run . . . very dark. I need to be careful of potholes. Yet running in the dark does come with a special solitude. For me, it's the calm after the storm. Unfortunately, I can still see the trash. As one of those partially responsible for the race, I feel guilty running by all the debris left behind. My first reaction is to grab a broom and trash bag, but I do want to finish the course before the following Wednesday.

I used to start the "night run" at 6 p.m., and depending on my fitness level that particular year, it could be a long and cold evening for my family and friends waiting for me on Boylston Street. In recent years, I've started running at 4, which means I finish around 7:30 or 8 p.m., depending on the headwinds, red lights, and amount of food I've eaten that day (which is mostly likely from the top portion of the food pyramid, as opposed to the healthy base). I've come a long way since 1977, when I was training with Bill Rodgers and went on a special "carbohydrate-depletion-loading diet." Now I just eat some chocolate-chip cookies and go! (Come to think of it, I haven't seen that 2:29 time since I started following the McGillivray diet plan. Maybe Rodgers was onto something . . .)

Rain or shine, many of the Hopkinton Marathon Committee members wait to see me start each year. Knowing how hard we've all worked eases the nervousness that I experience just before the gun goes off . . . yes, *the* actual starter's pistol. Once I put that first foot out in front of me, I am overwhelmed by a sense of relief and peace. The tough part of the day is over. Now it is time to "enjoy" myself and reflect on everything that transpired since I awoke at 3 a.m. As I get older, this now pleasurable part of marathon day is also becoming a bit more of a challenge, but the encouragement I receive keeps me going.

Jack Leduc, a good friend and a member of the Hopkinton committee, paints the marathon's starting line. Every time he paints it, he creates a new stencil design and includes the number of Bostons I've run. It brings me great joy to know I have friends out there who give their own time to make my run a little more special.

When I arrive in Hopkinton, a few of the same Boston and Massachusetts state police cruisers and motorcycles that escorted the leaders during the day are waiting to escort me the entire 26.2 miles. They're all tired from a job well done during the day, yet they come out on their own, out of friendship. By driving directly behind me with their lights on, they help me see where I am stepping and give me a great feeling of security. You just never know when a wacko is going to come out of the shadows and make a place in history at your expense.

Although nearly 20,000 people may have traversed the course only hours before, I enjoy going it alone. As I get older, however, the solitude I once appreciated has been replaced by the comfort of having one or two good friends with me as I run. This phenomenon began in 1996 when Jack Fultz, winner of the 1976 BAA Boston Marathon—more popularly known as the Run for the Hoses—decided to run with me. It certainly made the time go faster, and I appreciated the company. Jack and I crossed the finish line together, tied for last. And now Jack's claim to fame, as he so eloquently states, is that he is the only person to finish *first* in the Boston Marathon as well as *last* (though not in the same year!).

In recent years, my friend Josh Nemzer has also accompanied me the entire distance. He too is tired after a weekend of various marathon responsibilities, yet out of friendship and concern for my well-being, he laces up and gets me through it. I am overwhelmed by the Newton firefighters who, in years past, waited at the corner of Commonwealth Avenue, just before the dreaded climb up Newton Hills. It is difficult not to think back to just a few hours before, when I covered the same stretch on a lead vehicle. At that time, the road was filled with thousands of spectators, and the roar of enthusiasm could be deafening. They're all gone by the time I come through—except for the firefighters and even some police officers—clapping for the last runner and offering a cup of water.

Although traffic usually is light, the red lights certainly don't encourage me to run a "personal record" time. As I crest the infamous Heartbreak Hill, I ask a question that was most likely posed by at least a few thousand of the 20,000 who preceded me that day: "Why am I doing this?" For me, the real heartbreak of the marathon is not climbing the hills; it's descending them that can wreak havoc on a runner's body. I'm careful on the downhills, watching my strides, making sure I don't overdo it.

The last turn onto Boylston Street is so gratifying. In the distance are those friendly faces that kept appearing out on the course. The cleanup crew is the only other reminder that something spectacular happened here earlier in the day. At that time of night, Ed Jacob and his crew from Interstate Rental have already begun breaking down what took them days to put up, disassembling the finish-line bleachers, scaffolding, and tents, and clearing the road for the next morning's commute.

In the early years of my night run, there was no fanfare, no crowd, and no announcer—just my feeling of satisfaction as I crossed the line. Dead last. My time: 9½ hours after the gun.

Nowadays, as I run down Boylston, people stream out of restaurants, wondering what the heck all the commotion is. It's got the excitement of running into an Olympic Stadium. I have the entire road to myself; the police lights flash and sirens blare. One year, an officer who had escorted me all the way from Hopkinton jumped out of his cruiser and ran the last half-mile with me in his uniform and boots. And people think I'm crazy?!

Now, more than a decade since I began this nighttime run, there is a group of regulars who convene. Though the crowd does not number in the thousands, I am comforted when I see family and friends at the finish. Amid the trucks and the trash, they crown me, the last finisher of the Boston Marathon. In 1998, as I approached the finish of my 27th consecutive run, I saw my sons, Ryan and Max, holding up a break tape that Ryan himself had made. As I crossed the finish line, they placed a laurel wreath on my head. In Greek mythology, the wreath signifies victory as a result of overcoming great personal obstacles. We all probably deserve a laurel wreath at some point or another.

> What's the life lesson that you can take from any of your athletic pursuits? Dave's been able to stay true to something that he set for himself years and years ago: being able to achieve the balance. I don't think anyone can fully understand. We all work hard on the race. We're all spent by Monday. For him to get out there and put one foot in front of the other . . . it's a big day.
>
> *Josh Nemzer, DMSE colleague*

I never know what to expect when I cross the finish line. One year, former Boston Marathon winners Jackie Gareau and Rosa Mota held the official BAA break tape. After I finished my run a few years ago, I was walking into the Copley Plaza Hotel when I bumped into Johnny Kelley, the 1935 and 1945 Boston Marathon champion who was also a two-time Olympian (1936 and 1948) and finished second in Boston seven times. He asked if I had just finished the race, and he shook my hand when I told him it was my 32nd. "You are going to break my record, and I am not going to be around to see it," he commented.

"No, John, that is one record that will never be broken," I

replied. I'd have to run the Boston Marathon until age 79 to even *tie* his record of 61 starts and 58 finishes. There are some records that should never be broken.

Kelley ran his last Boston at age 84. At 84, I may give it a try, too, but it might be an achievement to just get out of bed. And first, I'd like to see how well the 84th birthday run goes.

One year, Johnny was too ill to come to the marathon, and he asked that I call him the moment I crossed the finish line. My only hope was that I would go fast enough to phone him before he fell asleep for the night!

I had first met Johnny years before that, in 1979—long before I had any idea of what an integral part of my life he and the marathon would become. I ran a road race in Chatham, Massachusetts. Prior to the start, Johnny came over to congratulate me on my successful coast-to-coast run. "I followed your run across the country last year, and I heard about your injured knee. I prayed for you every single day since, hoping that you would heal," he said with true concern.

I never let him forget that moment or those words. Johnny Kelley, who was already a running legend, came up to *me* to talk about my running. I told him what kind of impact that had on me. Sometimes we feel like we're in a vacuum, that it's just us against the world. When feelings are expressed, truly from the heart, it means a lot. I ended up winning that road race, and I kept in touch with Johnny.

> He was my hero before I met him. He was my hero while I knew him, and although he passed on, he will continue to be my hero forever.
>
> *Dave, the Eagle Tribune, October 17, 2004*

The running world, particularly the Boston Marathon, and my own life have experienced a huge void since Johnny Kelley's death at age 97 on October 6, 2004. One of the greatest honors of my life was being asked by his nephew, Tom Kelley, to be one of the pallbearers at Johnny's funeral.

Probably very few people know that Johnny was not only a runner, but he also liked to paint. He once presented me with a Johnny Kelley original of a runner alongside the ocean. I'm not sure if it's a self-portrait, but when I look at it, I like to think it's him enjoying some time on his beloved Cape Cod. Johnny was also known for always singing, especially "Young at Heart." This "mantra," if you will, truly described his life.

I wanted to honor this man somehow, and I directed a race named after him. It began and ended at the Vista Hotel in Waltham. The Jimmy Fund Boston Council helped me with the arrangements. We had an incredible crowd.

Johnny Kelley was an extraordinary human being and, of course, a great athlete, driven by many traits and ideals I recognize in myself. I don't mean to compare myself to this beloved running legend; however, we do share some commonalities, which I think were at the root of our bond. Johnny was from Medford; I am from Medford. He was 5-foot-5; I am *almost* 5-foot-5. He dropped out of his first marathon (at age 20); I dropped out of my first marathon (at age 17). Our best times for Boston were 2 seconds apart. We definitely had some similarities, but there is only one Johnny Kelley, and there will never be anyone who comes close to his legacy. There are thousands of great athletes out there, but I truly believe that what Johnny Kelley accomplished is the greatest athletic feat ever performed.

I am fortunate to have had the encouragement of my grandfather, in life and in death, during the early years of my marathon experience. I am deeply grateful for the support of one of the greatest running legends during my later years. Running at night is very difficult, but the influence of these heroes lights my way to the finish.

Almost exactly 26 years (there's that number again!) after I'd run my first 26.2 miles, there was something I needed to do. At the time, I was technical director of the world's most prestigious marathon, and my reputation as a race director had allowed me to be part of some very special events, yet I had some unfinished business. I drove along the route of the marathon and stopped when I came to the black wrought-iron gates of Evergreen

Cemetery—the point at which I'd been tempted to drop out of that second marathon. My friend Linda had suggested that I return for a visit to my grandfather's grave. My grandfather had encouraged me to live out my dreams, and everything I did back then was not only to make myself happy but also to make him and my parents proud of me.

As I walked into the cemetery office, just inside the enormous iron gates, I was struck by the file-card box that was still used to keep track of the gravesite information. It had withstood the grasp of the technology age. The gentleman behind the desk took my grandfather's name from me and thumbed through the cards until he came across one with my mother's handwriting on it. She had filled out all the pertinent information at the time of my grandfather's death. Seeing her writing transported me back all those years, as he gave me the plot number and I got back into my car and drove to the place where we had laid my grandfather to rest.

> Frederick A. Eaton
> Massachusetts CPL US Army
> World War I
> August 20, 1896–June 27, 1972

The marathon is an ideal metaphor for my life. It's challenging and difficult, but if you work hard and you're prepared, then it's manageable. I've run on that asphalt through heartache and also spent hours upon hours running alongside some incredible people. There are hills and valleys. The weather changes from year to year. Mostly, though, at the end of the day, it's up to me to get the job done.

CHAPTER 4

The Operations Manual

[Dave's] not somebody who goes into things lightly. He does his homework.

Rob Roy McGregor, DPM, marathoner;
Runner's Digest *radio show, June 20, 1978*

The view of the horizon from my desk at my first job out of college was mesmerizing. It served as a constant reminder that I was not meant for the monotony of a typical work environment. I wanted to be doing something different—something out *there*. With the ink on my mathematics degree barely dry, I had accepted a job at William M. Mercer, a benefits firm. Crunching numbers as an actuary was not my ultimate goal, but I was grateful for the opportunity and the paycheck. I love working with numbers, but that job and what was in my heart just didn't add up. My desire remained the same as when I was a kid: I wanted to be an athlete.

As a college senior, I faced the "what to do with my life" syndrome. I wanted to do something physically challenging, unique, and, most important, outside my comfort zone. An irony of my size is that I don't have small ideas, so when I heard about a friend who was riding his bike across the country, it opened my mind to the possibility that with proper training, I could do something similar.

Taking on the terrain of the United States using my own two feet was my kind of challenge. Medford, Oregon, and my hometown of Medford, Massachusetts, seemed like logical anchors for the run. They were on opposite coasts and nearly a straight shot from each other. The concept solidified during a trip out to California with my friend Ron Black. Just after college graduation, we purchased one-way tickets to the West Coast on the assumption that we'd find a way to get back home, which we did, even after the bus we were traveling on broke down in the middle of the Mojave Desert. We toured everywhere from San Diego to San Francisco and Las Vegas, and then contracted with a service to deliver a car back to its owners out east. During the 8-day drive, I paid close attention to the roads and elevations and the enormity of what I was contemplating.

I found strength in the knowledge that a handful of others had already taken on a transcontinental run, though there were lots of variables among them (such as start and end locations, support crew and vehicles, and funding). Similar runs had already been done by a Swede, a South African, an Englishman, and a few Americans, including Tom McGrath, a bartender from New York City who ran across in 1977. It was my turn.

"Why, Dave?"

Alan McGillivray, Dave's brother

I didn't have the abilities of a Billy Rodgers or a Frank Shorter, but I did have the desire to set a personal goal that would require the same dedication and grueling training of an Olympic athlete or professional competitor. Since I didn't believe I could go faster, I thought I would try running farther: literally cross-country. A run from the Pacific to the Atlantic would be my mini-Olympics.

Why did I decide to do it? Why not suggest the extraordinary, and then figure out how to make it happen?

I led a double life during those years of preparation: assistant actuary by day, and planner of my destiny by night. At times, I felt like Clark Kent, except that as Superman he wore a cape, while I was transformed by my running shoes. I kept my ambition close to the vest while I did my homework on what the actual time, cost, distance, and training commitment would be for a run from Oregon to Massachusetts. (My hope was that by running west to east, the state of Massachusetts would act as a magnet, constantly pulling me home.) Finding answers to these fundamental aspects of the endeavor and understanding its true scope finally earned me the right to publicly state my goal. It took 4 years.

Planning began with the basics: a foldout US map and a calculator. There were no computers or mapping software to conveniently determine which roads to travel on and how many days, hours, and nanoseconds the entire journey would take. It was all done with a No. 2 pencil, a pad of paper, and my fourth-grade ruler.

The number of days and the number of miles per day I chose to run was definitely a conundrum. I wanted to start at a Red Sox game on one coast and finish at another Red Sox game on the opposite coast, so I was tied to the team's schedule and would have to accomplish the run in 80 days. I calculated the total distance to be 3,200 miles—which meant an average of at least 40 miles a day—and took my personal fitness regimen to a new level. I would be doing nothing but running from June through August. In fact, the story of my run is really an essay on "What I Did on My Summer Vacation."

Planning was a full-time job, but then again, so was my full-time job! Each day at 5 p.m., the proverbial bell would ring and my floor of the John Hancock Tower, New England's tallest building, would clear out. I imagined people on the street below looking up at the massive structure and seeing only a few lights on in the darkness—one of them being mine.

I was working on my to-do lists for the run. Lists are the most important item I create to keep myself motivated and get things accomplished. If I write something down, I don't let it go until it's crossed off, even if I have to carry the item over to the next day. It's my own personal guilt complex.

I've kept a daily notebook since the tail end of high school. In fact, I still have them all. They're like a record of my life. Each is just a plain, small notebook with lined pages. I'd written the date at the top of each page, followed by a list of what I needed to accomplish. I made similar lists of essentials to complete for the run. Nearly every weeknight for months, I stood at the photocopy machine as the janitorial staff cleaned around me. They must have thought I was the most devoted worker at the company, when I was really just waiting for the precise moment to ask for a 2½ month leave of absence—without pay, of course.

> Here I am with my younger brother, and I felt bad for him.
> I thought to myself, "This kid is dreaming."
>
> *Bob McGillivray, Dave's brother*

My brother Bob is the oldest of us five McGillivray "kids." Due to our 7-year difference, the time we spent together in my adolescence was minimal, but he was my brother, and I wanted to share my plans about the run with each of my siblings.

One night, I invited Bob to join me for a beer at the Wursthaus in Harvard Square, a convenient stop for him on his way home from work. As I earnestly unveiled my plan for running solo from coast to coast, he never revealed that he felt a little sorry for me. He was concerned about how I'd deal with the disappointment of failure. He listened thoughtfully and never let on how unrealistic an undertaking he believed it to be. I don't blame him. My own negative thoughts surfaced more than once during the run, as I ascended a seemingly endless hill or ran in the intense heat of the desert.

Weeks before sharing the overall plan with Bob, I sought my parents' approval. I had created multiple three-ring binders with pages and pages of itineraries, maps, supply needs, contact names, potential sponsors—everything I could think of that would be an integral part of my effort. These books were the first in a lifetime of "operations manuals" that I create for every single event I produce, whether it's a 5-K race or an Olympic marathon trial. The creation of the op manual forces me to think about all aspects of a project, gather answers, and share the information with others who will be working on the event. It's all part of the preparation: The more that people know, the better they're equipped to help reach a goal.

In those notebooks, I tried to anticipate all of the questions my parents might have, both logistical and practical, about what it would take to pull this thing off. My desire was to give them a level of comfort and a minimum of worry by showing them that I had thoughtfully planned it all out. Playing devil's advocate helped me anticipate problems and questions along the way. For example, I wrote to the state police departments of all 15 states that I'd be running through. I gave them the route numbers of the roads I'd be traveling on and the exact dates (barring unforeseen circumstances) that I'd be spending within their state lines. I received favorable replies from most of them, though all were cautious to say, "Make sure you don't get run over!"

After several months, I finally felt ready to announce my intention. I carefully put the binders on the kitchen table where my parents would find them, along with a simple handwritten message: "Please read." Then I headed out for the evening. I chose not to talk about it face-to-face; I wanted the facts to speak for themselves.

When I returned later that night, I found a reply from them at the bottom of the note I had left for them. "David, we love you," it said.

That was it. They had read through everything and endorsed it. It was a tremendous relief, as well as an enormous boost to my spirit, knowing they approved. It wasn't until 20 years later that I learned that my brother Bob was not alone in concealing his doubts about my chances for success. Running across the country was an ambitious notion, even for the most well-trained athlete, and my dad just didn't see how I could do it. Yet he, my mom, and my siblings showed only their never-ending capacity for encouragement. I'm enormously grateful to them for allowing me the chance to believe that anything's possible, even when they were not quite as sure.

Truth is, even I couldn't be sure. Thanks to all of my organization and logistical planning, I had a solid body of knowledge about what needed to be done, but now I needed knowledge of my body: Was I in the right physical condition to cover the miles? I trained anywhere from 10 to 15 miles per day for several months and then planned a "trial" run from Medford, Massachusetts, to Rochester, New York, where my sister Susan and her husband, Graham, lived. Success with this litmus test would prove to me that a cross-country run was attainable.

The week before I ran the trial, I got into my car and drove all the way to my sister's house and charted out the exact 403.6-mile course. Every 40 miles—my projected per-day average for running across the country—I stopped at a nearby motel and booked a reservation for the following week. (Later, when I checked in as I was running, the managers would ask for my license and registration. I'd say I didn't have one. "Well, how'd you get here?" I'd point to my sneakers.)

I weighed 138 pounds when I left Medford at 8 a.m. on August 6, 1977. When I returned on August 12, I was 4 pounds lighter. I wonder if the usual reasons—dehydration and a high calorie-burn rate—were compounded by the fact that I carried the following items in a backpack for at least 200 miles during an August heat wave.

1. Maps (Massachusetts/New York)
2. Small flashlight (for running in the dark)
3. Radio (and batteries)
4. First-aid kit: bandages, tape, gauze, scissors
5. Vitamins
6. Vaseline
7. BenGay
8. Toiletries: toothbrush, paste, small soap, razor, deodorant

9. Clothing: sweatpants, hat, socks, shorts, T-shirts, underwear, extra pair track shoes
10. *Four Million Footsteps,* by Bruce Tulloh

I had no support vehicle, so I had to either carry my necessities or go without. Reviewing that list now reminds me of how naive it was to stuff 20 pounds of supplies into a backpack, then run with it during the hottest days of summer. Not surprisingly, that pack gave me problems from the first day; not only was it stuffed, but it didn't fit properly. I should've left some of those supplies at home. Given the choice, I might've ditched everything except Bruce Tulloh's book. Back then, *Four Million Footsteps* was my bible. Tulloh, a legendary runner from Great Britain, was best known for running barefoot. I intended for his words to provide me with inspiration, but the added weight of his book added only perspiration.

The list omitted a couple of other items I carried: a notebook and pencil. I kept daily logs of the temperature, my mileage, what I ate, and the time I went to sleep. I also calculated that it would take me 12 to 13 hours a day to walk my daily mileage goal. Knowing I could walk if needed provided a mental safety net.

My sustenance for the journey included Coke, candy bars, cheeseburgers, french fries, cookies, ice cream, hot dogs (which made me sick), doughnuts, iced tea, and candy. With food like that, it's amazing that I made it to age 23, let alone Albany, New York.

On day 4, my parents met me near the New York border. I took a break from the weight of the backpack and left it with them for the afternoon. I ran and walked about 15 miles in 2 hours, nearly twice my pace with that foolish thing on my back.

By day 5, my feet hurt so badly that I had to wrap them in bandages before I ran. This was the first time I had ever run mileage like this. It was a struggle to come up with the right formula. How much training was really needed? And could I handle the mental challenge of running solo for 80 days?

For 5 days straight, I ran west. My daily average of more than

45 miles showed me that my ultimate goal was realistic. I had nothing to prove by continuing on to Rochester for the full 400-plus miles, so at Schenectady, New York, I gave myself two choices: Either stay at a motel and run some more miles through Albany the following day before taking a bus home, or turn and run home.

I decided to take a bus back to Boston, for the same reason I decided not to continue on to Rochester: I had achieved my goal. Moments later, I bumped into a friend as I crossed the street to a drugstore for a "tonic" (that's "soda" in New England). Schenectady was hometown to Tony Torre, a fellow Merrimack College cross-country track runner. He invited me to his house the following night. Funny how I had no particular notion of exactly what I was going to do, but it all worked itself out.

So on day 6, I put in 40 more miles through Albany after all, including a 6-mile walk to Washington Park, along the Hudson River. I joined a guy who was spending his lunch hour jogging as part of an experiment testing the physical condition of US government officials. It must have been a big focus group, as there were so many people running through the park that it felt like I was running along the Charles River back home. I also ran to the University of Albany and did a few miles around the track with one of the students. In today's world, I doubt that people would be trusting enough to let a stranger start running with them. There are too many weirdos out there. Running from my home to a strange city hundreds of miles away, just to see if I could do it, might also put me in that category.

Day 7 ended the test. I ran and walked 5 or 6 miles to the depot from Tony's house. Still not having run enough, I ran home from the Boston bus station via Massachusetts Avenue. After seeing my folks, eating dinner, and catching up on newspapers, I went out for a 1½-hour run so that I could bring my total mileage to about 300 for the week. It was the most I'd ever run in my life.

The 7-day practice run was a microcosm of what I was going to experience a year later: intense heat, a lot of rain, and sunburn. I got lost, too, and at least once found myself in a more precarious part of Albany. I ran faster for safety's sake and did the same when chased by a few big dogs. Finally, there were those blisters. My body and mental fortitude had been tested. I was pleased with the outcome and the insight that I gained as I continued planning for June 1978.

Initially, the cross-country run was intended as nothing more than a personal challenge, but one Labor Day weekend, I was watching the telethon for muscular dystrophy and thought, "Wouldn't it be neat to present a check to Jerry Lewis himself?" I would be finishing in August, just before the telethon. I contacted the organizers, and initially they were interested. But after several months of back-and-forth, their concerns about me getting hurt were too great, and they said no. That was one of the first major setbacks I experienced. I could not understand the rejection: I was going to subject myself to the elements for 3 months and raise money at no charge and no expense and, hopefully, get them all kinds of publicity, and they said no. I was young, and at that time, I did not understand liability issues. What it boiled down to was the possibility that I would get hit by a car, a fear that nearly became a reality a few times along the way.

Focusing on a children's charity was of particular interest to me, perhaps because I had gone through so many growing pains as a child. My thoughts turned to the Jimmy Fund, a well-known New England charity that raises money for kids (and adults) with cancer. It also happened to be the official charity of the Boston Red Sox. Anyone who had ever sat at Fenway Park was familiar with its billboard on the right-field wall. When I was growing up, there always seemed to be a local Jimmy Fund bake sale or car wash—grassroots types of events—going on. Maybe a local organization would be more open to my idea than a big national charity was . . . ?

The answer was yes. After a phone call, followed by a high-spirited meeting, the Jimmy Fund organization enthusiastically backed my efforts. We agreed that I would talk up the Jimmy Fund across the country and spread the word about the important cancer research taking place in Boston.

Billions of fund-raising dollars have resulted from the marriage of athletic endeavors and charities in recent years, but in 1978, it was a tough sell.

> I remember Dave starting the process of trying to get corporations interested in sponsoring his charity run. He was meeting with some pretty high-level decision makers, and he was only 22 years old.
>
> *Ron Black, Dave's high school friend*

Other than the run to Albany, the absolute most challenging *pre*run aspect of my plan was that of finding a sponsor. I was young and unproven, with only enthusiasm and determination as collateral. But that was enough for me, and it would have to be enough to win the confidence of corporate executives.

I began by writing to recreational-vehicle companies and athletic corporations. I sent out *mimeographed* (knowledge of this term reveals one's age) copies of my timetable, route maps, estimated expense accounts, and full résumé. At first, the outlook was grim; I received offers of free sneakers, and that was about it. This was not a million-dollar event, but I did lack the resources to fund it myself. I mailed more than 25 letters. With each response, I learned that there are at least 25 different ways to say no.

The 26th reply came from a new magazine called *The Runner*, whose entire advertising campaign centered on the phrase "The Runner is coming!" The campaign already existed and was ready to launch. Since I was about to become "the runner," they decided my trip and I were a natural fit for the concept and agreed to back me.

I was flown to their editorial offices in New York for a planning session. The contract stated that *The Runner* would do the following:

1. Fly me and three companions to Seattle (for a ceremonial start at the Kingdome), and then from Seattle to Medford, Oregon (for the actual start).

2. Arrange for us to use one RV and one moped, both to be picked up in Medford, Oregon.
3. Donate $3,750 toward my expenses.
4. Set up all publicity and media coverage throughout the country.

A lawyer friend of mine took a look and approved the contract. All the pieces were in place, so we signed. I was all set—or so I thought.

Just 10 days before I was to board a plane for Seattle, I received a call from someone at the magazine. They had changed their minds about sponsoring me.

Had I heard correctly? I had spent 4 years of my life putting the pieces together; was it possible that just one phone call could bring it all to a screeching halt before it even began? The change of heart occurred when the magazine heard about a South African woman named Marvis Hutchinson, who had just completed a transcontinental run. Their thought was, "What's the big deal about your effort, McGillivray?"

That attitude illustrated to me that people had no idea (and neither did I, at the time) of what an undertaking this was. Just because it had been done before did not make it any less of a challenge. The magazine's philosophy translates to the likes of "What's the big deal about climbing Mt. Everest if others have already done it?"

The phone call momentarily paralyzed my thought process. *The Runner*'s decision also smelled of a very valid lawsuit against them for reneging on our agreement, but what would've been the point? I needed to put all my energy, or what was left of it, into finding another sponsor.

The Medford High School athletic awards banquet was that night, and I was guest speaker. I didn't feel much like going, but a commitment is a commitment. This was the same event at which I had received the Phelan Award, so I went. When I talked of the run and the fact that my sponsor had backed out that very afternoon, the crowed let out a collective gasp, as if they had all just been kicked in the gut.

One way or another, I was going through with the trip, even if it meant cutting back on certain necessities—namely, the motor home, the biggest expense and most valuable asset.

Just 1 day later, my brother Alan was playing softball after work: Alan's accounting firm versus their biggest client, which just happened to be an athletic footwear company called Pro Specs International. Alan most definitely had plan B in mind as he generously purchased drinks for the Pro Specs owner at the postgame gathering. The more the glasses were drained, the more Alan talked about my run and the jeopardy I found myself in without *The Runner*.

> I got home and started knocking on Dave's door at about 1 a.m., and I woke him up: "Dave, I got the sponsor! I got it! I got it!"
>
> *Alan McGillivray*

It was dark and way past the hour at which I'd gone to sleep. Alan was at the edge of my bed, "whispering" so loud that I thought he would wake my parents. As he shook me awake, I thought, "He's either intoxicated or hallucinating." I both requested and prayed that he'd let me go back to sleep. But he kept saying, "No really, I got it! I got it!"

Apparently, sometime over the course of the conversation, Al Spector, president and CEO of Pro Specs, had agreed to sponsor the run. Unsure himself if he had heard correctly, Alan called Spector first thing the next morning.

"Were you sincere about that offer of sponsorship?" my brother gently inquired.

Spector said, "Sure—get your brother and come down here."

We immediately drove down to Avon, Massachusetts, to the Pro Specs headquarters. After talking with Spector for about 5 seconds, I knew his decision to sponsor my run had nothing to do with the amount of barley and hops consumed the night before. He was a compassionate man with a heart of gold. He jumped in and saved the trip, as well as all of my dreams.

Pro Specs' generosity was unmatched, yet with my start date just a few days ahead, I had to be sure that their product, the Pro Specs Marathon 220 Track Shoe, could provide the support and stability I needed for 2½ months of running. I took the shoes out for a 30-mile test drive and also submitted them to my podiatrist to check support and strength.

During the week before I left, Alan and I drove back to Specs to iron out the details. Specs put together an entire sponsorship package in only a few days and agreed to underwrite all costs. We decided on an initial $4,000 to get us started. Jim Shapiro, president of the company, wrote out a check for the full amount, which Alan and I cashed at the nearest bank. Specs also gave us about 40 pairs of shoes, along with shirts, socks, and travel bags.

A day later, we met with Specs again and spoke with their public-relations firm in New York. At first, they weren't thrilled with my choice of the Jimmy Fund—it was too "New England." They preferred a charity with national name recognition. I was grateful that, after some discussion, Specs backed my choice. The Specs PR machine was in full force almost immediately, led by Mildred Vidgerhaus, a New Yorker who didn't take no for an answer. What they made happen under those time constraints was truly amazing.

Those few days—in fact, the few years of planning the trip—were a series of feeling sky-high one moment, only to land down in the dumps the next. The run took over my entire life, and as I got closer to June '78, I was unbelievably eager to just get out there and run. I prayed I would not get injured. Everyone was counting on me.

For most of the prerun prep, I focused on details other than my physical conditioning. I ran often, but not necessarily great distances, other than the trial run a year before I left. The reason for my lack of road miles was that my real training started during the winter of '78—as in, the winter of the blizzard of '78. Several feet of snow covered the ground for months, so I worked out at the Mystic Health Club near my home.

I had comfortably run four marathons that year, so it was not the mileage that concerned me as much as the terrain and elements I would endure. The desert was about 120 degrees, the same as the club's sauna, which served as a desert simulator; I regularly ran 10 miles at a time in there. Inevitably, some unsuspecting person would enter the sauna to unwind and see me in there, huffing and puffing, then exit in disgust a few moments later. Eventually, people got to know who I was and what I was doing and were more accepting of me and my apparent lunacy. My friend Jimmy Lyons, who worked at the club, even arranged for a raffle drawing among the members, with all proceeds going to the Jimmy Fund.

On the whole, though, I never ran more than 20 miles at a time. In fact, I trained less for the run across the country than for, say, the Ironman or the 24-hour run. Much more effort went into the planning and logistics.

Of course, I didn't ignore my physical condition. There were some minor aches that I wanted checked out before I left. First, I went to see a physician about pain in my arches. He treated me with a Myoflex machine, which sent minor electric shock waves through my arch areas to stimulate blood flow and speed healing. It sounded promising, but it didn't work. Not sure what else to do, I concluded that the best way to get in shape for the run would be the run itself. As I ran 40 miles each day, I would get progressively stronger. That theory could either make or break me.

Then I found Rob Roy McGregor, DPM, one of the very few medical practitioners who were experts in the field of running during the 1970s. A pioneer in the footwear industry, Dr. McGregor lived in the Boston area and had developed the Etonic sneaker, arch supports, heel cradles, and other cushioning devices designed to treat injuries and make shoes more comfortable. His expertise not only helped advance the running shoe industry, it also had a significant impact on the quality and success of my run. He diagnosed me with a minor plantar fascia strain in my right arch, which caused pain when I ran. He specially fitted sneakers to my foot, which I trained in well before Specs came on board.

Dr. McGregor went so far as to call Al Spector and ask if I could wear Etonics during the trip. He was concerned that if I wore Specs for the entire route, I might not make it. It would be like wearing a new pair of sneakers the day of a marathon (actually, nearly two marathons per day). Ten days before a 3,000-plus-mile run, I could not switch brands, no matter who the sponsor was.

I couldn't in good conscience tell the world that I was wearing Specs the whole way. Al Spector was very understanding. We agreed that I could simply say I was "testing" the shoe against others. Whenever possible, I would wear Specs in publicity shots. I also agreed to help the company with product development and improvement after I returned. In fact, that process began before I even left. The Pro Specs were a bit too stiff, so I put each shoe in a vice in my father's workshop and cut a groove in the outer sole, near the toe area. This one "enhancement" made them bend a little easier. Other improvements would be left to the Specs research and development team.

As I continued to check things off my list, I kept landing on the issue of a support crew. In this area of the preparation, I benefited from the wisdom of Tom McGrath. I went to New York to meet with him soon after he completed his own cross-country run in 1977. Tom emphasized the importance of choosing the right companions. For 80 days, these people would be my lifeline. Selecting those who would put my interests first was critical to my success. Boy, was that an understatement.

No one exactly jumped at the chance to go with me, perhaps because it was not the most glamorous of job descriptions. It basically boiled down to this:

> *Wanted:* Three men to live in a recreational vehicle for 80 days. Must be willing to do never-ending loads of laundry; withstand the smell of an RV housing three to four males (one of whom uses BenGay on a daily basis); grocery shop; find hotels and campsites, sometimes in the most remote places on earth; fill a gas tank; dump "other" tanks (assigned to the individual drawing the shortest straw);

maintain cleanliness of RV; contact local media and city and town officials; cook breakfast, lunch, and dinner; and be able to follow a runner more than 3,200 miles along narrow roads, busy interstates, and desolate desert and mountain roads wide enough for only one small vehicle at a time; and, above all, have a sense of humor. In-depth knowledge of the Three Stooges a plus.

A month or two before I left, I was a guest on the *Runner's Digest* radio show. During the interview, I mentioned my search for a support crew. Though no listeners called in, Tom Kinder, the show's host, spoke to me off the air and said *he* wanted to go. At the time, I had just one other support-crew member: Kent Hawley, a schoolteacher from Cambridge who had a desire to bicycle across the country and learned of my plan through a mutual friend. The school calendar prevented him from starting in June, so Tom agreed to come out for the first few weeks and cover for Kent.

At a whopping age 35, Kent was the oldest of the crew. He had spent 5 years in the navy. Himself a serious runner, he ran about 15 to 25 miles a day with me when he picked up with us in Utah. He also took photos and was responsible for the general cleaning and maintenance of the camper.

Jeff Donahue of Lowell, Massachusetts, at age 22, was the youngest of us. He had just graduated from Merrimack College with a marketing degree. Both of us were officers in the same fraternity; in fact, we had bumped into each other at a party, and he asked how the run was going. I said, "Great—how'd you like to come along?" At first, he thought it was a crazy proposition, but he called me a few weeks later and said, "Sure, why not?"

Jeff did the majority of the PR for the trip, other than what the Specs agency handled. He contacted local newspapers, radio stations, and TV stations in the major towns and cities we ran through and arranged press conferences and meetings with city officials. He also spent a great deal of time riding alongside me on the moped, carrying water, extra clothes, skin lotions, a radio, and so on, while maintaining a daily log of progress, mileage, health, weather conditions, and terrain for the 3-month trek.

Once the trip was under way, the guys came together as a team—and I learned I was not the only one with goals. A hometown friend, Danny Carey, age 26 at the time, was looking for a way to fill the summer before going back to school. His "run" duties included driving, cooking, and maintaining the motor home. But he also had a personal goal: He wanted to complete 100,000 pushups while we were gone. He did about 1,500 every day (a set of 500 each morning, noon, and night). One news article about the trip reported that Danny had done 45,000 pushups by the time I had run 1,250 miles. Must be something in the Medford water supply?

I ended up with four companions, though for most of the trip there were only three at a time. Tom stayed with us through Greeley, Colorado; Kent remained. I knew only two of the four prior to the trip. We were essentially strangers coming together for an intense journey, the likes of which none of us could anticipate. Why did I choose these guys? Because they were courageous and naive enough to say yes. I couldn't have done it without them.

My family's modest home on Belle Avenue became the logistical hub of my run universe. My support crew and I met regularly, partaking of my mother's chocolate-chip cookies while we discussed what needed to be done before and during the months away. I brought the guys to Dr. McGregor so he could teach them how to tape my feet, which added support and helped ease the pain. The strain was healed by the time I left, but I wanted to continue using tape to be on the safe side. Dr. McGregor gave us all the supplies we would need, including tape, anti-inflammatory drugs, vitamins, and padding for my shoes. His support, generosity, and expertise were a major factor in the positive outcome of my run.

I picked up more supplies at Bill Rodgers's running store, and one day I toured the Jimmy Fund Building at the Sidney Farber Cancer Center with Charlie Kilty, Ken Coleman's assistant. Ken had left for the day by the time we got back, so Charlie let me use Ken's office to return some of the never-ending phone calls. My home phone was ringing off the hook (as it has been for the past 25 years), and I welcomed the quiet place to work.

Ken Coleman and the Jimmy Fund also made it possible for me to start at the Seattle Kingdome during a Mariner's–Red Sox game and finish when the same teams faced each other again at Fenway Park, so I paid a visit to Fenway.

Even then, the Red Sox were a world-class organization. Bill Crowley, my contact there, and the team were extremely supportive. They booked and paid for rooms for Tom and me at the Seattle Hilton, and they gave us names of contacts at the Kingdome so we could iron out the details of running inside their ballpark. Arrangements were made for me to go up to the press booth after my lap around the park; I would be interviewed between innings by Ken Harrelson and Dick Stockton—I was really excited about that! We also ironed out the particulars for the August 29 finish. I stayed in contact with Bill for years afterward.

I also stopped by the Eliot Lounge on Commonwealth Avenue. My good friend Tommy Leonard, founder of the Falmouth Road Race, tended bar at this most famous of local hangouts for runners. Bill Rodgers was there when I arrived, and we talked about the run and how I would truly know I was home when I walked through the doors of the Eliot. It was a comfortable place, a "Cheers" of sorts for a lot of us '70s joggers.

The company where my dad worked threw a small going-away party for me. For weeks prior to my departure, employees donated their coffee money to my run and continued their fundraising while I was away. At the party, they presented me with $106 and a caricature of myself, drawn by one of the Sexton employees. On my way out, Ed Sexton, the owner, asked to see me. I went up to his office and we talked for a while. He then presented me with a personal check for $300. I walked out of the place with $406—the same number as Ted Williams's batting average. The money was a tremendous show of support, and I felt a bit like a Hall of Famer myself.

Just days before I left for Oregon, my girlfriend, Denise, and

I went to see the movie *The Goodbye Girl*. I have a way with metaphors.

My family helped me plan another farewell party so that I could say good-bye and thank you to all who had done so much for me. I anticipated beautiful weather for an outdoor affair, but—just as for the majority of events I've planned since then—the forecast was rain all day.

The day of the party—2 days before my departure—the *Medford Mercury*'s morning headline read, "Dave McGillivray's Dream Becomes a Reality." The article seemed to plug everyone who'd helped me, which pretty much matched the guest list. To ensure seating for the 60 to 70 people we expected, we borrowed chairs from a nearby funeral home—good thing I'm not superstitious.

It was a bittersweet evening. Among the guests from all aspects of my life—school, work, and running—were Dr. McGregor; Toni Reavis from *Runner's Digest*; Billy Rodgers (along with an *Esquire* writer following him for the week) and his wife, Ellen; Charlie Kilty from the Jimmy Fund; and Tommy Leonard from the Eliot Lounge. Several people gave me gifts and donations for the Jimmy Fund. My brother Bob and his friend George put together a slide show set to music. It was "dynamite," as I stated in my 1978 diary. ("Dynamite" is '70s talk for "the bomb"—both using explosives as positive references).

Sometime during that evening, surrounded by all the people I cared about, it hit me: I was about to leave home for the longest stretch of time in my 23-year life. The sadness was overwhelming, even though the party was great.

I didn't get to bed until nearly 3 a.m. The next day—Friday, June 9, 1978—was my last day home. I awoke and packed all morning. In the afternoon, I went for a run. I was anxious, and my mind was a roller coaster of emotions. I was ready to get started on my new routine. I wanted to know what running 40 miles a day, every day, would feel like while under the "supervision" of my companions.

Reporters called nearly every day before I left and while I was away, including the *Boston Globe*'s Joe Concannon. Paul Harber's reports in the *Medford Mercury* kept everyone at home apprised of my efforts. There were also weekly call-ins to the *Runner's Digest* radio show and updates during Red Sox games, along with spots on the *Calling All Sports* radio show and lots of other media outlets. All this ensured that the people I cared about were with me during the trials, tribulations, and personal victories of my months away.

The day I left for Seattle, my whole family (except Susan, who was still living in Rochester), gathered to see me off. Just as I was leaving the house, a reporter from the *Boston Globe* called. She had written an article about me about a month before and wanted to do a follow-up. Before I could tell her I had no time to talk, she jumped right in with the interview. My dad was already in the car, waiting to take me to the airport. I cut her short but gave her my flight number. I had a hunch she would show up at the flight gate; she got there even before I did.

The airport scene was difficult for me. Besides my family, others, including Joe Kelley, a very close friend and one of my professors at college, came to see me off. As the boarding call was announced for my United Airlines flight, I felt a surge of adrenaline: time to say good-bye. I looked into my mom's tear-stained face and tried to strike a lighthearted note, but my efforts fell flat. Two and a half months might be a long time away, but I supposed it would go by quickly—at least I hoped it would. After my companions and I boarded the plane, my dad and my girlfriend came running on to take some photos. (If anyone tried to pull that in this century, they'd probably be thrown to the ground and handcuffed within 10 seconds.) Then they left, the door to the plane was closed, and I sat there watching the terminal as we backed away.

Remaining optimistic would be a full-time job. I would give it my best, knowing that it would be a long, long way home. The preparation itself was an amazing experience that had consumed me, yet nothing could truly prepare me for what was ahead. I was about to learn that running 45 or 50 miles a day was only part of the challenge. The extreme heat and humidity, frequent swarms of bugs, bad roads, bad drivers, you name it—all waited for me.

> When I was on that plane, looking over the country that I had to run across, I was scared. I realized that now it's me, and no one else is going to stop me but myself. Everything is on my shoulders. If I make it, it's because of me, and if I don't, it's because of me.

*Dave, **New England Running**, October 1978*

It was 2 a.m. (5 a.m. Boston time) when Tom Kinder and I stood half asleep at the Seattle airport. I hoped I was just having a bad dream as I watched the luggage carousel go round and round without any sign of suitcases I could call my own. My run across the United States hadn't yet begun, and I didn't want to use up my energy worrying, even if my most critical personal belongings were seemingly lost. Empty-handed except for Tom's bag, we headed to our hotel.

Morning came too soon. We were due at the Kingdome to discuss my ceremonial start that evening, just prior to the Seattle Mariners–Boston Red Sox game. After a brief meeting with a Mariners public-relations guy, we were given a tour that began with the dugouts and ended at the 300th level—the highest seats in the place. At that time of day, it was empty, which was an awesome sight, considering that the facility was designed to hold nearly 60,000 people! In a few hours, I'd be hundreds of feet below where we stood, running around the bases as the scene was broadcast live back to Boston.

As if running from one coast of the country to another wasn't enough, Tom and I returned to the hotel and went out for one last jog. All day, I had said a few prayers to the god of luggage return. Though such a deity may not exist, my suitcases were indeed stacked at the front desk and waiting for us after our run. It was just a couple of hours before that first pitch. My grandmother Helen and some other relatives were also waiting for us. I had been gone only 1 day but was grateful for familiar faces. We all had dinner together, and then it was time.

We cabbed back to the ballpark, and Tom and I were escorted to the umpire's official press box, between the visitors and home dugouts. Seeing the dome lit up at night was a humbling experience. It was 250 feet up at its highest point. As I waited in the box, Red Sox players Jim Rice and Carlton Fisk came in with coach Don Zimmer. They were all fooling around, yelling at the umpires about bum calls the previous day. They kept my mind off of things for a moment or two.

At 7:32 p.m. on the button, the national anthem played, the hometown team was introduced, and then . . .

> The Red Sox still have a four-game lead over the NY Yankees, and we have a special event that we want to tell you about that is occurring right now on the artificial turf here at the Kingdome in Seattle. You know, of course, about the Jimmy Fund, which has been the Red Sox charity for all these many years. This evening, a 23-year-old marathon runner from Medford, Massachusetts, David McGillivray, is going to embark on quite a mission. He is going to run coast-to-coast, starting here at the Kingdome in Seattle, and, if all goes as scheduled, will end at Fenway Park on the night of Tuesday, August 29, when the Red Sox face the Seattle Mariners. We wish him the best.

> *Dick Stockton, Red Sox announcer, 1978*

As I took those first steps, I didn't listen to the rest of the announcement encouraging people to give to the Jimmy Fund. I was feeling the intense pressure I had myself under. There was also emptiness . . . perhaps a reflection of the stadium, whose occupants included a few Mariners fans and some pigeons in the rafters. I received a nice ovation from the small crowd, but I kept asking myself, "Who am I to be running around this place?" I was uncomfortable in the spotlight; I hadn't accomplished anything except flying in from Boston.

As I rounded third base, Tom was there, taking pictures. We were escorted directly up to the press booth to be interviewed during the broadcast. I needed to conserve every penny, so while there, I made a free phone call home. My dad sounded really upbeat after hearing the Red Sox announcers talk about my efforts. He videotaped the ceremony—and that entailed setting up his tripod, aiming his video camera at the television, and filming the screen: state of the art for 1978.

The goal of starting in Seattle was to gain some good exposure for the Jimmy Fund, and that mission was accomplished. All I wanted to do now was run home.

People wished me well as we made our way out of the stadium, and several asked for my autograph. I was bewildered by that for the same reason I had felt strange out on the field: I hadn't done a thing yet. I had no idea what to write, so I just signed my name as though signing a check.

Back at the hotel, Tom and I wanted to watch the coverage on the local 11 o'clock news, but as would happen so many times over the next 2½ months, we couldn't stay awake long enough. We needed the rest anyway; the next day, we would fly to Medford, Oregon, and take our first steps in the right direction.

CHAPTER 5

My Little Olympics

The human body has far greater powers of adaptability and endurance than most people give it credit for.

Bruce Tulloh, **Four Million Footsteps**

It was Sunday, June 11, 1978.

Tom and I flew from Seattle to Medford. When we arrived, Danny and Jeff were waiting for us with the motor home—our home away from home for the next 3 months. So far, so good. A member of the Oregon Sizzler's Running Club was also there to welcome us. We all drove to the Medford City Hall together.

During a small ceremony, I presented Mayor Al Densmore with a letter of greeting and a key to the city of Medford, Massachusetts, from my hometown's mayor, Eugene Grant. I received similar items from Mayor Densmore, along with a T-shirt from an annual mini-marathon that Olympian Frank Shorter had won the year before. A few local news crews were there to cover it. It wasn't a very flashy affair, but it was just what I had hoped for: nice and simple. At that point, all that stood between me and my goal was Oregon, California, Nevada, Utah, Colorado, Nebraska, Iowa, Illinois, Indiana, Ohio, Pennsylvania, New Jersey, New York, Connecticut, and Massachusetts.

At 1:10 p.m., as if I'd been holding my breath for months—years, even—I took the first step toward the east and allowed myself to *exhale*.

> He's been going constantly. Once David starts running, maybe he'll finally be able to get some rest.
>
> *Jacqueline McGillivray, Dave's mom*

Just 2 days earlier, I was quoted in the *Boston Globe* as saying that I was nervous to start on only "half a tank." The years of preparation, last-minute search for a sponsor, good-bye party into the wee hours, and jet lag rendered me fairly drained even before we began. With whatever I had left, I was ready to begin.

The mayor ran with us to the city limits, and three guys from the running club continued on for about 17 miles. Even with all my planning, I was not prepared for it to be so hilly so *immediately* between Medford and Klamath Falls, our first stop on the trip. That part of Route 66 seemed mountainous, reminding me of Mount Washington; the elevation just climbed and climbed. I couldn't believe it.

All in all, however, the first day went well. We stayed at a campsite and met a lot of interesting people, including a man who shared a portion of his daily catch of fish with us. It was the first of many food offerings we'd receive.

Personally, I wasn't very hungry. At first, I thought it was something I ate, but then I realized I hadn't eaten very much at all. It may have been the miles, or the altitude, or the massive amounts of vitamins I had ingested and would continue to take each day of the trip. Yet it wasn't the stomach pain or the surprise elevation that struck me most about that first day; it was the beauty of that part of the United States. It was my first time in Oregon, and I was astounded.

Only 79 more days to go.

The first day, he pulled off 28 miles, and we didn't start until about 1 in the afternoon. He anticipated he'd do only about 15, so we were just delighted with that. He was so eager, you couldn't hold him back. In spite of the mountains, he was cruising along doing 7-minute miles.

Tom Kinder, support crew,
Runner's Digest *radio show, June 14, 1978*

It was 2 days of an uphill climb to 5,000 feet. The irony was that I was climbing them faster than the moped was. I'd spent a lot of time training my body, but I didn't give much thought to what kind of shape the support vehicles would be in. The moped required daily maintenance and repair. After only 2 days of running, the RV's generator broke. Without it, we'd have no lights, electricity, or heat for those very cold nights in the mountains.

So Dan and Jeff drove the 70 miles *back* to Medford the next day, not only to fix the generator but also to install the air conditioner in anticipation of the desert. We had asked for that to be done before we left, but the rental place couldn't accommodate us. This meant that Tom and I would spend the day alone, without the benefit of the vehicle. We bought a sort of saddlebag big enough to hold a few pairs of shoes, a change of clothes, and some food and strapped it to the moped. We both hoped for dry weather. I hoped for no physical problems. So early in the trip, I was not looking forward to being cut loose in the elements, lest something go wrong with either me or the moped.

People ask me what the toughest part of the run was...the desert, the Rockies, the hills . . . my answer? The lack of pay phones to call home and hear a familiar, friendly voice!!

Dave

I knew the trip would be physically demanding, but in an age without cell phones and computers, the logistical communication issues were often more taxing than the running. The time differences, dearth of pay phones, and long-distance expense made this seemingly simplest of issues a real challenge that could sap valuable time and energy.

Every day, there were calls to make, and we were on a tight budget. I telephoned people only when I really needed to, but even the shortest to-call list was huge. It included the Jimmy Fund, the Red Sox, Mildred Vidgerhaus at the PR agency, and, of course, Al Spector. He was more interested in how I was doing than in the sponsorship angle of the run. People definitely came first with him. Same with the Red Sox: When I checked in, they were more concerned about my well-being than my arrival date. "Take your time," they said. The people in these two organizations really impressed me.

Communication between the RV, the moped, and me also presented a challenge. With Danny and Jeff headed back west to Medford, Oregon, while Tom and I continued east, we needed to find a central location to call and leave messages for one another. Calling my parents' house long-distance was too expensive, so we relied on the kindness of strangers. Jeff had already begun calling reporters that first night, and, luckily, a guy in Klamath Falls, the town we were running toward, wanted to do a story on us. He said we could all call his house the next day to coordinate a meeting place.

Tom and I ran through town and then stopped for ice cream between splits. The reporter caught up with us, and we talked for a while. Then we threw the moped in the back of his truck, which Tom then drove for about 10 miles as the reporter ran with me and continued the interview. I don't recall him taking notes while he ran; maybe that explains why his article stated that I was a computer programmer!

We ended that day in Newell, California, after covering 42 miles without the RV. The only pay phone—in fact, the only building—we could find for miles around was a drugstore, so we stayed put and at 3:30 p.m. called our reporter friend to give him our phone number and location. We waited until 5 p.m. to check in again and learned that Danny and Jeff were just leaving Medford; it would be another 2½ hours before they arrived.

There was nothing to do but wait. They finally showed up at 8:15. Tom and I had been waiting for nearly 5 hours. I felt badly about all that wasted time, especially within only the first 36 hours of the trip.

> What impresses me about [Dave] among all the things that he does is that at the end of the phone conversations I have with him, he says, "I'll tell you, Dr. McGregor, I'm going to make it." He has a determination. He has a mind-set that is organized and disciplined, and it's not foolish.
>
> *Rob Roy McGregor, DPM,*
> ***Runner's Digest**, June 20, 1978*

My attitude was all I had; it could make the good days better and the bad days worse. The mountains, the broken generator, the cold nights, and the little aches and pains were all a window into what I could expect as we progressed. I did my best to think of the miles I had already put behind me instead of all those yet to be run.

Interestingly, my quadriceps hurt *less* the *more* I ran. I heal better when I'm active; sitting around the motor home would make the condition only worse. My skin, however, was a different story; a few days out of the elements might have done it a world of good. My face was painfully burned and extremely sensitive to the touch. I had also pulled a muscle near my gluteus maximus as I veered out of the way of a truck that had come dangerously close to me. I was thankful for no blisters; I just had a bit of lingering stomach pain. My body needed to get used to the daily beating.

By the end of the first week, I could feel my endurance level strengthening. After just 6 days, I ran my first two *consecutive* 10-mile splits. Up until that point, I had never run that many miles back-to-back. The quad pain was quieting down, but as it healed, my right hip chimed in with its own discomfort. It was a symphony of body ailments, and it lasted from coast to coast.

The companions absorb the environment surrounding them; Dave sees none of it. His eyes are carefully scanning the terrain in front of him for his all-important next step.

Dan Carey, **Medford Daily Mercury**, July 25, 1978

The Sierra mountains were stunning, but I enjoyed the view only on the way up; on the way down, my focus was on the logging trucks barreling past me on their descent! I spent that day—in fact, the majority of the 80 days—leaping off secondary roads onto what little there was of a shoulder. It was tough on the knees. We weren't permitted to run on highways, though sometimes I'd sneak onto an interstate until the inevitable state-police cruiser escorted me off.

In Nevada, the temperatures soared. I constantly threw water over my head and on my face, arms, and chest. I ran without a shirt because I wanted to air out as much of my body as possible. By 2 p.m., the heat was almost unbearable. There was also humidity—man-made—from irrigation systems that sprayed the endless fields of corn, alfalfa, and cabbage growing next to the road. The air was so heavy that it made breathing much more labored.

Dave was strictly a junk-food kind of guy.

Kent Hawley, support crew

I'm often asked for advice on what to eat before an endurance event, and I confess that I may not be the best source of this information. In preparation for the trip, I surrounded myself with expert physicians and a great support crew, and I adapted a solid training regimen. The one thing I didn't change was what I ate—I just ate more of it.

There were no energy bars back then, but there was ERG (electrolyte replacement with glucose), which I drank in large quantities. I ate plenty of yogurt, but beyond that, the 40 to 50 miles per day were fueled by the following: fried bologna sandwiches, cookies, pudding, junk food of nearly any kind, an occasional bucket of chicken, ice cream, and pasta (legitimate sustenance).

Danny did the cooking, and when we needed groceries, whoever wasn't following me on the moped would go shopping. It took only a short time before the guys knew just what to buy. It was a standing joke that if people outside the motor home could see what I was eating, they would've been appalled.

To supplement whatever we had on board, we left no Dairy Queen or ice-cream stand unturned. After completing the miles per day, I would get in the motor home and quickly down a six-pack of Coke before I did anything else. That was the beginning of an eating-and-drinking frenzy that usually lasted an hour or two. Then we'd drive to our campsite or motel, and by the time I took a hot bath, Danny would have dinner ready. If dinner was chicken, I would easily eat 10 pieces. Milk was a big part of my diet but only at night. I'd drink it during the "late" night hours of 8 or 9 p.m., when the munchies would hit. I'd eat ice cream, cookies—whatever I could get my hands on.

One day, somewhere after the halfway mark, I woke up and discovered we were out of doughnuts, so I ate three oatmeal cookies, then between each 10-mile split, I had at least five or six Oreos. I ran 51 miles that day on cookies, ERG, and tonic. I'm not endorsing my food choices and have no plans to write a *McGillivray Diet Plan;* however, I did make it from California to Boston, running 45 miles per day, basically unscathed and with considerable weight loss.

At least I got plenty of nutrients in another form. The biggest part of the nighttime prep for the next day was my consumption of 30—three-zero!—different pills, both vitamins and anti-inflammatories. It took 3, sometimes 4 cups of water to choke them all down. It was a *chore.* By the time I reached Boston, I had consumed more than 2,400 pills. I don't remember them all, but they included kelp, brewer's yeast, zinc, calcium, and bee pollen. When I went to the bathroom after ingesting them, what came out of my body was in Technicolor.

From my perspective as a runner, the first week seemed like a lifetime. However, because there were few distractions at that high elevation—no real sign of anything other than trees—it gave the guys an opportunity to each find their niche. In addition to cooking, Danny drove the RV and, when he wasn't behind the wheel, worked toward his 1,000 pushups a day. Jeff called newspapers in the towns ahead and served as the great motivator for all of us. His quick wit and ability to keep things lighthearted provided comic relief when we needed it most. Tom alternated between running with me and riding the moped. These men were living proof of the truth in my personal mantra: "Surround yourself with good people, because it's tough to do it all alone."

As for me, the rhythm of the day went something like this: Upon waking at about 5:30 a.m., I'd stretch and apply BenGay to my quads. The RV reeked of the stuff every morning. Then I'd coat my face with Vaseline to protect it from the wind. I checked my feet for blisters and nails to be cut. Then it was time for toast or jam and a cup of tea with honey. I was out on the road by 6:30 a.m. I'd run 10 miles, rest 15 to 20 minutes, run 10 more miles, rest 15 to 25 minutes, and run another 5 to 10 miles, all before lunch, which was usually a pint of ice cream—my reward for accomplishing the morning's goals.

By noon, the sun was high in the sky, and I already had at least 25 miles done. In the heat of the day, I'd take an hour or hour-and-a-half break, maybe even nap in the RV, with about 15 more miles to go. It was a great feeling knowing that the largest portion of the day's quota of miles was done before lunch. It made the afternoons mentally and physically easier.

For the majority of the steps I took, someone either ran, biked, or rode the moped beside me. At the end of a 5- or 10-mile split, I'd go into the motor home to eat something and rest a bit, maybe take a 30-minute break. When I went back out and ran, the others would drive the RV ahead to the next 10-mile mark and wait. As I got stronger, the rest in between "splits" dwindled to 10 minutes. Around 2 p.m., I would run 5, rest a bit, run another 5, rest a bit, and then walk an extra 2 miles so I'd have something to put in the "bank."

We marked the road so we'd know where to return the following day—usually by tying a T-shirt to a tree. Sometimes it was a long drive back to our campsite or motel, so we kept track of the mileage on the odometer. The T-shirt was just insurance that we would start in the exact location, but sometimes when we returned in the morning, the shirt wasn't there. The question was, who would want a sweaty, dirty T-shirt that was tied to a tree?

Often when Tom followed me on the moped, he blasted the cassette player or radio. The music and company made the long stretches of highway more manageable. When the daily miles were done, we'd find a place to stay for the night, we'd eat dinner, and then, whenever possible, I'd take a bath, write postcards, and be in bed by 10 p.m.

One last-minute (but short-lived) change to the support crew occurred about a week into the trip, when we added one more to the roster. He didn't clean up after himself, but we couldn't say no—he was a 6-week-old puppy presented to us by a young girl at a campground. Danny volunteered to take care of him, so we welcomed "Specs"—named in honor of our sponsor. Specs was no bigger than the palm of your hand, which was great, considering there was barely enough room for the rest of us in our small container of a living space. It took only about a week (less for some) of stepping in poop or nearly squashing poor Specs to see that life on the road with four grown men in a confined area was too dangerous for the little guy. A few hundred miles later, we knew it was in our best interest—and his—to say good-bye, which we did in the same manner in which we acquired him. We gave him to a little girl at a campground near Craig, Colorado. A better quality of life awaited all of us.

> He would just get up in the morning, get his shoes on, and we'd be out the door. He'd walk for a few minutes, and then he was off and running. It astounded me that someone could do this day after day, no matter how hot it was.
>
> *Kent*

My greatest daily challenge was choosing the perfect pair of running shoes each morning. Just as a person might put together the day's outfit, I'd go to my shoe stash and try to decide what to wear, taking into account my mood and emotions. My shoes had to be just right. *They still do.*

In the course of each day, I'd wear three to four different pairs of shoes. Every time I changed, my legs felt a little more energized. Though it may not have been noticeable on a jog around the block, the differences in support were evident when I was running for 10 hours a day. Some shoes were worn in, some were new, some were Specs, and some were not (though I was always careful to wear Pro Specs during interviews). I went through about seven pairs of running shoes during the first 1,000 miles. I didn't wear them out; I simply "retired" them before they got to that point.

Starting the day on the right foot was a bonus, since something inevitably disrupted the rhythm of the miles, like the day the Jimmy Fund signs flew off the RV and we didn't notice until 14 miles later. Unexpected route changes were probably the biggest time waster. In Colorado, I came to a fork in the road with signs in both directions that said "Route 34 East," a 50/50 chance that I would choose the wrong road . . . and I did. It took me 3 miles of running and searching for signs to sort it out.

Then there was Hastings, Nebraska, where I made a wrong turn and ran another 3 miles out of the way. In Illinois, I tried to take what I thought would be a shortcut by avoiding a long on-ramp. Instead, I went straight and climbed up the side of an overpass bridge. At the top, I found only tall grass—they hadn't even built the darn road yet. So I ran back down to where I started. These extra miles might not seem like a big deal, but they certainly added up after a 45- or 50-mile day of running.

Motels were an issue—or, rather, the motel managers were. If they spotted the RV through the office window, they immediately got defensive about how many people were allowed per room. Our budget didn't allow us to get two rooms, so the guys took turns sleeping in the RV, although the managers rarely believed that we had no intention of sneaking anyone in. Some turned us away, which could mean another 20-minute or longer drive to find somewhere that was hassle-free. On at least one occasion, this scenario played out multiple times in one night, which meant we had to drive a considerable distance searching for a place that didn't turn us away! There were good people out there, too. In Iowa, we stayed at a motel that cost $10 per night. The manager donated $5 of the cost to the Jimmy Fund. We paid the other $5, which included air-conditioning and television. May as well have been the Four Seasons.

A most memorable spot was the Belly Acres Campground in Canby, Oregon. It was basically someone's front lawn. Across the street was a ranch where we could see some women riding horses and chasing cattle. We appeared to be in the middle of nowhere, yet a reporter driving by spotted the RV and stopped to do an interview, right there on the side of the road.

The RV was hard to miss. It attracted a lot of attention, and that was the whole idea. It was plastered with signs for the Jimmy Fund and Pro Specs. Even the horsewomen were coming our way—one of them recognized me from the news! She introduced herself as the cousin of Glenn Jobe, a fellow who had contacted me before I left Medford to see if he could run with us as we passed through his hometown. I couldn't get over the coincidence of her bumping into us, in the middle of nowhere, on her *horse*, and making the connection.

Glenn did meet up with us later, in the city of Alturas, California. At the time, he was training for the 1980 Olympic Biathlon, a run-shoot-run event. He joined me for 10 miles at a pretty good clip. Afterward, we drove him back to where he started and continued on our way. I later read that he went on to be ranked 14th in the world in his sport. Each encounter like that was a small miracle of distraction and enjoyment.

I reflected upon incidents such as that during my end-of-day soaks. (Being small came in handy—I was the only one who could fit into the RV's bathtub on the nights we weren't in a motel.) Soaking in a tub was not only great for my muscles but also provided quiet time to mull over the day's occurrences. I would speak into my tape recorder and make a verbal diary of virtually every mile, noting every remarkable event (and some unremarkable ones) along the way. In my early tapes, the sound of the bathwater dripping and the bathroom's echo provide unique background music for each day's musings.

Later in the trip, when I tacked on a few miles of walking to the end of each day, I would take the recorder with me. Emptying my mind of all that happened was a bit like therapy or confiding in a good friend, and it mentally prepared me for the following day. Even today, every time I run, I bring a recorder with me, though my current one is the size of a credit card. The one I used during the cross-country trek was heavy enough to actually increase my muscle strength as I carried it for 2 or 3 miles a day.

My thoughts ranged on everything from weather to RV politics. I figured that no one would ever listen to them but me, so I was very honest. Sometimes I gave my companions the recorder, and sometimes they took it without me knowing. Their perspectives were unique, humorous (mostly at my expense!), and not recommended for young audiences.

Runs inspire me, prompting my most creative thoughts for speeches or races. One day, I envisioned a way to save time and space: a wristwatch with a recording device—just hold it up, press "record," and commit thoughts to tape. I even went so far as to approach a few companies about the idea, but nothing ever came of it; though all these years later, someone else has made my idea a reality.

There's a Chinese proverb that says, "The palest ink is better than the best memory." I documented the run in more than just the tapes. Each day, I sent postcards to the Boston YWCA, which served as the mail stop for some running buddies of mine. We used to run along the Charles River, then shower and change at the YWCA (yes, there was a men's shower and locker room there). The cards were prestamped with places to note the date, day number, day's mileage, and location. I just had to fill in the details and write a paragraph or two about people, places, and so on—details I'd never remember weeks or even months after it was all over.

Memories fade, no matter how powerful the experience; you can't get back to that exact moment in time. So I documented it, partially because one day I'd hoped to assemble my experience into a book, but mainly because the run was a project of personal magnitude that would change my life forever. I didn't want it to fade away.

Meanwhile, my dad spent 80 days clipping news articles, which I keep in multiple three-ring binders. Sometimes reporters did great stories that really helped get the word out about the Jimmy Fund. Other times they didn't show up, be it for a press conference or a scheduled interview.

Even more often, they simply got it all wrong. Jeff called one particular radio station in Colorado and described every last detail of our run. Here's what aired later: Both Jeff and I were running across the country; our sponsor was Avon (headquartered in New York), as opposed to our actual sponsor, Specs (located in Avon, Massachusetts); and I had a total of 3,200 miles left to run, having already completed 12,000 miles—placing me somewhere in the middle of the Indian Ocean!

It's hard to fathom that one could be lonely on a trip with three other entertaining guys plus a slew of media attention and well-wishers along the way. But in the desert, there was nothing—for miles. The flat terrain was easy on my legs but tough on my psyche. As the weather got hotter, we decided to break up my running into two shifts, one in the morning and one in the evening, to avoid the unforgiving heat. The morning shift began at 4 a.m. in the darkness, and the evening shift began after the midday sun moved closer to the horizon. Mentally, running so early was much harder, despite the excellent weather. There was nothing to focus on but my breathing and my thoughts. Most days, I was on the road for about 12 hours, and then the guys would pick me up in the RV and drive me to the campsite or motel. I did nothing but run. After a while, the monotony got me down.

The desert is so quiet, I swear I could hear a car coming 5 miles away. There were no surprises out there—or so I thought, until we pulled over at a rest area near Reno. There we found Mark Renault, a fraternity brother who was in the process of moving to California. He knew our approximate whereabouts and drove out to find us.

Mark stayed with us at a nearby campsite, where we met some people originally from Manchester, New Hampshire. Their son was so excited about meeting us and hearing what we were doing that his enthusiasm renewed my own. To say thanks, I gave him a pair of Specs (we'd been outfitted with plenty of pairs in lots of sizes), which he asked me to sign. I remember watching the sunset over the mountains that night. We were at a place called Honey Lake . . . a beautiful, beautiful site.

> You'd wind him up in the morning, push him out the door, and he was good for it. The thing that amazed me about David: He never complained . . . ever.
>
> *Kent*

Sometimes I would question what I was doing: Why run 40-plus miles per day? Then I'd get letters from children who were donating their pennies, nickels, and dimes to the Jimmy Fund, like an entire fifth-grade class at the Gleason School, near my hometown, who sent me a letter and donation early on. Lots of kids, including my little nephew Michael, had hung a map on a wall to track my progress. It made me happy to think of him at home following along.

In sharp contrast to my loneliness on the road, the people back home were banding together, and my parents' house was always busy with phone calls and visits. In an effort to be efficient—and have some fun—my dad hooked the telephone up to stereo speakers and invited a small crowd of close friends to talk with me during a scheduled phone call, listen to cassettes of my radio interviews, and see some slides. My mom told me it was the first time she had made chocolate-chip cookies since I left. She called it David McGillivray Night at Belle Avenue.

The Medford support constantly grew stronger. In early July, the chamber of commerce sponsored the Dave McGillivray One Dollar Per Mile Jimmy Fund Drive, to raise $1 for every mile I ran. They printed flyers and put them up all over town. Medford businesses and individuals all donated. The VFW Post gave $500, and an anonymous $25 donation was made in honor of seven-time Boston Marathon Champion Clarence DeMar, who worked as a printer in Medford. The St. Francis parish, where my parents belonged, also had a collection in my honor.

In addition to running numerous articles, the *Medford Daily Mercury* included a small box in the sports section, in which Paul Harber reported my location, the weather along the route, how many miles I'd run, and how many were left to go. He even let people know my next mail stop and encouraged them to write. The city was doing so much for me; I sincerely hoped that I could bring it on home.

> Considering McGillivray's present pace, extended rations of running probably won't be required [as he gets closer to home], although there's no doubt that he would be up to the challenge. Luckily for friends and relatives of McGillivray, the Atlantic Ocean prevents him from running past his destination.
>
> *The* **Yuma Pioneer,** *Yuma, Colorado, July 20, 1978*

I never considered the run a race, so my pace didn't matter. The trick was to figure out ways to make time go faster. We focused on items strewn on the side of the road to keep things interesting. There were so many coins. I didn't always take the time to stop and pick up the scattered change, but I did sweep up some as I ran by. Though it may not have been "significant" in terms of amount (maybe $50 to $75 total), it was a significant effort to stop midstride every time I saw a coin. But every little bit would help the Jimmy Fund, so why not?

We also found tools: wrenches, screwdrivers, all manner of things. Kent created his own toolbox with the collection. There were lots of eight-track tapes and cassettes, too. Seemed like people got fed up with them and simply tossed them out the window.

The guys and I played our own version of the license-plate

game: We didn't just spot the plates; we actually *found* them. For some reason, license plates were also major roadside artifacts. We collected one from nearly every state. Funny; I've been driving for a long time and have never had one fall off . . .

Then there was roadkill. You name it and we nearly stepped on it. From the biggest creatures to the smallest, we saw and smelled animals in nearly all stages of death, including denial. I was shocked by the number of carcasses on the road. Rattlesnakes both dead and alive were prevalent, especially in Colorado. Then there were the "dog" days of Pennsylvania. I've never seen so many stray animals in my life.

Roadkill comes in many forms. A day before we arrived at a mountaintop motel, a truck took a hairpin turn a little too quickly, which meant death for the 500 boxes' worth of cantaloupes that ended up strewn all over the road. At check-in, we were given a big stash of the fruit, which on our food budget was much appreciated.

> For the next 8 days, the Medford, Massachusetts, native will rise at 4 o'clock in the morning darkness and run east. He will face the dangers of skyrocketing temperatures, iconoclastic rattlesnakes, the Great Salt Lake Desert, and earthquake fault areas.

Medford Daily Mercury, June 20, 1978

As I went through Frenchman, Eureka, Keystone, and Ely, Nevada, rattlesnakes were an issue, but nosebleeds were the surprising problem. I'd never had trouble with them before. Perhaps it was the elevation of the Pancake Mountains, a misleading name for an elevation of 6,517 feet.

Somewhere past Frenchman, we completed the miles for the day and were looking for a place to park for the night. We pulled off to the side of the road, but when we looked out the back window, we noticed that Jeff was no longer behind us on the moped. Somehow he took a wrong turn and was lost for nearly an hour.

That same night, we encountered an even more serious situation. A car pulled down the same road and parked a short distance ahead of us. The driver started beating on the girl in the front seat next to him, then left her behind and staggered out of the car and up a hill. We ran over to see if she was all right. In spite of her bruises, which were many, she didn't want any part of us.

Quickly, we drove all the way back to the tiny town of Frenchman to a gas station, where we knew there was a pay phone, to call the police. If she wouldn't let us help her, maybe they could. The gas station was closed, and the phone was inside. With no other business or town in sight, we had no choice but to go back and check things out again ourselves. By the time we returned, both the guy and the girl were standing outside the car, talking. Who knows exactly what transpired, but it was a mental souvenir I'd rather not have collected.

The bad and the good of Nevada continued as we ended a 42-mile day at an old mining town situated way up in the mountains. We were on the old Pony Express route at the Pony Canyon Motel. Bill Emmerton, who was running from Missouri to California by way of that road, had stayed at the same place just days before us. The manager gave us a reduced rate and invited the other guys to crowd into my room if they desired— kindness we didn't find too often at lower elevations. We stayed there the next night, too, and after a run of 42 miles up to an elevation of 7,500 feet, I was enormously grateful for the "upgrade" we received to the room with the bathtub.

Just outside Eureka, Nevada, I told the guys I'd meet them in an hour about 8 or 9 miles down the road. The terrain continued to be one way—uphill—and I could feel something go in my left knee. At first, I thought it was temporary, but the pain got worse and worse. Eventually, the RV caught up to me, and I learned that the throttle had broken on the moped and needed to be fixed. We were literally in the middle of nowhere. So we drove back to Eureka for repairs. At least the ailing moped was cured; I was not so sure what might help my knee.

The morning run was interrupted by an NBC reporter who

pulled over after seeing the RV plastered with signs. He stopped for a 10-minute interview, then wished me luck and went on his way. (Probably my worst interview; my knee was really hurting.) Later in the day, somewhere between Eureka and Ely, at my 40-mile point, a guy drove by and asked me if I wanted someone to run with. I thought he was kidding, but before I could respond, he jumped out of the car and was in stride right beside me. His wife drove behind us while he ran the day's last 2 miles with me. Turned out his interest was also piqued by the decorated RV. Similar scenarios played out many more times during my cross-country run.

My knee pain worsened the next day. We awoke at the usual time, and I went out and ran 10 with Tom. We planned to do another 7 or 8, but by the 5-mile mark, I simply could not continue. The pain was excruciating. It felt like a warning—that I might face permanent damage if I kept on going.

The guys picked me up, and we drove 30 miles to the hospital in Ely. It was 9:30 a.m., and we were told we'd have to wait until 2 p.m. to see a doctor. I called Dr. McGregor, hoping for some quicker answers. He suggested I take a muscle relaxant he had sent with me and advised me to stay and see the doctor, who could better analyze the situation. I was to call him back if the ER doctor suggested any powerful drugs. During all those hours waiting at the hospital, no one vocalized the thought we all obviously shared: that I might not make it to Fenway in time or, worse yet, make it at all.

> No one would have crossed the ocean if he could have gotten off the ship in the storm.
>
> *Charles Kettering, inventor*

The doctor who "treated" me basically told me that the body wasn't meant to run on this type of terrain, and I needed a few weeks of rest. Well, I knew by listening to my own body that rest was just the *opposite* of what I needed. After all, my quad pain had improved the more I ran. I could not conceive that the best therapy for my knee was to do nothing, so I asked the guys to bring me back to where we'd left off.

When we arrived at the T-shirt, they threw me out of the motor home, and I started to run. As expected, the pain returned, but I knew I was strong. The key was to take a mental step back and pinpoint the cause of the problem. If I could figure it out, I could run.

I thought, "Well, I'll just try something different." Running the usual way was not doing me any good. Up until that point, I had been running against traffic, on the left side of the road. So I switched sides and ran with traffic. I did another quick 10 without discomfort, but the pain returned after another 5. Still, I ended up with 32 miles that day . . . a tough 32.

Throughout the night, I took the pills and iced the injury. I was a bit stiff in the morning, like always, but didn't really feel too badly. I ran 10 without trouble, but as I neared 12 miles, the pain slowed me to a walk. That alone was like arsenic for my ego. We ended around 37 miles west of the Utah border and stayed at a town called Major's Place, which consisted of a bar, a couple of gas pumps, and, most important, a pay phone. I checked in with Dr. McGregor, who advised me to continue icing and taking pills—but never weighed in on whether or not I should stop running. That wasn't his role. I also called my folks; my mom was uncharacteristically quiet. I had also spoken to her the day before from the hospital, and I could tell she was worried about me.

> When I saw David go out on the road and run, I knew one of two things: Either he would finish his run to Medford or he would have to be taken home on a stretcher. That's the only way they could stop him.
>
> *Dan*

The days prior had basically consisted of mountains and valleys. Climbing and descending over and over again wreaked havoc on my back, shoulders, arms . . . everything. I applied cold packs and took muscle relaxants. The knee pain must have been a result of the severe crown of the road, coupled with the extreme number of miles, because after a few days, the pain subsided. Eventually, the other knee started to go, so I switched sides again. For the rest of the trip (and ever since), I alternated the sides of the road; so *far*, so good. I could have folded it all up and gone home, but instead, I took a chance and gained some new insight into my own body.

We went for 2 days without seeing any towns. After 9 days and 360 miles, we were out of Nevada—and boy, was I glad to wave good-bye. My ailments were all but gone. I remember being thrilled about our first full day in Utah, not so much because we were in Utah, but because we were finally *out of* Nevada! We had also crossed a time zone, which put us 1 hour closer to home.

With 90 miles between cities, we knew we'd be spending the night in the desert. My knee still bothered me a bit, but Tom ran with me through the flatlands. The heat was intense, but the beautiful scenery took my mind off the negatives. In fact, as my knee healed, the difficult part was holding back on the miles.

The guys and I talked about milestones along the way—things we could tick off our list, such as when we hit the 1,000-mile mark; reached the halfway point; and entered Colorado, our fifth and longest state. These represented small victories; they were my mental reward for getting it done. The minute we hit an anticipated mile or crossed a state border, that single achievement provided immediate gratification.

The nights were difficult, especially if I had an injury, however slight. I was in a constant state of worry that a small injury would blossom into a much larger one. For instance, my knees bothered me again in Utah. I iced them both and just hoped that the next day they'd be okay. Another time, I stubbed my toe on the stairwell of the RV and worried that it would swell up and present a problem the next day. The littlest thing could potentially slow me down or stop the whole run.

By Utah, I started to get a little down. The running was getting tougher, and I was homesick. Provo was to be our first mail stop. Getting a letter was just as valuable as going to a pay phone; both provided a means of connecting with others.

I received letters and cards from local schoolchildren from Medford. Both friends and strangers mailed donations. Dr. McGregor sent running shoes, tape for my feet, and pills for my various pains and ailments. The mail-stop logistics became very important, down to the exact day and location of where we would be passing through a particular city, not only because I looked forward to those stops so much but because the dates and locations were also printed in the local paper.

Of the 15 letters waiting for me in Provo, a particularly special one came from a little boy named Robbie McGillivray. Robbie wrote because he had read about me, "the Runner," in a newspaper. He himself had walked 20 miles for the March of Dimes and described how his feet had hurt him. He was concerned that my feet "must hurt an awful lot too." He ended by telling me how proud he was to share the same last name. A letter like that was fuel for my soul.

That day, I also received my mom's daily diary, with tidbits of what was happening back home. It was as much about keeping her mind occupied while I was away as it was about keeping me connected to home. Some sample passages:

> Saturday, June 17, 1978: I was so relieved that you called Denise this morning. I know it's hard for you to call, but you said you'd call Friday night, and I couldn't understand why you didn't.
>
> Tuesday, June 20, 1978: I went to church and prayed for you. Everyone I meet is praying for you. People you don't even know. All the hospital was talking to me about you. I'm so proud to be your mother. Of course, I always was.
>
> Tuesday, June 27, 1978: Today was the sixth anniversary of Grandpa's death. I know he would have just loved all the excitement your run is causing. Maybe he would have gone with you. I'm praying for you every day, David. I know you will make it with his help.
>
> Friday, July 7, 1978: I went down and got my hair done,

and I'm quite the celebrity now because I'm "David's Mother," the mother of the kid who's running across the USA! Also went to the library, and the woman at the desk asked me if I was "the runner's" mother.

When we were in Delta, Utah, a knock on the motel-room door woke me up from a deep sleep. "Special Delivery—mail is here." *More* mail?! No, a male: Kent Hawley. He had flown out west a few days early to visit family. It was almost dark when he spotted the motor home after pedaling the 400 to 500 miles to catch up to us. It was our 20th day; we were officially a quarter of the way home, and it was good to have him aboard. He got right into a routine and usually ran 20 of the day's miles with me.

Citius, Altius, Fortius (faster, higher, stronger)

Olympic motto

Other than my knees taking turns being stiff, by the time we hit Utah, I felt like I was gaining strength. In fact, it was hard to refrain from running more than 50 miles when I felt good, but the guys held me back and told me to wait until *after* the Rockies, and I suppose they were right. On the Fourth of July, I ran 45 miles, my longest distance since the start. Along the way, several people stopped to ask if I needed a ride. I was even offered a saddle horse by a farmer passing by in his horse and buggy.

Finally, on July 5, we hit the 1,000-mile mark, a *big* goal for me. Making it that far and being healthy proved to me that I had planned correctly and would show everyone at home that this wasn't a fluke. I didn't want to make an event of it. I just wanted to hit the mark and move on.

I stood by a pay phone with the usual list of contacts in my hand. WEEI Radio and others were waiting to hear from me on that particular day, but it didn't seem right to call anyone before I shared the news with my parents. Plus, I had been particularly homesick the night before. Independence Day is a big deal back home, and my thoughts were turned to the Esplanade, that piece of real estate along the Charles River where the Boston Pops Orchestra plays every July Fourth, followed by an incredible fireworks display. Since I couldn't share that celebration with my family, I decided to surprise my dad with a phone call to his office.

Throughout the trip, it was he who was most on my mind. I would think about him and get choked up. Perhaps it was because of the letters he wrote to me. I had never before received a letter from my dad because I'd never really spent time away. I wanted to succeed for him.

> There are probably quite a few people who are in as good a shape as Dave is, but there are very few who have the mental discipline that he has.
>
> *Jeff Donahue, support crew member*

My companions watched out for me as best they could. You really need people who are very, very interested in keeping you on your feet and about *your* well-being, as opposed to being concerned about how much fun they're having. It was a demanding situation and difficult at times, but they all knew what they were getting into and accepted that before we left. Even after 4 weeks of the routine, it was hard to adjust to the running, the distinct personalities, and the living conditions. But they all came through for me—and for each other.

We were just shy of the 1,200-mile mark in Mable, Colorado, just a few days before reaching the Rockies. As we approached them, we were 41 miles ahead of schedule, and my body had acclimated to the stresses I was putting it under. Gradually and for no evident reason, the ongoing pain in my hip and kneecap went away. I had great respect for the climbs we were about to make, but I was also interested in what it would be like to be in the thick of them, in the moment. I was about to find out. The next day was Dinosaur, Colorado.

Mentally and logistically, there was an enormous lift to my

spirits as we reached the Continental Divide, 7,988 miles above sea level. We hit it two more times because of the way the road wound along, but that first "hit" was such a comfort. The second was at Poodle Lake; it was so beautiful, with snow up there in July. Just knowing that all the rivers from now on would flow to the Atlantic Ocean and not the Pacific reminded us that we were getting closer to home—not to mention that the water in the toilet was finally flowing the way it should.

> With calf muscles tightening, he rounds the horseshoe curves, barely keeping from the edge of the 2,000-foot drop.
>
> *Dan, Medford Daily Mercury, July 25, 1978*

Rabbit Ears Peak was probably the second-toughest climb of the Rockies. (The most challenging was Estes Park, only a few days away.) It was a 7-mile climb up to 9,400 feet without a break—no plateau or anything. I did 41 miles, and I was very happy with that day. I had expected to lose ground in the Rockies and make it up later in the prairies. But with our 40-mile-a-day pace maintained, we'd be home before we knew it.

When asked to describe Colorado, Teddy Roosevelt said, "The scenery bankrupts the English language." We couldn't have said it any better. We spent the day at the top of the mountains, taking photos to send back home. Danny and I wore our Mystic Health Club shirts, then I changed into an Eliot Lounge shirt. Then we used the tripod for a lot of different shots (including *Rocky* poses) with the snowcapped mountains in the background. Everyone took pictures of everyone else. A lot of travelers at the top asked to take a picture with me because they saw the RV and wondered who "the runner" was. That was the first time since we'd started that I didn't feel the mental burden of how many miles I had to go to get home; I didn't even think about home. I almost felt as if I was a regular tourist. After finishing my miles for the day and enjoying the view, we all hopped into the RV for the truly frightening part—the ride down.

As we went east, I grew stronger, but the vehicle's health became more questionable. Knowing that the brakes were due to be retired, I was on edge. I kept my eyes closed the entire way. What if I made it all this way, and then something happened to the RV? Or, worse, something happened to us in it?

In Kremmling, Colorado (population: 1,578), we found an auto-parts store. After several phone calls, they found brake parts in Denver and said they could have the RV fixed the next morning. The guys went grocery shopping while the mechanic started to work. I really wanted to run 40 that day and had only 37.4 complete, so Kent drove me out on the moped. I ran back to our motel but wanted to do more, so I continued 4 miles more outside of the city, then rode back on the back of the moped with Kent—a rare treat.

The next day, Kent and I got up early and hopped on the moped again, and he drove me back out to where I had left off. The others stayed in the motel room, caught some extra sleep, and went for breakfast, as they had to wait for the brakes to be fixed. We thought it would be finished around 10:30 a.m., so I ran the first 10. We obviously didn't have the RV to rest in, so Kent and I walked a bit, and then I decided to stop and lie down on the side of the road, in the breakdown lane.

All of a sudden, a Volkswagen came to a screeching halt. A guy jumped out of his car, stethoscope in hand, thinking that I was either dead or had suffered a heart attack. Kent immediately calmed him down and told him I was just grabbing some rest during my run across the country. We had a good chuckle about it afterward, but it was nice to know that there were still people out there who cared and didn't just drive by folks apparently in trouble, not wanting to get involved.

Jeff and Danny caught up with us in Granby, Colorado. The RV had new $370 brakes, but I didn't care how much they cost, as long as they worked! It turned out the brakes were not the only things that needed fixing, however. The following morning, we all sat in Craig, Colorado, at a Kampground of America, as Danny tried several times to start the engine. It wouldn't budge, so we finally opened up the hood. I checked the distributor cap to see if it was moist, and then we took the air filter off and checked the choke. Bingo. Once the choke was opened, the engine started right up. But I got off to a late, 7:30 a.m., start and spent the rest of the day playing catch-up. We finally made up for the lost time and found ourselves with a flat tire on the moped. That was easily fixed, thank goodness, and the people in the Steamboat Springs bike shop who worked on it were kind enough to charge us only $1—they contributed their labor to the Jimmy Fund.

A few days later, at a campsite farther on in the great state of Colorado, we once again could not start the van. This time it was the battery. The night before, we had stayed at a campsite without an AC outlet, and as a result of keeping on the lights and everything else for most of the night, we had drained our power. It took us a while to figure out a solution, since we were in the middle of nowhere. Eventually, we jumped the dead battery with the RV's auxiliary battery. (Later, in Pennsylvania, the fuel pump broke.) That morning was my latest start of the trip. I didn't take my first step until about 8:15 a.m. It was all a set-back, but we were lucky nothing more serious or expensive needed to be done.

> I think that the mental approach that Dave has is what is going to get him through, because he believes so strongly that he can do it. There is a woman named Diana Nyad who has been getting a lot of media lately because she is going to swim 103 miles from Cuba to Florida, and she's been doing things like running 12 miles every day in 74 minutes, plus swimming for 7 hours a day after that, ingesting about 5,000 calories per day, and swimming 24-hour swims. I think what we're finding out is that if we have no preconceived mental ideas that we can or can't do something, then perhaps we have not even come close to what our limits are.

> *Toni Reavis, **Runner's Digest** host, June 20, 1978*

At one point, we explained our trek to an older couple, and the woman asked me if I was going to run up to Estes Park. When I told her yes, she kindly informed me that if I tried to run up to Estes Park, I wouldn't make it alive. That was the kind of attitude I was up against. A lot of people told us that the Midwest would be 110 degrees, and I'd be crazy to try to make it through. They told me that the desert and the Rockies were going to be the toughest thing I'd face in my life. Yet there we were, with just 1 full day remaining in the mountains, and I was okay. It just confirmed to me the importance of taking a wait-and-see approach to each challenge.

At a tollbooth 2 or 3 miles past Grand Lake Resort Area, I spoke with a very kind ranger who explained what was ahead: a climb the equivalent of two Mount Washingtons. As we spoke, he noticed my Etonic shoes. We talked a bit about Dr. McGregor and how he had designed the shoe, and he took my name and address, saying he would give me a ring if he ever decided to run the Boston Marathon. That friendly exchange was typical of my encounters along the way, although Tom McGrath had described experiencing the exact opposite just a year before. Maybe my crew and I were just lucky, or maybe, as we put more miles behind us, we would meet more of the kind of people Tom had.

Even in the Rockies, we maintained more than 40 miles per day. All along, I had built up a reserve because I assumed the Rockies would slow us down, but that never happened, even at Trail Ridge Pass. With an 8 percent incline, it's the longest continuous ascending road in the United States, beginning at 8,000 feet and rising close to 13,000 feet, all within 8 or 9 miles. No plateau to catch your breath and no stops. I'm not sure what was more painful: running that seemingly endless climb, or the muscial "accompaniment" as my companions loudly sang along with a tape of John Denver's "Rocky Mountain High."

Physically, going *up* the mountain range was almost easier than going down (just like Heartbreak Hill). I was in good shape, my lungs fully adjusted to the altitude. My only problem at that point was a strain on my left upper quad. Running downhill gave my upper quads a real beating, especially my left one, plus I had strained a calf muscle on the same leg. I was afraid of damage to my knees and ankles as I pounded down the mountain, so I took it slow, lest bad tactics at that point should prove catastrophic for the entire run.

During the first 24 days on the road, it rained only once. That all changed very quickly in Colorado. In that part of the country, meteorologists use the word *severe* when describing rain and lightning storms, and they mean it! While climbing one of the most mountainous regions in the area, Jeff and I were out in the rain, and then the thunder and lightning started. There was no need for us to count one-Mississippi, two-Mississippi; the lightning and thunder seemed to occur together, at once rattling our bones and our nerves.

Weather aside, the road itself was scary. There was no shoulder. I had to keep jumping off to the side for fear of getting hit by a truck driver who couldn't see me through the driving rain. It was one of the few and most vivid memories I have of being genuinely frightened for my life. I wanted to hang up the whole endeavor a few times because of the danger involved, but I knew once we got through the Rockies, things just had to get better.

The climb in Estes Park was all uphill, though "up mountain" might be a more appropriate term. Had the route through the park been closed (due to snow), it would've taken us 100 miles out of our way to go around it. It was a very, very tough run, but right on the other side of it was Greeley, where there would be mail waiting for us—a great reward for finishing one of our toughest climbs. Greeley was also significant because Tom was going to leave us soon after we arrived there. Though I was very disappointed to see him go, his departure brought change to the daily grind—phase two of the run.

Recalling the older woman who told me that if I ran up those mountains, I would die, I checked my pulse and, much to my happiness, found I was fully alive. People thought I wouldn't even make it 1,000 miles, and there I was, with some of the most difficult parts of the run behind me and very close to the 1,400-mile mark. That's the way my whole life has been.

The nearly 2 weeks in Colorado were difficult, but as we continued on to Nebraska, we were nearly to the halfway point. I knew things would seem a little easier. The closer we got to our final destination, the more excited I hoped everyone would get. I was homesick and couldn't wait to finally run into Medford Square, and I counted on the enthusiasm of my three companions to carry me along.

Running for 80 days was tremendously taxing on my hamstrings; sometimes they got so tight, I couldn't touch my toes. Even more challenging was the continued sense of loneliness that I experienced at different degrees during various parts of the trip. I went 150 miles through the Great Salt Lake Desert without seeing a town.

Emotional boosts came from even the smallest things, like the night Danny and I listened to a Red Sox–Royals game, broadcast from Kansas City. Even though the Red Sox lost, it gave me incentive to keep running toward Fenway. I even felt rejuvenated after Kent gave me a haircut in between splits. Another day, I learned that Massachusetts governor Michael Dukakis had heard about my run and wished me well. That was very cool. I never knew where it would come from, but I found something to make me smile just about every day.

"Grasshoppers Greet Marathon Runner"

Sidney (Nebraska) **Telegraph** *headline, July 26, 1978*

From eastern Colorado to western Nebraska, I received a warm welcome from most residents—all except the little green ones. There were millions of grasshoppers. *Millions.* I encountered 5 straight days of grasshoppers. With every step, they were all over me. It was phenomenal in a horror-movie type of way. They would jump at my face, legs, and chest, and then fall off. One even jumped into a water bottle as Jeff handed it to me from the moped. Every step of Nebraska was a crunchy one, almost like running on Rice Krispies. The only blessing was that grasshoppers don't bite. I felt bad about stomping the little guys—I really did—but I didn't have much choice. If one landed underfoot, there would be one less. Finally, the rain came and lasted for nearly a week. After that, the grasshoppers didn't seem as prevalent, and I got a little break. So did they.

> Make sure you bring a fly swatter with you, because after running 50 or 60 miles a day or something, you're in no mood to put up with them.
>
> *Tom McGrath*

I wish I had a penny to donate to the Jimmy Fund for every fly that inhabited the motor home, expecting a free ride across the country—but not if we could help it. Swatting at flies became a sport. We each had our own special technique. Dan Carey became "Fly Man"—he was really out to get them. They drove us nuts.

We were 1 day away from Cambridge, Nebraska, the halfway point of my trip—time to celebrate. But as we looked at the map, we realized that the trip was not 3,180 miles, as I had estimated; it was more like 3,400 miles. Misidentified and closed roads, wrong turns, and other unforeseeable circumstances brought the mileage up to about 200 more than we had planned. We also encountered several places that I had to run "around" instead of "through."

The realization of those extra miles was disenchanting at best. I just wanted the most direct route possible. I had no ambitions of breaking any mileage records. The only thing I had committed to was running from Medford to Medford— 3,200 miles. At first, I was really angry. I felt as though I should stop running after 3,200 miles, then get in the RV and drive the rest of the way. I didn't owe anyone those extra miles.

When reality set in, we all understood that it was going to be 3,450 miles—an extra 200 that equated to 4 or 5 more days of running! I decided I needed to increase my daily mileage and developed a new routine: Every day after I finished my 40-some miles, I would get a can of tonic and walk along with one of the guys, putting 2 or 3 more miles behind me. That also allowed me to talk with each of the guys one-on-one and address any personal concerns.

Over the course of 80 days, the extra miles could make or break whether or not I got home in time. If I was only a few days behind schedule, I'd be thankful for having tacked on those miles. I got so carried away that I found myself ahead of schedule, which was just fine; it would be easier to cut back than to add miles at the end of the trip.

It was at that juncture that Macadoo "Magellan" McGillivray figured out how to save us 40 to 50 miles of running. My dad cut New Jersey, New York City, Connecticut, and Rhode Island from my plan and instead sent us through the hills of Pennsylvania to ensure that I made it to Medford on August 29. He took down one of the many posters plastered all over the city of Medford that stated I was running 3,200 miles across the country. He changed the mileage, made copies, and redistributed them wherever he could: truth in advertising.

Also at the halfway mark, my dad drew me a celebratory picture of the United States, featuring a stick figure holding an American flag and running through Nebraska. It said, "I hope you're not as skinny as this guy!" Underneath the map, it said, "This is the *left half.*" An arrow on the other side said, "But this half is *left.*"

> We were out on the road at about 4:50 this morning, and it was pitch black. All you could see on all sides of you was a foggy mist. You could hear cows in the distance. The dark clouds just kept coming our way. Then they passed over us. It was kind of an eerie moment. The wind kicked up, kind of the quiet before the storm. And as we wound toward Beckelman, the rain started coming down and lightning was flashing all over. Thunder was rumbling. The rain continued and got worse as we got closer, and as we passed through it and out into the open plain, it really began to pour.
>
> *Jeff*

Today I think sleep is overrated. However, back on the trip, nothing had a greater impact on the outcome of a day than a good night's sleep—or lack of it. In the Midwest, especially Nebraska, the storms were spectacular, and the thunder was bone rattling. In a McCook motel—the equivalent of the "No-Tell" Motel back home—the sounds from a couple in the room next door rivaled any of the storms. Without an air conditioner to turn on to escape both the noise and the summer heat, I tossed and turned all night. I was not about to say anything to the manager—I was in a strange town with strange people, not a situation in which to make waves. Kent and I both woke at 4 a.m. but were so drained from lack of sleep that we decided to take a 30-minute nap in the quiet of the motor home before beginning our miles for the day.

By our 30th day on the road, I think the guys were getting a little loopy. We were out on the road and saw a lot of cattle behind a barbed-wire fence. One of my companions climbed the fence and another followed. I yelled at them not to go any farther, warning them that the cattle would come after them. But it fell on deaf ears; one of the guys began mooing. This, of course, started a stampede directly at the two of them. They got out of there just in time, much to my amusement.

Lincoln, Nebraska, with 100,000 people, was the biggest city and first state capital we ran through. In a wonderful welcome, Mayor Helen Boosalis presented me with a key to the city, and we held a press conference covered by United Press International (UPI).

The reporter was using the latest technology: An optical scanner moved across the photo, picking up tones that it sent over the telephone line. The tones were then converted to impulses, which were picked up at the other end. The words came over just as though they were being typewritten right there, only they appeared on a video display (a monitor!). Finally, the story was printed out on a Teletype machine at about 100 words per minute. (I asked the reporter if he would shove *me* in the telephone line so I could get home faster.) It was incredible. Nearly 30 years later, we call it a fax.

If impatience is considered a fault, then it is his only one.
For the Runner has battled nature every day for 6 weeks
and he, so far, is the victor.

Dan

Just outside Lincoln, my most harrowing episode occurred.
During our first 10 miles, Kent and I came up to a railroad
crossing. An endless line of train cars crawled by very *s-l-o-w-
l-y*, and I just could not wait for the 10 or more minutes it would
take them to pass, so I hopped onto the coal car and climbed to
the other side, getting all sooty. Suddenly the train gained speed,
going south, when I was supposed to be running *east*! I had to
decide whether to stay on board, only to lose mileage and time,
or risk injury by jumping. I crawled through two cars and
jumped off—I felt like Jesse James. I rolled right into a gully.

People in their cars were stunned, to say the least, to see this
half-naked guy in shorts going through the trains. Kent was
smart enough not to follow me. So even after risking my life, I
still had to wait for him until the train went by. The next time I
saw a slow-moving train . . . I decided to wait.

By the 39th day, we were in Arapaho, Nebraska. The next
day was our revised halfway mark—only 40 more days to go.
We'd tallied 1,692 miles at that point, so we figured that our
total was somewhere in the vicinity of 3,400. We were once
again on target for our August 29 return.

For the first 40 days, I had run without too much incident. I
was surprised by how good I felt. As we entered Iowa, I got
inexplicably tired. In fact, at one point I simply couldn't take
another step and had the RV pull over so I could rest. It was the
first day Kent didn't run with me; perhaps that was part of the
problem. I ran another 13, and then the rain came. Despite my
fatigue and the weather, I managed another 9, until the moped
Kent was riding on got a flat tire.

The guys took the moped on board the RV, and I told them to
meet me up ahead in Funk, Nebraska; very fitting. I thought
that perhaps getting up at 4 a.m. was too early. There was no

reason to run 50 miles per day. I was so tired that I sometimes ran with my eyes closed and talked less with whoever was accompanying me. I also began having problems with my middle metatarsal under my right foot; perhaps an overuse injury. It felt as if I was running with a wad of tissue under my sock.

Just 1 day before, I had run 52 miles; perhaps that's what fatigued me. (A "lightbulb" statement, yet after running so many miles each day, 52 didn't seem to be too bad.) My hamstrings were tight, and it felt as though I had a strain in my arch area from overuse. I decided to focus my attention on my arches. (Things sort of broke down one after another, but at least they didn't all break down at the same time.) When I called Dr. McGregor about my foot problem, I learned that he was going to Paris for 3 weeks and would not be back until just 3 days before my return home. Knowing I wouldn't have his services anymore lowered my spirits even further.

The first day in Iowa was boiling hot, with lows in the 90s, even as the sun was going down. It was sunny and difficult to run. The rolling terrain was a challenge; though it didn't seem overly taxing to the eye, it was never flat and after a while would take its toll if I wasn't careful. My hip bothered me, too, though not as much when I was running as when I sat down afterward.

In the midst of all my discomfort, some guy stopped his car and handed me a pair of socks. He had seen me on TV, and since he worked for a sock store, he sought me out, thinking—and rightfully so—that I could use an extra pair. At day's end, I ran a bit with Danny, and we met some folks who lived on a nearby farm and invited us back to their house for supper and to stay the night.

The Petersons' home was in Red Oak, Iowa. We met their two kids, a boy and a girl, and their animals—and I mean lots of them. There must have been 20 kittens, some goats, a horse, dogs; you name it, they had it. They cooked us steak, potatoes, and corn. They were so generous, but I wasn't in the best mood to accept their hospitality, and I felt bad about that. I was very, very tired from the day before. We stayed in the RV, which we had parked on the Petersons' property, and it was a tough night.

Tom McGrath had told me, "Sometimes when the miles are done for the day, you'll just want to go back to a motel room and be by yourself." That's how I felt then. I needed to catch up on my tape cassette and postcards and everything else. My mind just couldn't relax and enjoy.

At times, the road through Iowa was just one continuous cornfield: corn on the left; corn on the right. Then, when there was no more corn, there were pigpens near the side of the highway—dirty, smelly pigpens. Inhaling that odor while running in the heat was terrible. The amusing part was that as we ran by, the hogs wouldn't make a sound. Then we would start to scream and holler, and they'd take off like anything. Jeff and I got a big kick out of that. Amusement can be found most anywhere when you're running 40 miles a day!

Iowa was not the most pleasant state to run through. One reason may be that there were no real breakdown lanes, and what they did have was not tarred but gravel, which was too difficult to run on. So we ran on the hardtop, but then we had to jump off to the side every time a car went by. If the car steered clear, we could stay on the road, right on the white line.

I am from a state with a national reputation for bad drivers; however, Iowa should definitely be considered as a successor to the title. It was somewhere near Ottumwa that Kent and I nearly lost our lives. For some reason, several people tried to run us off the road. They beeped and yelled and made obscene gestures. Most folks didn't think their car should have to share the road with a pedestrian. One time, two kids came by in a truck, and as they approached, they opened their door and tried to hit us with it while they were traveling at 45 or 50 miles per hour. I didn't want to believe they were aiming for me. Maybe the sun was in their eyes and they simply did not see me, and their wheel was just naturally turned in my general direction. But that still didn't explain why their door was open. It was the most outlandish thing, but it proved what we already knew after so many miles across the country: There were definitely some kooks out there.

Later, in Pennsylvania, my friend Dave Nichols came out to

run with me. As we ran along those busy roads, every so often he would quickly grab me, pull me to the side, and say, "Sorry, Dave, but I thought that truck was going to hit you." My extreme caution of the first few weeks had greatly diminished by then. I'd seen so much that my fear of traffic was gone, which could've been a lethal mistake. I couldn't use all my mental energy thinking about "what if" anymore; I just needed to keep putting one foot in front of the other.

In Sheraton, Iowa, Jeff learned that Alan Tardy, who was running from San Francisco to North Hampton, Massachusetts, had stayed at the same motel we were at. *The Runner* magazine—the *almost* sponsor of my trip—had told me about him. We got his home address and telephone number, and Jeff called and spoke to Alan's mom.

We found out that Alan was 23, same as me. He started off at about 138 pounds, same as me. He was running for a charitable organization. He was averaging 55 to 60 miles per day and intended to cover close to 4,000 miles—an awful lot, and he was doing it all alone. "I could never do it that way, but more power to him," I thought. Jeff gave Alan's mother my mom's number, and a few days later they spoke with each other and swapped "my son is running across the country" stories—not something you can do with just anyone!

By Hastings, Iowa, I decided to no longer get up at 4 a.m. and run in the dark. Lack of sleep and lack of daylight were getting to me. I'd been thinking about changing the schedule for a few days, but the clincher came when I was running along in the dark early one morning and noticed an unusual minty smell and tingling on my legs. I had slathered my legs with toothpaste instead of BenGay. No question: I needed to alter the schedule a bit.

For the entire trip, I would run, get to the campsite or motel, eat, go straight to bed, and then start all over again the next morning. I wanted just a bit of time for myself at night. I thought maybe I could see a movie, but that proved unrealistic. All I had time for was to run, eat, and sleep. I imagined that a lot of people thought that my companions and I were out partying for 3 months, but it was anything but that. Pulling ourselves out of society for a summer was tough, but it was the name of the game, and that's what I got myself into.

I created rituals to keep myself engaged. For example, every time I ran past a church, I made the sign of a cross. And I knew that every Saturday at 4:30 p.m., my mom was in church. Jeff was usually riding beside me on the bike, and once a week I would say to him, "Why is this time so special?" And he would say, "Because your mother is in church." And I'd say, "Yeah, that's it." I knew she was spending at least part of that time praying for me to come home. That thought helped a lot.

On July 27, we broke the 2,000-mile mark. It was our 47th day, and my mood was sky-high as we picked up my brother Alan from the Burlington, Iowa, airport. He brought along a care package with cookies, and not just any cookies: my mom's chocolate-chip cookies, the ultimate in comfort food. Those cookies were a staple of my diet, as well as my friends'. They'd come to my house and risk third-degree burns to eat them just as quickly as she could get them out of the oven.

Usually, I was the one interviewed, but this time, at day's end, I grabbed my cassette recorder and asked the questions in an exchange between Alan and me.

Dave: This is July 31, 1978, our 51st day on the road, and with me, at my motel right now, I have my brother Alan. I'd just like to ask him a few things. Alan, how do you feel about being with us at this time?

Alan: Really super. The last 51 days, I've been trying to imagine, along with Mom and Dad and everyone else, what it's really like, and you just don't know until you come out and live with it. I've been here just 1 day and I've seen a lot so far, and I know you're going to make it.

Dave: You say you're going to be with us for 7 or 8 days. What do you think you'll be doing?

Alan: Well, I hope to be one of the guys and take a little bit of the workload away from them, because they've been going at it for 50 days now, and I just hope that I can help in any way.

Dave: Four weeks from tomorrow, hopefully, I'll be done with my run, and you'll be with me for one of those weeks, maybe a little more. It almost seems like I can subtract 1 week because just having you with me is like bringing the whole family here; I have a little of my own flesh and blood with me. I know there will still be the aches and pains—I'll have those up until the last day—but psychologically, mentally, it'll be 1,000 percent better than it was ever before, because you're here. . . . I just hope it all goes well so you get a good impression of what's been going on, and you can go home and tell everyone that the guys are doing okay, that Dave is okay and everything is going super, and that we'll be home in 3 weeks. . . . It's great to have you, buddy.

Alan: Thanks. I wasn't sure what type of condition you would be in. . . . You say on the phone that everything is great, but you just really don't know until you see it. Aside from a few pounds lost, I would say that you look as good as the day you left, and psychologically you seem to be as high-spirited as the day you left. It's just supah ["super"]! Fifty days on the road, 2,240 miles; just seems like you're feeling excellent. I don't see any problems the rest of the way as long as you can keep away from the injuries—just like any other sport.

Dave: The ball game is not over until the last out. No matter how sky-high I feel the rest of the way mentally, I still have to continue and take that last step. . . . I could never fathom running 1,200 miles a few years ago, and now we're saying "only 1,200 miles to home." It's like a magnet effect: The closer you get, the stronger the pull is. It's like the third-quarter drag type of thing, and having someone like you here with me during that third-quarter drag just slides us right into the fourth quarter.

There were two great milestones back-to-back. On Monday, July 31, we came to the Mississippi River—a definite cause for celebration. We were officially in the East.

It was funny to wake up and see my brother next to me. It had been a long time since we had slept in the same room, and in a sense it felt like home. Alan settled in quickly and immediately started running a few miles with me every day and doing a lot of the bookkeeping. Having him around helped me tremendously.

Outside Chicago, I felt very strange. I wasn't physically injured, but the extreme fatigue I had felt earlier continued to plague me. I didn't know if it was symptomatic of my diet, my shoes, or the fact that I'd run more than 2,400 miles. I needed to get my zip back, but it wasn't going to happen that day. The Chicago Heights traffic missed us by inches, and I mean *inches*. There was no sidewalk. It was nerve-shattering.

The day Alan left didn't help matters. He'd been a lot of fun and a great inspiration, just as I knew he would be. He kept the guys going with his trivia questions. He would be out again with my parents at the end of the trip, just 2 weeks from the day he left. That also happened to be my birthday—another cause for celebration. If I could just stay physically fit, I'd be set.

As we neared the Indiana/Ohio line, it seemed as though the media started to go nuts back home. Finding a phone became more of a priority so I could call in to the local sports shows and newspapers. My anxiety mounted with the attention, especially after learning that the PR agency in New York was beginning to book me for national media appearances that were scheduled for the morning after my return. My legs were fatigued, but they got me where I wanted to go. Mentally, though, I had to give a little extra effort. I just hoped I had the energy to make it all the way.

McGillivray has run in blistering heat and crackling thunderstorms, across the trackless deserts and over the rugged Rockies, through the monotony of Kansas and Nebraska, across the Mississippi at Burlington, Iowa, past the University of Notre Dame in South Bend, Indiana, and by late Thursday had made it through Cleveland, one of the few persons to run through Cleveland and live to tell about it.

*Ray Fitzgerald, the **Boston Globe**, August 13, 1978*

My biggest opponent as an athlete, and now as a race director, is the weather. For the first 2 weeks, nearly every morning I was greeted by the rising sun—a product of running toward the east. Then the rain that traditionally follows me wherever I go finally found me. There were days I ran all 40-plus miles soaked from head to toe. Sometimes it was a warm rain, and sometimes it chilled me to the bone. Often, the storms out west were so intense that the driving rain left us with zero visibility. I'd just stare at the pavement, follow the line, and pray that a tractor-trailer didn't hit me. There were only one or two times when the only option was jumping in the RV and sitting it out.

By the time we got to Ohio, I'd had enough of the rain. I stripped down to my underwear (briefs, not boxers), grabbed a bar of soap from the RV, and took a shower in the downpour. People passing by thought I was *nuts*. I didn't take offense. Little moments like that renewed me. The rain could either drown me or help me stay afloat by adding a little levity to the life of four young guys who had spent the past 60 days in an RV, stayed at campsites and in cheap motels, and were now in the middle of nowhere in a rain that would have impressed Noah.

One morning, I had just run my first 5 or 6 miles alone, when a police cruiser approached me. An officer pulled up beside me, with no lights flashing, and asked if I was "the runner." He let me know that my bicycle friend was on his way, as well as the RV. Then he handed me a copy of *Runner's World* magazine! He and his partner were runners, and one of them had run Boston. He asked me to sign the magazine, the August issue with Lynn Jennings on the cover. I wrote my name right over her face. A lot of people asked me for my autograph on the trip, but this was the most interesting one. I was expecting a reprimand, not an autograph request.

A lot of truckers also asked for my autograph. They were going cross-country, too, and they all had CB radios. They called me Marathon Man. At rest stops, they'd come over to see how I was doing. Apparently, they told each other where I was so they could either be aware or give a beep as they drove by. Many news articles said that truckers treated me badly, but in fact, they treated me better than did the others on the road.

On August 10, I did my longest accumulated mileage of 1 day. I didn't intend to run all those 57 miles, but the RV was late in catching up with me, so I had no choice but to keep going. By the time we reached the motel in Norwalk, Ohio, something was wrong with my right knee—some stiffness below the patella. Later on in the night, it got worse, and Kent, who had studied physical therapy, massaged it a bit and stretched it. We put ice on it, but it continued to hurt badly. A good soak might have helped, but the motel had no tub.

By the next day, I couldn't bend the knee very well, and there was a sharp pain. Kent and I decided that I should try to run on it, but that if the problem continued, we would have to call one of the podiatrists that Dr. McGregor recommended I contact while he was in Paris. I ran the first 10 extra slowly; bending my knee even slightly caused too much pain. The slow pace added to my misery. I iced it again that night, but the next day the knee was still no better.

About 2 weeks from home, three little boys came up to the RV at a campground. The youngest of the three brothers showed me what looked like an appendix scar. He told me he had just had a cancer tumor removed. Meeting this young boy and thinking about all he had gone through became a focus of mine for the remainder of the run: It wasn't just for kids in Boston; there were young cancer patients all over the country. Although I was keenly aware of why I was running, seeing this child made each step I took that much more meaningful, and the pain I was feeling seemed numbed by the reality of what cancer patients of all ages endure.

I knew that my discomfort was nothing compared to that of a truly dire illness, but I have to admit that my knee still hurt—

and Pennsylvania was right around the corner. The prairies and flatlands were over. From then on, it would be an undulating run—not a good time to have a knee injury.

In fact, on August 19, the hills I ran were the worst I've ever faced. I was afraid to tell that to my dad, because he's the one who directed us that way. My dad was like our personal navigation system. We'd call him to review the route, and he'd say, "You're going to go 10 miles, and the road is going to turn into a dirt road." He was accurate and did cut miles off the trip, but sometimes the shortest distance between two points is not always the easiest or the fastest—as was the case with his suggested route through the hills of Pennsylvania.

> I appreciate your enthusiasm about running, but if you cause a traffic accident, I'm going to arrest you.
>
> *Pennsylvania state trooper*

Just outside Corry, Pennsylvania, a police officer came up to Kent and me and gave us a lot of grief about the alleged traffic we were causing. He was downright mean. I spoke politely back to him, and I think he felt bad that he'd been a little rough with me. I was already running on the edge of the road; there was nothing else I could do.

In contrast, just a few miles down, we were parked along the same road, and a woman nearby asked what we were doing. She disappeared inside her house and came out a minute later with some chocolate ice cream. Goes to show you that you just never know: Some people bend over backward to help you out and wish you well; others scream at you and tell you to get off the road.

During one of our check-in calls, Jim Shapiro of Specs International told us that the money for the rest of the trip was waiting at a bank in Warren, Pennsylvania. We picked it up the next day and found they had wired us $1,750. I couldn't believe it! We needed only $800. I told Jeff to set aside the extra $1,000 for an emergency, kind of like the extra miles I'd been banking. I hoped to return the extra money.

As I got closer to Massachusetts, I began to have trouble falling asleep. As I neared the journey's end, it was hard to think of anything except the fact that I'd be home in 2 weeks' time. From then on, it was just a numbers game with days on the calendar. The more my parents talked about my homecoming in Medford and the party being planned at the Irish American Hall (Danny's father had procured the space, which was donated), the faster I wanted to go, and I *could not* go any faster. At that point, my mileage was up to 50 miles per day—my limit, as I learned from the knee problem that arose when I did 57.

In Warren, Pennsylvania, we had no idea which way to go. I went straight, and the RV followed right along. We were scheduled to meet up in the middle of town with a guy in a mobile radio station. A lady saw me and jumped out of her car to tell us she had just heard on the radio that I was supposed to be interviewed, and she wanted to let me know we were running in the wrong direction. Kent and I hopped into the RV and drove as fast as we could to the right spot, but we arrived just as the host signed off for the morning. His program was only 20 minutes long, and he had ad-libbed everything when we didn't show. We had even heard a bit of it as we raced toward his location.

As I ran back through the city, one girl asked me for my autograph, and a guy got out of his car, shook my hand, and wished me good luck. Another guy came out of his house and took a photo. It was a pleasant surprise. People were yelling encouragingly and beeping. It was a nice town with really nice people. In fact, in 2004, Warren made it into the *Guinness Book of World Records* for having the most people ever in one place wearing Groucho Marx glasses. My kind of place.

To climb steep hills requires slow pace at first.

William Shakespeare

On August 15, 1978, we were at the Denton Ski Area in Pennsylvania, more than 2,400 feet above sea level. We were only about 20 miles from the New York border—the perfect place for me to hit the 3,000-mile mark of the journey. A radio reporter interviewed me at that point, and the guys were yelling out the window of the RV: "David, what do you think of the *next* 1,000 miles?" They were nuts.

There were still 420 miles left to go, about the same distance as in my "trial" run to Albany. It was all coming together. If I did 50 miles for the next 5 days, I'd have 175 left—just 20 miles a day for the last 8 days. Mileage-wise, I could afford to be careful, and I intended to be, because the outside of my left tibia had begun aching. (The only time I really upped my pace was the next day, when we were in the middle of nowhere—a place we were in *a lot*—and I passed some car that was beaten in with broken windows, just sitting on the shoulder of the road. There was blood all over the place—blood in the car, blood on the car, blood all over the road. I don't know what happened, but I looked in and there was no one in there, so I just kept on running—*fast*.)

I thought I'd damaged my body, and it would take a few days to recover—but there'd be no recovery period, since I had a few more days of exactly the same type of terrain ahead of me. It was me versus the state of Pennsylvania, and I used every ounce of guts I had to get through it. Kent monitored my pulse. It was steady, so that was a relief.

There was a bright spot on our way to the next mail stop in the city of Mansfield. It was during my 30-mile break. I was in the RV, making plans for it to go ahead while I continued running, and I looked out the window and saw two friends from home, Dave Nichols and Diane Perry. It was a huge surprise; I leaped into the air (and nearly hit my head on the van's low ceiling). Having those two with me was a big lift: the first sign that we were close enough to home for people to drive out to meet us. Davey walked several miles with me, and Diane ran 18— another great boost. Dave brought me a copy of a *Boston Globe* article describing the whole run and updated me on events at home and how excited everyone was—and that, in turn, psyched me up. The last 6 miles, Dave drove the RV, something everyone who visited wanted to do.

We ended up in Troy, Pennsylvania. Dave had made a set of six or seven signs with different messages, which he had intended to put out *before* I saw him but didn't get the chance. So when I finished my 50 miles for that day, he just placed them on the side of the road. The signs featured snippets from the *Globe* article: "Trackless Deserts," "Blistering Heat," "Rugged Rockies," and "Sore Feet." As Dave and Diane were about to leave, I gave them each a pair of Specs, plus some money for burgers over at the Dairy Queen. It was the least I could do after the effort they made to come all the way out to see me.

After that, it was back to business. I made my final call to Bill Crowley at the Red Sox to confirm plans for the 29th. I was to show up by 7:30 p.m. The game would be delayed for half an hour to ensure a full house, which was quite an honor. Alan and Bill had been working together to arrange for tickets for friends and family, as well as for what would happen on the field. Bill knew I was in Troy, Pennsylvania, and I asked, "How do you know that?" He said, "I'm following your every step." So I said, "Oh yeah, what did I have for supper?" And he said, "I don't know what you had for supper, but you probably just had ice cream." That was true—I had just finished a frappe!

The next day, Kent and I ran more tough, hilly roads. At one point, we pulled over to rest, and a family in a camper came over and started taking pictures of me. The woman told me she had just seen the UPI story about me in a local paper. She showed us a picture of Kent and me running through Lincoln, Nebraska, and the accompanying article. About time they ran it—it had been written weeks before—but how ironic that she was reading about us at the very moment we came hoofing along.

In the final days, I also had to keep my emotions in check, because I still had a job to do. At that point, the whole run was a lesson in self-restraint. I felt like a racehorse just before the gate is opened. I could see the finish line—and I wanted to bolt for it. However, I needed to pull back on the miles, or I'd get to Fenway early and ruin the planned finish.

I tried to continue to simply appreciate the trip for what it was on each particular day, but it seemed phenomenal that we were only 10 days from home. Meanwhile, people continued to offer us beers and ask for autographs. One day, a girl stopped and talked to Jeff. I went on ahead, and she told Jeff that she thought I was pretty cute. Always good to hear, especially after spending nearly 3 months with four guys!

Soon after we left Pennsylvania (good-bye, "shortcut") and entered New York, a dog started chasing Kent and me. Kent yelled at it, and some guy yelled at Kent. We just kept going. We had to stay safe and avoid trouble when we were in foreign territory, such as rural New York. Running on the road means you have no protection. We were in no condition to fight, and we could blow the whole run. It was aggravating to always have to back down, but we adhered to that approach, and it served us well.

In Monticello, New York, Danny and I ran 8 together. His goal for the trip was to run 10 miles consecutively, something he'd never done before. We intended to run only 6 but couldn't find the shirt that the guys were supposed to put on a pole to indicate the 6-mile mark. We did 51 miles that day, putting us just 90 miles from the Massachusetts border. We got a motel with a balcony overlooking a mountain range, most likely one I'd have to run over the next day.

In that part of New York, we saw many Hasidic Jews. Some stared at me as we went by their houses, and I can't say I blame them. I don't think they knew what to make of me, but there was no reaction at all. No smile. No wave back. I was a little disappointed, but I just waved and ran.

At that point, my calves were tired and tight. Every day was a struggle. My hips and gluteus maximus area (both sides!) were really sore. It felt just like when I was in the hills of Oregon, but now we were so close to home that I almost felt like saying, "Oh, the heck with it." But there were still 200 miles left to go, and the people I missed so much were on their way!

It was August 20 (2 days before my birthday), and the next day would be the single best day of the trip: my parents and Alan would drive out and meet us. My thoughts also turned to my grandfather, whose birthday was this date. All these years later, he was still with me, and I was still running.

In the darkest contrast to my unadulterated joy about seeing my family, Kent called his mom that very night and learned that his father had passed away on July 10. I felt so bad for him and encouraged him to do whatever he had to do to take care of himself and his family, but he assured me that he was okay.

We awoke at 5:30 a.m. to get ready for our final day of 50. After that, I would do "only" 20 or 22 miles each day. I ran just a bit faster, in anticipation of reuniting with my mom and dad by day's end.

On my fourth set of 10, we came to the Hudson River. As Jeff and I were approaching, a guard at the bridge said, "Hey, you can't go over there—no pedestrians allowed." I pretended I didn't hear him and just kept going. As I was running along on a narrow strip of sidewalk, two Hudson River Authority security guards came up to me and told me to get off the bridge and go back to where I got on, or they'd arrest me. I appealed to them and told them that if I didn't run across that bridge, it would break up the continuity of the run. They were sympathetic to my needs. Though a portion of my run was broken up due to construction, I still made it across to the 40-mile mark.

Eight miles later, I recognized the blue Honda Accord the moment it pulled up alongside me. I was finishing up somewhere just outside of Albany, New York. As I raced toward my mom, my dad, and Alan, I could have sworn I smelled chocolate-chip cookies. Sure enough, as I leaned in to kiss my mom, there was the package beside her on the front seat: the traditional birthday batch of her cookies.

We had a big celebratory dinner that night—a feast that my mom had cooked ahead and we reheated in the RV. There were gifts, a cake with candles—the works, which I shared with Alan; that day, August 21, was actually his birthday. It wasn't merely a birthday party, however; it was also a celebration of being reunited and being close to home. I also shared my excitement with listeners on the *Runner's Digest* radio show.

Host: Dave has crossed over the Massachusetts line and is in the commonwealth. . . . Are you excited now—about the fact that your goal is in sight?

Dave: I'm very excited about it, and you know it's been a long time coming. Running through desert and mountains, it's been difficult to try to grasp the idea that maybe I might make it, and now I have all the confidence in the world. I have around 60 to 80 miles left to go. And I'm very excited to help raise money for the Jimmy Fund of Boston, which is the charitable organization I am running for.

Host: Did you ever find, when you were going through the mountains or out in the desert . . . that the body was not feeling too well, that you might have been losing water or something like that? Did you ever find yourself near delirium at all?

Dave: Um, no, not really. I've been totally amazed at the strength of my body throughout the whole trip. I was never totally fatigued to the point where I was losing my mind or anything such as that. My companions just kept me on my feet, kept me going. Two of them, Kent Hawley and Danny Carey, were right beside me all the way. They kept me going, and I really never got to the point where I was delirious. I must say I was very, very fatigued at times. Doing 50-plus miles per day, obviously you do get totally exhausted . . .

Host: In traveling through the country, have you noticed a change, not only in the different regions and the climate, but also in the people as you go from state to state, region to region—some being more friendly than others? Or perhaps the difference in accents? Are parts of the country different between east and west, north and south?

Dave: Amazingly, it almost seems like it changes as soon as you cross the line, especially geographically. You know there is a definite difference in each state and in people's attitudes and their customs and everything. Going across the country at a snail's pace, you're more aware of something like that than you would be zipping through it at 55 miles per hour. There was a difference, and it was nice to be able to notice that.

Host: We'll all be excited Tuesday night when you come through Fenway Park. But I'm sure it will be a very special and a very private moment for you, knowing what you've accomplished and what you've overcome and for the reasons that you did it.

I didn't get up until 6:30 a.m. on my 24th birthday—the latest I'd slept on the whole trip. Good thing, too, since I'd been up in the middle of the night. I had woken up around 1 a.m. and realized I'd fallen asleep without taking my pills, so I got up, swallowed them, worked on my feet a bit, and grabbed a snack. Then I fell asleep again and "overslept," but after all, it was my birthday. We deserved the extra rest. We were right on schedule to be home by August 29.

Entering Egremont! Incorporated in 1761

Massachusetts highway sign

A bit disappointing—all those miles and no "Welcome to Massachusetts" sign! But I had just run the best 10 miles of the entire journey. My dad was behind the wheel of the RV, and Alan was by my side when we crossed the state line. After 72 days of doing nothing but running, I had finally returned to my home state. The feeling was indescribable. Danny continued on with me, and we did 8 miles and walked a few. I ran 42 miles that day; my goal was to do 24. We stayed in Great Barrington that night . . . Great Barrington, *Massachusetts*!

We all went out to eat to celebrate my birthday. The guys presented me with a baseball cap to replace my favorite Mercer hat, which I had lost out west somewhere. We stayed up late to listen to a Red Sox game. In a phone call earlier that day, Ken

Coleman told me he planned to announce on the air that I was running 24 miles to celebrate my 24th birthday, but I was too tired to stay up to hear it. The thrill of the day—entering Massachusetts, plus having my folks with me—had overwhelmed me. Only 175 miles to go; now, that was a *happy* birthday.

The state line also marked the start of some other work. Invitations needed to be sent for the party that my mom and dad were hosting that Thursday night. Paul Harber at the *Mercury* wanted to come out and interview everyone. I also contacted Massachusetts state trooper Dan Donovan to apologize for not notifying him that we had rerouted the course. He was expecting me to come in from Connecticut. No problem, he said; we would get a police escort from Hopkinton to Medford and Medford to Boston. "Trooper Dan" has been a friend ever since.

With all the calls to be made (thankfully, now local), Kent and I didn't get out on the road until 9:30 a.m. We ended on Route 20 that day, the same way I ran to Albany a year earlier. Everything was familiar. My parents headed back home, and in less than a week, I'd be there, too. There was no more intense pressure on me. I could do less than 20 miles a day and still make it to Fenway on time. We were right on our doorstep.

> [My greatest memory will be] the feeling of how everyone back home in Medford and Boston has come together and raised money for the Jimmy Fund. . . . If we can help just one little kid, one child with cancer—if we can save one person—then in my own heart, I know it's all been worth it.
>
> *Dave, **WBZ Sports Final** radio show, August 27, 1978*

With home only a few zip codes away, I downshifted my daily mileage from 50 to 25 to 30 miles. My friends Mark Comfort and Joe Petrasso came out to meet me along Route 20 in the western part of the state. They were two of many who ran with me during the final days. Mark was a younger running buddy of mine in high school. He lived down the street and would just show up at my doorstep at 6:30 in the morning, and we'd go for

11 miles. (I don't know why 11, but that was the number.) Later, Mark enlisted in the Marines and was killed in a friendly-fire incident—a sobering example of why those of us who are *here* should live each day to its fullest.

It was a real boost having Mark and other friends by my side as I worked my way toward familiar territory. The run was the best US geography lesson I've ever had. I learned about mountains where I didn't think there were any. I saw cactus where I didn't know they grew. I discovered how selfless and how selfish people can be, and that people are as different as the geography from state to state.

I now had 85 miles left and 5 days to do it in, an average of about 17 miles per day. I wanted to get as close to home as possible, as soon as possible, just in case. While Kent and I were running, someone in a bookmobile stopped to shake my hand. Another couple drove by and threw an ear of corn at us. What was that for? Just another strange thing to add to the list.

Running took a backseat to administrative housekeeping during those last few days leading to Fenway, which were spent mostly on the phone with reporters and friends, writing postcards, and gathering my thoughts for that final lap. I still woke up around 5:30 or 6 a.m. so I could get it all done. Even today, I'm an early riser; I like the calmness of the morning.

The Friday before I finished, I called everyone I could think of, including Bill Crowley, and confirmed last-minute details such as where to park the RV at Fenway, and reviewed tickets. Crowley had reserved 100 bleacher seats for my friends and family, press passes for my support crew, and eight box seats for my parents. The rest of the calls included the state police, the *Today* show, and the *Mercury*.

I also checked in with Jim Shapiro at Specs about the PR issue, which had been bothering me for several weeks. It seemed that the PR firm was planning my life's schedule. I wanted to be advised on everything before they made definite plans. I was more than willing to go on *Today;* however, I didn't want to leave the Boston area until I felt my job was done as far as the press there was concerned. Jim said he'd figure out the quickest way to get me to New York and back. By the time we hung up, we had squared everything away, and I felt much better.

We stayed in Wilbraham and spent the day in Sturbridge. I ran 20 to 25 miles, and then the guys all went for haircuts. Danny's parents showed up with an apple pie that was designated "for David only." That evening, I did an interview with Bob Lobel, a local sportscaster, on his *Calling All Sports* show. Joe Kelley came by, and we talked for hours.

Like those first few days at the start, my stomach was upset a bit, mostly from the anticipation and excitement. There was still a lot to do. I made personalized plaques for my support crew, sent postcards to the YWCA, and wrote a letter to the Olympic Torch Committee. I'd learned from a *Globe* article that they were seeking runners to carry the Olympic torch to start the 1980 Winter Olympics, so I submitted my name.

For the first time in my trip, everything was all coming to life. At the same time, I was anxious to get it over with; so much could still happen in the remaining 60 miles. I ordered a stack of pancakes at the motel restaurant and reflected on what it would be like to run into Fenway. Sitting there, alone, I got very emotional. I was feeling so many things all at once: relief because I was so close, and if I had to crawl the remaining miles, I could and would; sadness because a life-changing journey was about to end; nervousness because I wanted to say all the right things when I spoke at Fenway; and pride because we were only hours away from completing our commitment.

Three days before the finish, as I was running the first 10 miles with Kent, my brother Bob and his friend George caught up with us. It was the first time I'd seen them. My brother opened up his shirt to expose a T-shirt with a photo of me on it! George was wearing the same one. Apparently, my whole family was sporting them.

Somewhere past Auburn, we stopped so I could change into my Specs. Bob and George were snapping photos like crazy from overpasses and bridges. I was so happily distracted, I completely missed a turn and went 2 miles down the wrong road. The RV caught us and drove us back. I ran the last couple of miles in the right direction on Route 30 and ended up around North Grafton. The total for the day was close to 22 miles (some going the wrong way). Only 40 miles to home . . .

We booked a room at the Holiday Inn in Worcester. Lots of folks came up and joined us for pizza, including my cousin Jimmy Connelly, who worked for the *Worcester Telegram* and had sent some reporters to meet us. Paul Harber arrived, and my companions and I gave him an exclusive interview.

Physically, I felt good. I had done a lot of pickups—bursts of running fast—during that day's 20 miles. I wanted to get my speed back but was careful not to injure myself.

Our final motel stay was at the Newton Holiday Inn. The weather was beautiful, but rain was predicted for Tuesday, of course. I finished up with 21 or so miles. My mom brought the bathroom scale with her. I had lost 9 pounds. She also mended my shorts, which were starting to rip.

Then, with only 3 days remaining, I reached the start line of the Boston Marathon. I was *home.* I met state trooper Bill Coulter, our police escort for the day. I took off from Hopkinton around 12:30 p.m., and by 1:30 I was running hard, trying to stretch out my hamstrings and back quads, as well as get in a little speed work. At Natick, we stopped for the day and had a cookout at nearby Lake Cochituate. The atmosphere had that party feel to it. People who saw the RV and had followed the run via radio and newspaper accounts came over to congratulate me.

Officer Coulter, a runner himself, asked me for my autograph. I signed his *Worcester Telegram,* right above the article about the run. Now Billy Coulter is a friend who inspires *me;* he has completed 10 Hawaii Ironman Triathlons and run even more Boston Marathons.

> What McGillivray has done to dramatize the exceptional continuous work of the Jimmy Fund will remain a landmark for years to come. All who can should participate in this, the successful conclusion of his sterling effort, not merely as a tribute to what he is giving of him-

self, but as evidence of concern with the research under way to conquer one of man's most dreaded diseases.

Paul Harber, Medford Daily Mercury

At 4 p.m. on August 29, I arrived in Medford. People told me to expect a big welcome, but it was beyond anything I had imagined. The cheers and church bells and sirens as I sprinted to the finish at city hall were deafening. I climbed the steps and shouted to the thousands of people gathered that I was finally home! It was like my own ticker-tape parade. The town square was packed with thousands of people. I felt like a hero. Mayor Eugene Grant was there to greet me, and Bill Rodgers crowned me with a laurel wreath. Among the local business leaders and politicans was Marvin Adner, MD, head of the Governor's Council on Physical Fitness. A decade later he became the BAA's medical director—and has been my marathon colleague since.

I was presented with a check for $5,100 from the Medford Chamber of Commerce and another for $1,000 from the Mystic Health Club, whose members also gave me a 5-foot-7 trophy adorned with a winner's cup and a runner holding a laurel wreath. The height of the trophy was supposed to represent my own, and who was I to tell them they were too generous with their measurement!

I handed the checks to Dr. Emil Frei, then head of the Sidney Farber Cancer Institute, there to welcome me home on behalf of the Jimmy Fund. Then Mayor Grant, Al Spector, and dozens of others ran alongside me from Medford to Fenway Park. The guys ran, too, since the RV had decided that home was an excellent place to finally break down (it eventually had to be towed from in front of city hall). Man versus machine—and man won.

To accomplish great things, we must dream as well as act.

Anatole France

I had just turned 24, and if I lived to be 100, I still couldn't adequately describe what I felt as I ran those laps around Fenway. Following a short press conference afterward, I joined my parents in a box, where, after running for 80 straight days, I finally got to sit and simply watch the game.

I received the following a few days after that unforgettable Fenway night.

> Dear Dave,
>
> I am compelled to write a letter to a stranger, which for me is a bit unusual. I watched a most amazing event on TV last night—of course, the culmination of your incredible run. I watched with my 27-year-old husband, who is recovering from the run of his life, a confrontation with cancer. I point this out only to express the viewpoint we shared as we watched someone close to our age involve himself so unselfishly for a cause so awesome. We both got the same feeling as when we watched some of the moving events in the last Summer Olympics. I wish you all the best in your endeavors. For if it weren't for individuals of the same caliber as you, I'd be a widow at 26 instead of a grateful optimist.

That letter is my Olympic gold.

CHAPTER 6

The Journeys

Thank goodness that feet last longer than tires do.

When I was growing up, we spent our summers on Nuttings Lake in Billerica, Massachusetts. We would stay there all summer while my dad, Francis "Macadoo" McGillivray, commuted to his job at the can company in Everett. The summer house was officially named the Merri-Macs, but we all referred to it simply as "the camp." It was built in 1927 by my grandfather, along with some help from my dad.

Each Labor Day weekend, the lake's Sunnyside Improvement Association put on a series of sporting events and games to end the season. Most of the attendees were summer residents, and the three-legged race, canoe race, and pie-eating contests were our way of saying good-bye to summer. There were road races, too. According to my dad, I was around 5 years old when I entered the boys' race for my age group—probably about 100 yards. It was my first race ever. And I won! It's probably my only win that's captured on film, and certainly the only one filmed on 8 millimeter.

> He was this little boy who had so much energy, he would just go, go, go, go all day long. At night, he would fall asleep in the living room. When he was done, he was totally wiped out. He was exhausted.
>
> *Susan McGillivray West, Dave's sister*

Doing my best is always my ultimate goal. I may not be the fastest runner out there, but being prepared makes every task easier, especially the more challenging ones. In between the start and finish is where the unexpected happens. With each mile, I've learned to survive hardship, value friendship, and, most important, think both literally and figuratively about where to go next and how to get there—though at times I have definitely detoured. These journeys have taught me things about life that go deeper than I ever would've imagined possible.

My athletic endeavors—a 24-hour swim, a 24-hour run— may seem a bit over the top, but boiled down, they are simply goals born of a desire to create my own personal challenges, and what's wrong with thinking *big*? Though my challenges are athletically focused, others might desire to make a risky career change in midlife or overcome a fear of trying something new, like learning to drive. Personally, I believe my greatest act of endurance would be to sit still in a chair for more than 5 minutes. I'd give it my all, but I'm not sure I'd succeed.

I am my harshest critic and certainly my toughest competitor. I'm always looking for a way to push, push, and push myself some more, until I believe I've reached my maximum potential. I would argue that the majority of us never really know what we're capable of because we either don't take chances or don't try hard enough. Giving up is easy. Persistence and Preparation are essential; you just don't know unless you try.

In 1979, I read a *Sports Illustrated* article by Barry McDermott, who "discovered" the Ironman event while covering a golf tournament in Hawaii. He produced a 10-page account of the race, which was in only its second year at that time. I devoured every word describing this new competition: a 2.4-mile openwater ocean swim, followed by a 112-mile bike race, and finishing up with a 26.2-mile marathon run. I had tremendous wonder and respect for the athletes who pioneered the event.

At that time, I was working as a public relations "ambassador" for Pro Specs. They encouraged me to travel to races wherever and whenever I could, wearing their gear and promoting the company. It was the first time in my life that I tasted the freedom and joy of a vocation that mirrored what I most loved to do. I spent my days training and setting my next athletic and charitable goals.

Since I had already run across the continent, I believed—rightly or wrongly—that I was capable of doing anything from an endurance point of view. Yet at the time I learned about the triathlon, the dog paddle was about the extent of my swimming skills, and I didn't own a bike. Anyone else might have viewed the lack of mastery or equipment for two of the three disciplines as a deterrent to doing a swim-bike-run event.

A few months after I'd read about the Ironman, I drove over to my friend Hal Gabriel's house for his annual road race. I happened to have the article in the car and showed it to him. Hal is a longtime running friend—a running *machine* is more like it.

"Hal, look at this event!" I said, excitedly tapping the pages depicting athletes torturing themselves to cross the finish line of this gut-wrenching event. Without batting an eye, he immediately replied, "Wow, *we* can do that!" Another friend, Paul Sullivan was with us, so we got him hooked, too. The three of us trained together, swimming at the YMCA and the Tufts University pool, where we enlisted a friend, Tufts swim coach Don Megerle, to instruct us.

What made the Ironman different, right from the start, was that it was the first endurance event I did that was just for *me*. There was no fund-raising required, no media or sponsor obligations; I was liberated to train hard with no distractions. I felt a bit guilty at times, thinking I could have turned it into another charitable project, but I soon realized that sometimes I needed to give myself permission to focus on the athleticism of it all. It sounds selfish, but it was refreshing to take a "break" and focus on the same reasons I loved to compete in my youth: strictly for the sport of it.

At that early point in Ironman history, the event was held in late February. Wintertime may not have been an issue for an event held in Hawaii, but it made for grueling training for participants from colder climates. New England winters are not empathetic to athletes, and the winter of 1979 was no exception.

Back then, if I entered a road race, I knew who the competition would be. Most everything I did was local. I always strove to fare well against my peers. But in Hawaii, I would know only Paul and Hal. Close friends though we were, Hal and I competed against each other—quietly and sometimes not so quietly—as well as against our own standards of excellence.

That's probably what drove us to train in adverse conditions. It was like a game of chicken. Neither of us wanted to be the one to say, "Let's not train today; it's too cold" or "I'm too tired."

> We trained, and we were focused. We went out one day that was 15 degrees with a windchill of 20 below zero. We biked 50 miles. That was 20 years ago. . . . Now I won't even go outside to get the newspaper on a day like that.
>
> *Hal*

In January 1980, after just a little more than 6 months of training, we were on a plane to Waikiki, then home of the Ironman (the next year, it moved to Kona). We had only a slight understanding of what we were about to experience. Ninety-eight percent of my goal was to simply finish the event. The other 2 percent was to see how fast I could accomplish that other 98 percent.

My track record with travel is pretty bad but very consistent. There's always a variable that makes it a challenge. In fact, just getting to Hawaii from Boston was a true test of human endurance. A storm whipped through the Hawaiian Islands just days before our flight. Severe weather shut down the airport on Oahu, the island where the race was held. It was the first time the airport had been closed since World War II.

Our enormous 747 jet was rerouted to the Big Island of Hawaii. It was a rough landing; on descent, the overhead compartments popped open, and luggage rained down on us all. Hollywood could not have scripted a more nail-biting scene. To exacerbate the situation, we were grounded for 3 hours. The fierce wind rendered it unsafe to try to make our way across the tarmac to the terminal, so we were all confined to the plane. Total travel time: 21 hours—not the ideal way for body or mind to spend the last few days before a demanding physical event.

Thankfully, Hal and I had made it safe and sound, but his bike did not fare as well. It never appeared in the baggage claim area. Hal, always good in a crisis, immediately began executing a contingency plan. With only 3 days before the competition, he stopped nearly every person on the street of Waikiki and asked if they had a bike he could borrow. He didn't care if it had a banana seat, streamers coming out of the handles, or three wheels. He intended to find a loaner just in case his never showed up, and he collected the names and phone numbers of several potential donors.

The night before the competition, the airline delivered Hal's bike to us. It was a wreck. It looked as though it had done some flying of its own in the cargo hold during that nightmare landing. Still determined, Hal took it to a bike shop that evening. Miraculously, they were able to fix it, and with not a moment to lose.

Much has changed during the 25-plus-year history of the Ironman. At that time, to protect participants from the potential dangers of the long-distance athletic demands, race organizers weighed everyone just before the swim and again at scales along the course. If you lost 10 percent of your body weight during the race, you could be disqualified. Hal was and still is one of the healthiest, most active human beings I know, and at that time, among the biggest eaters. He consumed about 7,000 to 9,000 calories a day— and never gained any weight! The night before the race, he and his wife, Elaine, spent $50 on juice and even more on food for his self-made water stops, to stoke him with enough calories to fend off weight loss. And it worked: Hal may be the only person in Ironman history to gain weight from checkpoint to checkpoint.

We also had other logistical business to attend to before the race. In those days, the Ironman had no aid stations along the route to supply water and, say, bananas. Procuring sustenance was every man (and a few women) for himself. Each triathlete was also responsible for putting together a support crew. Hal and I had flown over early, not to search for a bike but to allow time to find a local who was willing to spend at least 10 hours following us around the race. Each participant was like a moving target, especially with 112 miles of biking and 26.2 miles of running. The job of a traveling "pit crew"—to track the athlete's whereabouts and be right where needed to provide hydration— was a very tall order.

Hal, charismatic and industrious guy that he is, almost immediately found two young women to help him out. Elaine was truly his support, but the local girls' car and knowledge of the island would be valuable for his racing success.

I, on the other hand, just grabbed a phone book the day we arrived and started randomly calling people on the island. The cold-call method probably wouldn't work today, now that the world, and people's trust in others, is so different than it used to be. But back then, before the world of telemarketing, it worked great. After a handful of calls, I found a man who agreed to be my crew. The night before the race, I took him and his daughter out to dinner. As agreed, he showed up at my hotel the next morning at 5:30—in a small Honda Civic. There was no roof rack, and my bike couldn't fit in his car. I had to get in, put my bike on the roof, and hold it there while we drove to the start.

On race day, the storm that wreaked havoc with our travel was still lingering in the form of high tides, strong currents, and heavy winds. As a result, the ocean swim was canceled, and the swim portion was moved to a nearby canal. I made it out of the water and hopped on my bike, but my support guy was stuck at a red light, so I pulled over in the shade and waited. It took half an hour for him to finally catch up to me with some much-needed food.

Today, the day of the event is a local holiday, with roads closed and people lining the streets of downtown Kona. When I participated, however, the course was nothing short of dangerous. The traffic was terrible—it was like biking 100 miles on a busy interstate. The fans were enthusiastic, though one guy threw a beer can at Hal, who nearly crashed as he swerved to avoid being hit. At 20 miles per hour, a fall from a bike could be disastrous.

I was ahead of Hal during the swim and starting on the bike, but he caught me 50 or 60 miles into the 112-mile ride. (After changing for the run, I realized I had put on a singlet with no bib number, so I had to turn around and go back for the right one—another small setback.) Then I caught him 10 or 12 miles into the run, and we shared a water bottle. It was a great moment for both of us. That first year, out of a field of 108, I finished 14th and Hal finished 17th. Hal is my senior by about 15 years, but if he'd had the advantage of youth on his side (minus the times he stopped to eat!), I think he could've won the darn thing. My time was around 11 hours and 30 minutes. Not bad.

> The connections you make are part of the lifestyle of being an athlete. If Dave is president, I'm vice president of the club. He and I shook hands and then embraced on the beach in Oahu after we finished. These priceless moments define what you're breathing for.
>
> *Hal*

The year 1980 was also when ABC's *Wide World of Sports* aired the event and introduced it to millions of viewers. There were 106 men and two women who participated. Dave Scott won the event. He and I became great friends, and 20 years later I became his sports agent.

It takes a lot to make me "awestruck" about anyone. But one of my few "idols" was also at Waikiki that year as an ABC commentator. The triathlon was a small event, and the media were right in our faces and very accessible. So when I saw Diana Nyad standing near me, I had to introduce myself. For a decade, Diana was the greatest long-distance swimmer in the world. In 1979, just a year after I finished my cross-country run, she stroked the longest nonstop swim in history, 102.5 miles from the island of Bimini in the Bahamas to Florida. She and I became friends and kept in touch for a long time afterward. I have so much admiration for her and what she has accomplished.

The stories of the Ironman are ones of human courage and sacrifice, but there are also many lighter tales. For example, in one of my later races, I was in the transition area (where athletes switch from swim to bike, bike to run) down by the Kona Surf. I got off the bike and grabbed my "bike to run" bag with all my gear in it. One helpful volunteer continuously yelled out our next instruction: "Just run down to the changing area." He pointed me toward some rooms within a building just off the parking lot of the Kona Sur Hotel. I ran right in. Time was of the essence—until I realized I had been directed into the *women's* changing area, a room filled with 20 female triathletes, all in various stages of, shall we say, "transition."

The women didn't even notice me. With 7½ hours of swimming and biking behind us, we all had one goal: Change fast and get back out for the marathon. Part of the challenge of a triathlon is that the race clock never stops, so, in the interest of efficiency, I decided to stay rather than waste time searching for the correct gender-filled area. I believe that plan worked against me; my transition time was probably the longest of any participant that day.

> October 1982: The race owners move [the Ironman's] date to October to give athletes from colder climates better training conditions. Evidence that the race is maturing, cutoff times are introduced. Contestants must complete the 140.6-mile course within 18½ hours. Race organizers begin coordinating the race with the full moon to assist runners after dark.
>
> *Ironman Triathlon World Championship, History,*
> *IronmanLive.com, July 15, 2005*

Like thousands of honeymooners before us, I went to Hawaii with my first wife, Susan, after our Columbus Day weekend wedding. The draw was not the lava sand beaches or the deep teal of the water, however—it was the fact that at that time, 1988, the Ironman had been moved to the Saturday nearest the October full moon, allowing those of us in colder climates to train during summer and early fall. So, in typical McGillivray fashion, my new wife and I flew to Hawaii for anything *but* rest and relaxation.

Susan, an aerobics instructor, was in great shape, but the intense heat and incredible physical demands of the Ironman can take a toll on even the best athlete. Sue finished in an impressive time of 12:04 but wound up in the hospital for dehydration. (So much for starting out the marriage on the right foot.) My massage therapist, Tia Bentley, whom I had brought along, had been hit by a bike several days before the race, and, strangely enough, she and Sue ended up sharing a hospital room. Sue was treated and released, and we flew home as scheduled. Tia, however, spent a month in Hawaii while she recovered.

Though I competed in eight of them, the Ironman was not destined to become one of my "streaks." In 1989, my mom, Jacqueline McGillivray, was diagnosed with cancer. Getting her cured became my focus, leaving little time for training or anything else. My family and I saw her through her long illness. The next year, my first child, Ryan, was born just a month before the Ironman, so I never did make it back to Kona as a participant.

In the years that followed, however, I spent a good deal of time getting to know the Ironman as I've gotten to know so many other athletic events: from the inside out. I've visited Hawaii several times in the fall just to observe the complexities that go into organizing an event of this magnitude. I believe that the athletes are the backbone of the sport, and the race directors and management teams are the heart and soul; only by understanding each other's challenges can we survive and prosper.

One of the greatest professional affirmations I've received was during the Ironman's search for a new race director a few years ago. I was asked by a few people close to the race if I would consider taking the job. At the time, several years after my divorce, I'd recently remarried, and though the idea of moving to Hawaii had a romantic ring to it, it required sacrifices that my new wife, Katie, and I were not ready to make. As they say at the Oscars, it was great just to be nominated.

I've considered competing again, but it ultimately comes down to personal incentive. I no longer give myself the time to stay as fit. Between work and family, there's no time left to devote to the amount of training required.

It's been more than 15 years since I turned that last corner onto Alii Drive, on the Big Island of Hawaii, and experienced the indescribable feeling of crossing the finish in front of a crowd that seems to generate enough energy to power the sun. Someone who's never been to Kona might assume that the majority of participants are lifelong athletes—world-class swimmers, runners, and cyclists. Truth is, before they became "athletes," they were simply people who decided to do something remarkable for themselves, perhaps to celebrate a milestone or to laugh in the face of Father Time as he decreed them middle-aged. The Ironman triathlon makes you feel alive in a way you never imagined possible. Someday I may ask my body to shift into Ironman mode just once more to see what I'm made of these days.

> The New England Run has a most interesting aspect. [David McGillivray] is performing his feat in a triathlon fashion: running; swimming, and bicycling a 1,400-mile course. The itinerary somewhat resembled the grueling Honolulu "Ironman Triathlon," which David competed in on January 12, 1980.
>
> *Princess House, Inc., sponsor of New England Run; company newsletter, 1981*

After first experiencing the Ironman, I came down with triathlon fever, and it just wouldn't break. Plus, I was still looking to benefit the Jimmy Fund and raise that $1 that might solve the puzzle of childhood cancer. So in October 1981, I came up with my own version and called it the New England Run, even though running was only a third of the endeavor. It was actually a month-long triathlon. But at that time, and even today, "triathlon" is a relatively unknown term in the realm of the general public, plus I didn't like the sound of "New England Triathlon," so I just called it a run for simplicity's sake.

My swim-bike-run event through six New England states included a daily goal of completing a 1-mile swim, an 80- to 100-mile bike ride, and an approximately 20-mile run. It worked out to roughly 1,522 miles in 30 days and started at Medford High School, a place close to my heart. I had trained for the Ironman in that pool, and I still lived in Medford at the time.

A lot of people get grounded in Medford, a very tight community where everyone knows everyone. It's changed some over the years, but it once had a reputation as a "tough" community where you had to earn your stripes. I certainly earned something during those years. As I stood in that high school gymnasium, on the very floor I was not permitted to play on as a member of the basketball team, I thought about how far I'd come. Here I was, addressing an assembly of 4,000 students who listened intently as I described how I would swim, bike, and run all over New England. Then I took off and ran the first leg with the cross-country team. Anything is possible.

By far the biggest challenge of that journey was the daily swim. Some days I found a lake; others, a river; and yet others, the Atlantic Ocean. And some days I was in need of a divining rod as I searched around for water—any body of water that could help me achieve my goal. I hadn't mapped out that aspect, so if I was biking or running along and saw an opportunity for a swim, I would just stop and do it. Most of the time, the swim played out in a hotel pool—not too glamorous. I'd do 400 circles in a kiddie pool if need be. I just had to get it done.

There was a stretch in New Hampshire in which I biked 100 miles to the base of Mount Washington, ran the 8 miles up the mountain, turned around, and ran back down in the rain. Then I biked from Mount Washington to Lake Winnipesauke, jumped in, and swam for 2 miles. The water in that lake was so cold, it seemed more appropriate for ice-skating than swimming.

Fall was not the ideal season to be swimming in New England waters, but I wanted the run to take place during the school year. Following my travels gave kids an opportunity to learn about geography and fitness as well as about the Jimmy Fund. I even self-proclaimed September 30, 1981, Quarter Day in New England. I asked the kids at the schools supporting me to bring a quarter to school on that day and planned my route so I could collect their donations. We raised thousands of dollars, and transporting all those coins to the bank gave me a new appreciation for paper money. The superintendent of the Randolph, Massachusetts, public schools helped set up this part of the project, and the town held a special celebration for me the night before I finished. They made me feel like I was one of their own, just as so many had along the way.

> You are not doing this for nothing, you know. There are millions of kids around here that need you. You have to be

pretty weird to do something like this, but I know how much you care about those kids.

Child commenting on the New England Run

Going "down the Cape" is a New England expression that usually conjures up summertime images of the beach; warm, humid days; and "lobsta" rolls. I ran and biked the Cape and made it to Woods Hole, a wonderful village on the southwest tip, on October 10, but the water temperature of Cape Cod Channel was just 50 degrees then. My great friend and eternal navigator was, and still is, Ron Kramer. There was no one I trusted more to get me through the infamous current of one of the toughest channels in the world.

Ron had one goal for the day, and that was to get me safely across Nantucket Sound. He had his boat and had amassed a support crew to help with navigation as well as serve as lifeguards in case I got into trouble. Those aboard included Hal Gabriel, BMac (a.k.a. my brother Bob), Jack Flanagan, Kent Hawley—and my dad, who was a great comfort to me.

Everyone thought the water was too cold to swim in. They didn't want Ron to allow me in the water, and negative tones floated around the boat for most of the early morning. "Don't do it," my trusty crew advised.

> Dave had trust in me, and I knew he was looking to talk about what to do. So I suggested we get off the boat and take a walk to hammer it out and discuss it. Basically, Dave's thought was, "I've got this commitment, and I'm going to do it." He was steadfast with it. I was comfortable with it, but I knew the water would not be comfortable for Dave.
>
> *"Captain" Ron Kramer*

Being stubborn—I mean, focused—is not always a trait I'm proud of, but I had promised myself and others that I would swim from Woods Hole on Cape Cod to Vineyard Haven on Martha's

Vineyard, no matter what the water temperature was at the time.

I basically said, "I'm running the show, and we *are* doing it!" I wasn't trying to be full of myself; I just wanted to meet my objective. I also had complete trust in Ron to get me through whatever happened. I was finally able to convince the others that it was worth a try. Someone suggested I wear a wet suit, but I felt like that would be cheating. (I did, however, slather myself with petroleum jelly, which I'd read can insulate the body in cold water.) So we took off, and I dove into the water.

I've never been so cold in my life.

> When he jumped in, I didn't know the temperature of the water. When I found out it was 50 degrees, I realized it was impossible for him to complete the swim. He tried his darnedest but soon turned blue from the cold water. The crew fished him out and had him laid out inside the cabin and covered him with blankets. He lay motionless on the deck of the boat until they warmed him up.
>
> *Francis "Macadoo" McGillivray, Dave's dad*

I don't remember much except the moment I looked up from the water and saw my father peering over the side of the boat clearly worried about the safety, and perhaps the sanity, of yours truly. *He* knew I was in trouble, and *I* knew I was in trouble. I had been in the water for only about 20 minutes, but that's all it took. The chill went right through me, and I suddenly found myself physically "trapped" inside my body. I was unable to speak and couldn't even tell if my arms and legs were doing what I was asking of them. For a second or two, I thought I was going to die in the water. And I thought, "Well, if I've gotta go, then at least my dad is out here with me."

From the vantage point of the boat, the guys could see me exhibiting signs of hypothermia. My energy and my stroke seemed greatly compromised. At that point in my life, I had very little body fat, so it didn't take long for the dangerously frigid water to have an enormous effect on me.

Jack Flanagan dove in, got me in the lifeguard hold (arm across chest), and brought me to the swim platform. I was shaking and shivering and silent when they got me on board—very lethargic, I guess, and semi-comatose. They immediately wrapped me in towels, rubbed me down to warm me up, and dried me off. Ron quickly cranked up the heat and covered me with blankets.

> It happened right off the entrance to Falmouth Harbor as we were heading off to Vineyard Haven, so I called the dock master and told him we needed an ambulance waiting. As we pulled in, the ambulance was there. They took Dave to the hospital, where he remained for about 2 or 3 hours.
>
> *Ron Kramer*

I'm not sure if I even took the time to remove the hospital ID band from my wrist before I resumed my adventure. My body temperature had gone from the blue zone to the red zone; I felt great again and basically said, "See ya, we're outta here!" then left for a 20-mile run from the hospital parking lot to a school in Martha's Vineyard. The kids were waiting for me, eager to present me with money they had raised for the Jimmy Fund. I couldn't let them down.

The children greeted me with signs and posters that had obviously taken them a long time to create. They had also raised a good deal of money. Those young people had put a remarkable amount of energy into everything, and I was glad I got to them on schedule.

> McGillivray, renowned for his staying powers, displayed just how resilient he really is when he recovered from the bite of trying to swim 4 miles in 50-degree waters and ran 22 miles around Martha's Vineyard.
>
> *Medford Daily Mercury, 1981*

The next day we got back in the boat and returned to Woods Hole. As we pulled away from the dock, I looked up at Captain Ron and uttered the words made famous by a former actor, now governor of California: "I'll be back." I knew that in the not-too-distant future, I had to return and face the strength of the current and the frigid temperatures until I prevailed. Whether driven by pride or a goal not accomplished, it didn't matter; I wasn't going to let it slip away.

The next day was spent running, biking, and swimming between Falmouth, Hyannis, and Eastham. I purposely back-tracked through East Dennis so I could stop by Johnny Kelley's house. We ran a "brisk" 10 miles, as one reporter put it. At the time, 73-year-old Johnny was training for the New York City Marathon. It was difficult for me to keep up with him!

Johnny wasn't my only interesting partner; this event was particularly wide-ranging in terms of the support I received along the way. For example, I also ran with the members of Walpole Prison Yard Runners' Club, which I'd founded. They wanted to help the cause, so we arranged to run a 10-K within the Walpole (Massachusetts) State Prison yard. The inmates gave a few hundred dollars of "cigarette money" to the Jimmy Fund instead of using the money to purchase the very thing that causes so much cancer. My entire support crew went within the walls and ran alongside these men. When the 6.2 miles were covered, the crew and I exercised our freedom to leave, but we hoped we left behind some light in that very dark place.

> They have different jobs, different homes, and different goals in life, but they were all on the Cape yesterday for the same reason.

Edward Moran, Cape Cod Times, October 10, 1981

As with the cross-country run, I had a motor home and crew of invaluable people who supported me during the New England Run, as a way to be involved with the Jimmy Fund. In addition to those on the boats, I was aided by friends like Kent

Hawley and brothers Eddie and Bill Burke. Ed's 3-year-old daughter Jessica, a Jimmy Fund Clinic patient, had died of a brain tumor 8 years before the New England Run. The Burkes helped me on many journeys before and after this one. Years later, more of their family members, including Ed himself, developed cancer. Steve Quinn, a young guy with a keen knowledge of cycling, accompanied me on the bike and rode alongside me for some of the run portions, as did Dave Laprise. We had great photographers along for that trip: both my brother BMac and Lindsay White, a part-time UPI photographer who arranged to join our crew. And I greatly appreciated the public-relations efforts of Leo Callahan, a reporter I'd befriended in Bermuda, where I was putting on a series of children's races sponsored by Pro Specs.

The New England Run ended at Schaeffer Stadium (now Gillette Stadium) in Foxboro, Massachusetts, at a New England Patriots versus Houston Oilers game. I ran across the finish line tape with two Jimmy Fund patients, Tara Orlowski and Brendan Newman, and Johnny Kelley, who had driven up to be part of the finish. I felt so blessed to share the moment with two children who might benefit from the past 30 days of fund-raising, as well as a running legend who was a hero to me.

The 30-day "run" was in many ways more of a physical challenge than the cross-country run. I covered 1,522 miles, which broke down to 518 miles running, 29 miles swimming, and 975 miles cycling—and raised more than $60,000 for the Jimmy Fund. I also learned a lot about the power of a team effort.

One year later, I returned to Martha's Vineyard, the scene of my unfinished business. I chose the weekend just before the Falmouth Road Race, hoping the crowds gathered for that event might help my fund-raising effort. Once again, I was accompanied by Captain Ron, as well as several friends and support crew, including Coach Megerle from Tufts, Hal Gabriel, Kent Hawley, and Paul Daley, known to friends as "the Ghost" due to the pallor of his skin—though in later years, his DMSE colleagues would kid him about appearing at an event, getting the work done, and then disappearing without a trace.

Ron and I thought it best to swim in the opposite direction

and finish in Falmouth. By his own admission, it was one of Ron's few navigational errors. He put me in the water right off of West Chop, an area notorious for a very strong current. I went in the water at 9:24 a.m. and was out at 9:34. Next I started from the beach, caught the current, and went nowhere. Then it was back in the boat and back in the water at 9:43 for another try.

Ten minutes after that, I had more problems with the current; I wasn't even going in the right direction anymore, and I noticed the same buoy go by me a few times. I didn't know if had gotten cut loose—or if I'd already been there. Coach Megerle jumped in and swam with me until I got past it, and then I was fine. Hal and Paul also joined me in the water for a while.

At 1:45 p.m. I was done. It was a 7-mile swim—a very tough 7 miles. I spent most of the time treading water and not making any headway. As Ron explained it, that section of Nantucket, Woods Hole, has one of the worst currents in the world. If you look far east of Nantucket and Chatham, it's wide, and as it goes west, it narrows to a funnel, creating a confluence of current and turmoil in the water. It's no wonder that the Vineyard was the site chosen to film *Jaws*—although I think the water itself is much scarier than the great white.

I literally crawled out of the water and onto Falmouth Heights Beach. The good thing was, there were thousands of people on the beach. Among them were my mom and dad, Eddie Burke, and Tommy Leonard; so were Alberto Salazar and Craig Vergen, first- and second-place winners of the Boston Marathon, now in Falmouth for the race. As for me, mission accomplished—but the next day, I felt strong enough to run in the Falmouth Road race.

I think the 24-hour run was one of his toughest endeavors. On the final leg, he didn't know where he was going. Team members all agreed that he was in very bad shape, but he surprised us all when he snapped out of it and motioned to his crew to get going. My wife and I were really worried about him up to that point.

Dave's dad

This time, in 1980, *they* called *me*. The Wrentham (Massachusetts) State School, dedicated to the needs of the mentally retarded, had heard about me in the news and thought I might be just the guy to help them raise some extra money and awareness of their noble cause. I came up with the concept of running 120 miles in 24 hours throughout 31 cities and communities in southeastern Massachusetts: the "Run for Our Dreams Marathon." I don't know what the heck I was thinking when I proposed the 24-hour format, but I feel fortunate that I lived to tell about it. Most of the run was okay, but in the final hours, I gave yet another support crew and my parents a big scare.

Among my support was Hal, who ran the first 50 or 60 miles with me. Ron also ran 75 of those miles. The day we started was rainy and cold (of course!). At the end of each 10-mile split, we took a break. I had a few massage therapists with me, too. We picked up Michael Robinson, a podiatrist, 80 or 90 miles into the run, but by then we were more dead than alive.

About 100 miles into the trip, I stopped for some food, water, and just a few minutes of rest. But when I was ready to hit the road again, I headed in the wrong direction. My friends, and especially my parents, realized I was delirious. They were all around me, saying, "David, wrong way, turn around." It's even captured on video, which is astounding for me to watch because I don't remember any of it. It's clear that even though people were talking directly to me, I didn't hear them or pay attention. For just a few brief moments, my mind had betrayed me. In the end, I rallied and finished and was just fine.

It was another Foxboro finish, this one during the half-time of a Patriots versus Miami Dolphins game. The run raised more than $10,000, which back then went a lot further than it does now—very much like my legs. It made me feel good knowing that I helped the school in some small way. And just like always, my success was due in large part to the support of my friends and family who, for 24 hours, brought the mission of the Wrentham State School to the forefront of many people's minds.

Most people give money to the charity of choice in a much easier way: They simply write a check. Dave *believes* in what he's doing and is willing to walk the walk—or perhaps I should say "do the run"—himself. He's not a sort who claims credit without doing the work.

Bill Rodgers, marathon winner and running legend

After the 24-hour run, since I was in the triathlon mood, I decided on a 24-hour swim as my next fund-raiser/challenge. I trained in the Medford High School indoor pool, and school officials were kind enough to allow me to hold the event there, too. It was good to be home.

One day, while I was training, a swim instructor named Tim Barry came in. As he tells it, he said to his boss, Dick Lennon, the Medford High pool director, "Who is that guy?" after noticing that I had been doing laps for 4 hours. He wondered what the heck I was doing.

"Why, that's Dave McGillivray," answered his boss. "He's going to do a 24-hour swim here to benefit the Jimmy Fund."

"Well, he's not going to make it swimming like that!" commented Tim.

Tim says that I was swimming like a fish out of water, thrashing around. He came over to the side of the pool, introduced himself, and asked if he could help me out. I'm always open to improvement, so of course I said yes. Apparently, he took it upon himself to help me because he wanted to prevent me from drowning—my form was that poor. We started working in 2-hour increments and gradually worked up to 4 hours per day—which was probably more tiresome for Tim, who'd just walk back and forth and urge me to take a break.

After training with Tim for a while, it was time for the actual event, which took place in fall 1983. I started around 2 on a Friday afternoon, while school was still in session, so students and friends could swim laps with me. No one else stayed in the pool the entire time, but everyone who did a mile here or there boosted my spirits. As I swam in my own roped-off lane, I'd look up and see visitors, including Mike Andrews, director of the Jimmy Fund. Mike succeeded Ken Coleman in that role, and it meant a tremendous amount to me that he stopped by to show his support.

After every 50 minutes in the water, I'd get out and wolf down 10 or so of my mom's chocolate-chip cookies. My massage therapist, Margaret Karg, would work on my shoulders for 5 minutes, and then I'd jump back in.

My biggest boost came from Olympic swimming champion John Naber. In 1976, John captured four gold medals and a silver in Montreal. He also broke four world records. He and I met when he was doing some network commentating at the Ironman in 1980. At the time, he was sponsored by Speedo, a company with whom I had some close contacts. So when I told Speedo about my swim, they flew John out to Boston.

He came to my house the night before, and Kent Hawley, now one of my roommates, cooked us a spaghetti dinner. We were hanging out with John Naber—unbelievably cool. The next day, John spent about 30 minutes in the water with me. Swimming side by side with one of the best swimmers in my lifetime was a thrill. He's 6 feet 4 or 5; it took him about five strokes to do the pool from end to end, and it took me about 500.

I had underwater speakers put in at both ends of the lap lane, and the music saved me. There's nothing like swimming and listening to the soundtrack of *Saturday Night Fever*, although I could really only hear it if I was close to the speakers.

A few weeks earlier, I'd helped my landlord carry a refrigerator up three flights of stairs. Somewhere between ground level and our destination, I tore or pulled something in my shoulder—something important. I was a mixture of pain, frustration, and nerves before I even swam one stroke of that fund-raiser, because I knew there was potential for problems. I recall waking up the morning of that swim and acknowledging, then completely denying and ignoring, how bum my shoulder actually was. I swam anyway, which probably made the injury much worse.

It was 1,884 laps. Each lap was 25 yards. My total distance was nearly 27 miles—basically, I had swum a marathon. For reasons both obvious and not so obvious, the swim was different from my previous events. With running, I break down my ultimate goal into "splits" of specific, doable mileage goals. With the swim, I just swam laps until I had to either ingest or "expel" sustenance. It wasn't very scientific, but it worked.

As I'm running the marathon course, people will often say, "I don't know how you've done this so many times." Sometimes I think to myself, "You think running it is hard? Try swimming it!"

I had done a 24-hour run and a 24-hour swim, so the natural progression led to a 24-hour bike ride. The first event was tough on my feet, the second was hard on my shoulders, and this next one—well, let's just say that gel seats were not in the mainstream in the '80s.

In 1986, I decided to ride my bike for 24 hours around Spot Pond in Medford to make the effort a true swim-bike-run. By that time, I had created the Bay State Triathlon because I wanted athletes in New England to experience the rush of pushing oneself to the body's limits in a multidiscipline sport. So I combined my own efforts with those triathlon participants and rode my bike for 24 hours along that course. I was alone at first on the 5-mile loop but suddenly found myself with 500 companions for 3 or 4 hours.

A lot of friends came out to keep me company, though I must admit there was one whom I sent away. My friend Tim decided to ride his bike alongside me—problem was, his bike was a Harley Davidson. I thanked him for supporting me, then asked him to leave. It was just too loud for someone who'd already spent 12 hours on a bike.

The race went off without a hitch, as did the ride. I rode 385 miles (77 laps) in the final leg (this one for the Jimmy Fund) of my fund-raising triathlon: a 24-hour run in 1980, a 24-hour swim in 1983, and a 24-hour bike in 1986—3 years of transition time between segments. Whew.

The English Channel is a unique and demanding swim, considered by many to be the ultimate long-distance challenge. It isn't just the distance that is the challenge but more the variable conditions that you are likely to encounter. These may vary from mirrorlike conditions to wind force 6 and wave heights in excess of 2 meters. The water is cold;

there is a good chance of meeting jellyfish, seaweed, and the occasional plank of wood. It is one of the busiest shipping lanes in the world, with 600 tankers passing through and 200 ferries/Seacats and other vessels going across daily.

ChannelSwimmingAssociation.com

My ill-fated trek to England to swim the infamous English Channel in 1988 stands out as the only event I have ever planned and prepared for that I did not complete. In fact, I never even started.

After my 24-hour swim and some experience with open water/ ocean swimming, I looked forward to testing my endurance on another continent. I joined the Channel Swimming Association; according to their Web site, they have organized and regulated all "official" channel swims since 1927, and their record books go back even further. They provided me with information and contact names of those who could help me accomplish the task.

I opened up the Jimmy Fund–English Channel Swim bank account and started collecting donations. I also assembled a small team of people to help me. We made countless phone calls to England and also met with the US Coast Guard, gathering as much information as possible about the channel tides and other conditions.

First and foremost, the best time to attempt the swim is July through September, with the most ideal conditions in August. You can't just fly over and jump into the water; it's basically required that you stay at least a week to allow time for getting a clear day to make the crossing.

The English Channel is 21 miles as the crow flies; however, it's more like 30 miles the way I swim. The actual "course" usually starts near Shakespeare's Cliff, between Folkeston and Dover, England, and finishes near Cap Gris Nez between Boulogne and Calais, France. Beginning at Shakespeare's Cliff is fitting, since the big question for me was "to swim or not to swim."

At the time, I felt I could slug my way through it. Tim Barry coached me, as did Coach Megerle. Through Tim's gentle advice and instruction, my stroke gradually improved. Apparently, I didn't do everything I was told, but I eventually got there, though it took a lot of work and time.

I brought my personal boat captain, Ron Kramer, over to England for the attempt in August 1988. Thanks to our experience at Martha's Vineyard, I knew I could trust him to look out for me while I was in the water.

A woman from the channel association introduced us to a fishing-boat captain who would serve as my guide boat and then take me from France back to the white cliffs of Dover. We also met a terrific coach named Tom Watch. He was the English equivalent of Billy Squires, the founding coach of the Greater Boston Track Club who worked with me and many successful athletes, including Bill Rodgers, Greg Meyer, and Alberto Salazar. (Coach Squires called me Long Run, for obvious reasons.) We told Tom we'd stay for a week, and if the right conditions presented themselves, we'd give it a shot. He invited me to train the next morning with three of his swimmers.

We met on a beach between Folkeston and Dover, right along the straights of the channel. It was a cool, misty, foggy day; it felt just like Nantucket. Ron and Coach Tom stood together on the beach. The coach, the weather, the accents . . . I felt like I was in my own version of *Chariots of Fire*.

> It started to rain so hard that we had to get out of it, so we took a walk away from the water. The two of us took shelter in a World War II bunker. Tom was in his sixties, kind of weather-beaten, as he smoked a cigarette and watched his three swimmers and Dave, who were swimming in the channel about 100 yards away. Dave had taken maybe two dozen strokes when Tom asked me if Dave had a problem with his right shoulder. I was shocked at this as I replied, "*Yes,* he does."
>
> *"Captain" Ron*

Tom knew I was hurting. My swimming strokes were not even. Ron was amazed and impressed that he was so astute, he could pick that up from half a football field–length away. The injury of carrying the refrigerator still plagued me, probably because I didn't give it the healing time or care it required. In fact, it hurts me even today.

I later learned that Tim, my swim coach at home, had doubted that I could swim through the shoulder pain for the 15 or 16 hours it would take to cross the channel. But even if he had shared his opinion with me then, I most likely still would've flown all those miles just to prove him wrong. But I never had the chance to do so. The weather never cooperated, nor did my shoulder. After about 20 minutes, it would really bother me. Coach Tom tried to help me out but to no avail.

We stayed at a bed-and-breakfast in Folkeston. One morning when Ron and I were in the lobby, about 10 guys came down for breakfast. They all had deep-brown skin—Middle Eastern, maybe? And each man was an amputee or partial amputee. We could not imagine what so many disabled folks were doing in this little out-of-the-way B & B.

We struck up a conversation with a few of the men and learned that they were Egyptian and all there for the same reason: They were going to swim the Channel, in relay fashion. Ron and I were blown away. It took guts and courage to attempt the swim even under the best of circumstances.

More people from Egypt have swum the English Channel than from any other country, they told us. In 1920, the Olympics were held in Cairo, and the king wanted his nation to excel at some sport. Himself a swimmer, he started a youth program that has produced generations of great Egyptian swimmers. The channel represents the pinnacle of swimming goals for their country, so many of them come over—and succeed. Ron and I watched in awe as this exceptional group of men, many hobbling on crutches, crossed the street and followed the path down to the beach, where they slipped into the water and swam with impressive agility and grace.

While in England, we met lots of people who shared our goal. One kid, Mark Newman, about 17 at the time, was a great swimmer and attempting his first channel. We all hoped to make the swim together, but for 8 days straight, we experienced the same foggy, damp, cold, misty weather that reminded me of that fateful first swim attempt at the Vineyard. Every day, the water temp averaged about 50 degrees. I'd get out after training and shake and shiver for several hours afterward. Even worse, in Ron's opinion, was the absolutely disgusting smell of the fishing boat that guided us. We had an incredible experience for those 8 days, but in the end, it was really disappointing to return home without having accomplished, or even attempted, the goal.

Mark Newman stayed until the weather improved, and wound up setting a record. I think he swam the channel five or six more times after that, though since then, his record has been broken.

For me, never starting was almost worse than trying and not finishing. I felt like a bit of a failure because I had made a commitment that I hadn't fulfilled. Following through with commitments has always been my goal. I have a certain stubbornness about getting things done.

Honestly, do I have the desire today to do the amount of training and make the sacrifice necessary to earn the right to make an attempt? No. But maybe a relay format would work—and I know just the people I want on the team.

I am often asked, especially by children, what my greatest accomplishment is. I tell them it's my next one—and although it's important to remember what we have accomplished, it is more important to keep doing more.

I never intended to start running and never stop. It just fed on itself. The same goes for the charitable aspect of my athletic journeys. In a way, my life is a quest to prove the theory of perpetual motion. I don't intend to stop until something stops me first.

North Medford Little League, Hosmer Tigers, 1966. Coach Matta, upper left; Coach Henry, upper right. John Hosmer, sponsor, and Vin Rivera, assistant coach, also in the back row. That would be me, front and center. Photo by Bob McGillivray

Running a 2-mile indoor race for Medford High School at Phillips Andover Academy, Andover, Masachusetts, winter 1972. Coach Lou D'Angelis counts down the seemingly endless number of laps left to go. Photo by Medford High School

Reaching the top: I made it all the way up the Rocky Mountains—with my support crew. Front (left to right): Tom Kinder, Kent Hawley; rear: Jeff Donohoe, me, Dan Carey. The tougher challenge awaited—running down the mountains on the other side. Photo by Tom Kinder

Heading out of the Rocky Mountains in Colorado during the Run Across America. The motor home is parked on the side of the road as I run past. Note we spelled *Athletic* wrong on the top banner and drove all the way across the country with no one ever saying anything! The banner below blew off a number of times, as evident by its condition. Photo by Kent Hawley

Crossing the Mississippi River: This marks a major milestone—and the point of no return—in the Run Across America. Photo by Kent Hawley

Run Across America—Pennsylvania. Almost home, I reflect on the past few months and contemplate the final few weeks. Photo by Kent Hawley

Fenway Park, August 29, 1978. Finish of my solo 3,452-mile Run Across America, in front of 32,000 Red Sox fans. Bill Campbell, Red Sox pitcher, throws me his cap from the dugout. Photo by Bob McGillivray

Oval Office visit, March 1980. Bob Hall and I met with President Jimmy Carter in the White House during the East Coast Run. When we explained we were raising money for the "Jimmy" Fund, the president's eyes lit up. Photo by White House Staff (unidentified)

With Bob Hall, wheelchair marathoner, at a celebration in Fenway Park a few months after our 1981 run up the East Coast for the Jimmy Fund. With us are four members of the Boston Red Sox: Jim Rice, Dwight Evans, Dennis Eckersley, and Dick Drago. All four ran a lap around Chain O' Lakes Park in Winter Haven, Florida, a few months earlier to kick off our run. Photo by Bob McGillivray

Finishing the New England Run in what was then Schaefer Stadium (now Gillette Stadium) at the halftime of a New England Patriots football game. With me are the legendary marathoner, Johnny Kelley, and two Jimmy Fund patients, Brendan Newman and Tara Orlowski, as we are welcomed by 60,000 fans. Photo by Bob McGillivray

Meeting my biggest fans: My father and mother at the 27-mile point of my 32nd birthday run along the Boston Marathon course. Photo by Bob McGillivray

Running in a 10-K race I organized inside the Walpole State Prison yard. Armed prison guards watch from the towers above. Photo by Bob McGillivray

Running in a local road race for the Greater Boston Track Club, wearing (for the first and perhaps only time) the coveted #1 bib. Photo by F. H. McGillivray

In front of my house in North Andover, Massachusetts, with 4 miles to go of my 40th birthday run, August 21, 1994. Of course, it is raining out. Photo by Bob McGillivray

Finish of the 2002 Boston Marathon Night Run: Katie Lynch, wearing a laurel wreath that I presented her that morning after her own "run," returns the favor that evening. Photo by Bob McGillivray

My family (left to right): Me, Katie, Elle (20 months), Max (12), Ryan (15), and secretly one more on the way! Photo by Bob McGillivray

CHAPTER 7

My Birthday Suit

Most people treat themselves on their birthday. Maybe they toast the
moment with a glass of champagne, slice an extra piece of cake, or
light up a cigar. Not McGillivray. He beats himself into the ground.

Rob Duca, **Cape Cod Times,** *August 16, 1999*

It started as a desire to accomplish something—something outside the norm. On August 22, 1966, I was wearing my sneakers
but had no particular place to go. I headed out the door and
toward Spot Pond. I decided on the 5½-mile lollipop loop
(named for how it looks on a map) from my house and back.
That kind of mileage would be a new experience for me on the
day I turned 12 years old. I had never before run, other than the
usual strides inherent with being a young boy, like those taken
between bases or running down a basketball court.

Turning 12 was a big deal to my small self. I wanted to do
something that would be challenging—truly challenging—and
give me a sense of accomplishment for the day. Back then, there
was no higher aspiration for me than to prove myself an athlete;
although I was still convinced that "sports" applied only to team
sports such as basketball and baseball. But for now, what better
way to test my stamina than with a run? So off I went.

I returned home feeling pretty good. I felt even better when I found that Grandpa Eaton had dropped by to take me out for ice cream. He and I walked up to Buttrick's, *the* place for ice cream in that part of Medford. As we walked, we talked about the miles I had just completed. My grandfather was impressed, but I wasn't satisfied that I had done something memorable enough.

As I thought about it a bit more, I got the idea to do another loop so that I could accumulate 12 miles for the day, or 1 mile for every year of my life. (Everything in my life is all about the numbers adding up.) I liked the equation: Miles Run = Age on Birthday = Goal.

By the time my grandfather and I were done with our mint chip, I had decided to go one more time around the pond, plus a mile, to get the total mileage I was after. At age 12, a few scoops of ice cream was all it took to fuel me for what would become my inaugural birthday run. I was a little tired, but the desire to achieve something unique that day outweighed the discomfort of any lactic-acid buildup from that first go-round. As would be the case with so much of my running throughout my life, it was the mental muscle that helped me to attain what I was after.

My grandfather waited for me to finish up, same as he would do at several other turning points in my young life. He seemed to quietly understand my need for a sense of accomplishment. The only thing that might have made the experience better was a great pair of running shoes, which I don't think existed back in the 1960s. The leather sneakers I had on were not exactly ideal for running in the heat, plus they seemed to weigh a few pounds each.

I had no idea then that what began on a whim would follow me forever after. I'm 51 years old, but I don't feel much different than I did back then. A lot of it could be genetic—at age 85, my father is more active than most of my contemporaries—but I'm a believer that state of mind has even more to do with it than state of body. I was brought up to say "I can," never "I can't," and I lived with two parents who made the most of their lives.

In fact, to me, a birthday is actually a celebration of parents, not a child. My birthday is a tribute to my mom and dad and the love and commitment that went into raising me. It's not I who deserves a present each August—it's them. The greatest gift I could ever give them and my other loved ones—particularly my wife and children—is to be as healthy as I can be. I never want to be a burden to anyone. I believe we all have an obligation to keep ourselves in the best possible physical shape so we can be self-reliant. It's a big reason I run today.

Breaking the distance down into two equal loops made that first run attainable, and although it was not done that way by design, I've followed that tactic ever since. At ages 13, 14, and 15, I set the same goal and met the challenge on each birthday, but it was a lot of miles for a young boy. By 17, I had begun running marathons, which brought my athletic conditioning up to a whole new level. After that, the birthday runs got a bit easier, as they were always under that 26.2-mile distance. Now that I'm more than half a century old, I'm running an ultramarathon distance on my birthday and reconsidering the "rules" of this commitment that I made to myself.

Though now a trademarked slogan, "just do it" is a philosophy I've always tried to live by. It's a simple approach that is sometimes the only way to get anything accomplished. I wanted to run, so I did it. In fact, I mostly kept the endeavor to myself. It wasn't a secret, but it wasn't something I brought up in conversation, either. Back then it was easier to expose my goal *after* I had accomplished the task. That way, I didn't disappoint anyone but myself if I didn't succeed. So every year, I would "quietly" go out and run my neighborhood streets to celebrate my life. I just wanted the personal satisfaction of knowing I was getting stronger every year.

Now, as I gain confidence in whatever task I'm doing, I take the opposite approach. If I want to enhance the commitment and keep myself motivated, I announce my goal. Having others aware of my intention keeps me true to my word, especially on the days when I wake up and think, "Not today; I just don't think I can do it today." It's then that I gain tremendous strength from those around me who offer encouragement and support.

These runs have served as a diary of my life, though I say shame on me for not documenting where I was each August 22 and who I ran with, for no one's interest but my own. The first years, I just went out and ran the miles. As I got into my late teens and early adulthood, I looked forward to the solitude as a way to plan the coming year. Most people do this on New Year's Eve, but I usually make my resolutions in August. It gives me something productive to do as I pass the same landmarks with each loop, over and over and over again.

Initially, I'd just go out the front door and return home several hours later. I'd cover the miles early, before most people were even awake. No matter what else was going on that day, running was part of my birthday routine. By my twenties, I began to "celebrate" in locations other than my home.

I was on a business trip in Manhattan the day I turned 22. I ran 17 miles through Central Park and around New York City— that was all I had time for before catching my plane back to Logan. By the time we landed on Massachusetts soil, it was already dark; nonetheless, as soon as I got home, I dropped my suitcase and went back out to complete my last 5 miles in familiar surroundings. It didn't matter to me whether or not I did the miles consecutively, as long as all 22 were run on August 22 before the clock struck midnight. I had to run 6-minute miles to reach that goal, but I did it. Those were my rules at the time.

"Happy Birthday, David McGillivray, Wherever You Are!"

Patriot Ledger headline, August 23, 1978

My 24th birthday was a little different than any I'd celebrated before. I was about a week away from completing my run across the country. That was one birthday for which I had truly overtrained! In fact, running 24 miles would be a bit of a rest. And though my intent was to do only 24, I got so caught up in the excitement of having my family with me and of crossing the Massachusetts border that I continued on. I ended with 42 miles for the day and made a mental note to run only 24 when I turned 42. But with memory being the first to go as we age, I forgot to stop at 24 when the time came.

Just before my next birthday, a friend of mine from Merrimack College, Mike Beeman, asked if I'd join him on a charity run in New Hampshire. It just happened to coincide with my annual run, and I figured Mike could use the company, so I did it: 25 miles on a track, or 100 laps, also known as "loops." One hundred loops: around, and around, and around. *Loopy* is more like it; that's how I felt when I was done. That was the first and last time I chose a track as the venue for the birthday run.

I ran 60 miles when I turned 26, not because I was delirious but because I was training for my 24-hour run, which would take place just a few months later. (I hoped to "bank" those miles for later but so far haven't used them. I'm thinking maybe now is the time to cash in!) By then, my birthday miles were the equivalent of a marathon, so I headed for familiar territory and ran the Boston Marathon course.

I spent a decade of birthdays running that route, each year altering the start to suit my needs. At age 27, I started at the 1-mile mark, then ran back to the start and ran the entire route. By 37, I started in Natick, ran to Hopkinton, and then headed back to Boston. That was too many miles away from having a true "home base," however, and simple issues like water and bathroom facilities became logistical problems. So at 38, I ran around the neighborhood in North Andover, where I lived with my family, with my own house serving as a pit stop.

My friends and family are curious about when this birthday gig will come to an end. But why does it have to stop? I can tweak the rules a bit and still get the same result. One continuous run was tough, so as I got older, it was time to divide and conquer. I broke up the mileage into smaller splits of 5, 7, or 10 miles: same goal, different approach. Others may see the obstacles, but I try to focus on the excitement of the challenge.

With an August birthday, I'm almost guaranteed a scorching-hot day every year. I stole a page from the run across the country and decided to head out earlier to beat the heat. I'm not complaining, though; the heat is better than battling the wind of a nor'easter in the fall or subzero temps in the winter. If I had been born during one of those seasons, I may never have started this in the first place.

Another change in "format" came at age 40. Until then, I always did the run on my actual birthday, but that year, I broke the string. I wanted to celebrate in a big way, though I know a lot of folks just pray that 40 will come and go without much notice. My birthday was on a Monday, and I decided to do the run on a Sunday. The weekend closest to August 22 was also the weekend of the Falmouth Road Race on Cape Cod, considered by most New England runners to be as important as *the* marathon.

The party was scheduled for the evening so everyone could finish the race and drive up afterward. During the day, however, it was eerily quiet. I ran alone because basically everyone I knew was running Falmouth. By the time they crossed the finish line, I had already completed 36 miles of my personal race, which I had begun at about 6 a.m. In between splits, I put up two 20-foot tents in my backyard. Setting them up alone was almost as challenging as running the 40 miles I needed to complete by day's end.

When the guests arrived around 4 p.m., we (about 80 of the 150 guests, including my dad) ran and walked my final 4 miles together. The course began and ended at the foot of my driveway. And, as is the case with most DMSE-produced events, it started to rain *really hard*! When we finished, we all sought shelter (and sustenance) under the tents.

My repertoire includes not only race planning but party planning. I had put together a slide show, videos, and games, including my trademark "Pin the Mustache on Dave." More than a decade later, my signature mustache is long gone, but my memories of that day remain vivid.

Increasing age turned the birthday run into an all-day endeavor, beginning in darkness and often ending in rainstorms or sweltering heat (or, more likely, both). As the years passed, I worried that my little run had become a full-fledged event and possibly an imposition to those who felt they needed to accompany me. For more than a decade, my friend Dave Laprise cleared his calendar to run big portions with me, and several other friends have done the same. By moving the run to Saturday or Sunday when my birthday fell on a weekday, no one, including me, had to miss work. Breaking with tradition was hard at first, but once done, I appreciated the freedom of choosing more-convenient dates.

> But his toughest run was unquestionably at 41. Coming off a devastating divorce, McGillivray was at [his brother's rental house] in Harwichport when the day approached. When his alarm rang at 6:00 a.m., he pulled the covers over his head and went back to sleep. At 7:00, 8:00, and 9:00, a voice in his head kept shouting, "No, no, no. Not this year."

> *Robert Duca, Cape Cod Times, August 16, 1999*

On my 40th birthday, I had a great day; a year later, everything was falling apart around me. It was my mental shape, not physical ability, that almost did me in. That year, as my first marriage ended, was the most painful and challenging one of my life. Keeping up my birthday tradition helped me hold myself together at a time when I faced countless uncertainties. The day of that run, I was feeling particularly down and didn't get out of bed as early as usual. The clock was ticking later into the day, and I still hadn't laced up my sneakers. With my friend Bob Barnaby's help and a lot of faith, I finally got started, and as I racked up the miles, my mood improved. Still, it took everything I had. In some ways, that birthday run saved my life. It forced me to keep going.

> He's taught me that within the context of your plan, just modify, but still do something; still get out there. . . . His message is that what you're doing is not only good for yourself but for others as well.

> *Josh Nemzer, DMSE consultant*

When I turned 45, I planned my birthday run within the parameters of the Falmouth Road Race, using the home of my friend Kevin Cummings, who was renting a house near the course, as the base of out-and-back runs. At 2 a.m., my friend Josh Nemzer and I started at the Falmouth finish, as another friend, Mike Thompson, followed in a van to light our way. Getting hit by a car or stepping in a pothole were greater dangers than the miles I faced. Later, Tom Licciardello and his wife, Lyn, joined us. I ran the race course in five 6-plus-mile loops, then ran to Woods Hole and back. I scheduled it so I could finish the final 7 during the actual race and wind up with everyone else.

While I was flexible with timing, I did have this rule: The miles must be run *before* my birthday, up to 2 weeks before the date. This way, if I start the run but for some reason can't finish it then, I still have time to accomplish the goal. It takes the edge off the pressure I put myself under every summer.

The window of time is mostly a mental cushion; the first time I came close to actually needing it was at age 47, when an injury nearly prevented me from accomplishing my goal. A recurring calf problem just wouldn't quit. My massage therapist recommended magnet therapy—a noninvasive method of applying magnetic fields to the body. It seemed to bring relief and gave me enough confidence to attempt the run. My friend John Mixon and I did a series of loops in my neighborhood. It was raining hard—what else is new?—and with only 4 miles left, my calf muscle suddenly seized up and stopped functioning. I could hardly walk, let alone run, but I limped the last miles in agonizing and frustrating fashion.

I did break my self-imposed rule once, and that was at age 49, when I was delayed due to a run-in with a folding table. I planned to do my birthday run the day after the 2003 People's Beach to Beacon 10K Road Race in Maine. The day of the race, it began to pour (of course!), so I set up the water tables at the start. As I picked up one of the 6-foot tables, it fell on my foot and broke a toe—the first fracture of my life. I had to postpone the 49 miles until mid-September.

That morning, I was accompanied by my own "pace" bunny, a.k.a. Josh, who joins me on many of my runs these days. He must have been the prototype for the bunny you see on TV. He just goes and goes. We headed out around 4 a.m. and finished at 3:50 p.m. Josh could have done the 49 miles in his sleep, while numerous times throughout our run that day, I wished I had not been woken up from mine!

As always, this "celebration"—if that's what you can call running for 12 hours—was accomplished by running, jogging, and shuffling through seven 7-mile splits (or laps) around my neighborhood. Bob Barnaby, who has helped me continue this streak over the past 8 years, joined us for 11 miles. The highlight of this particular run was when my wife, Katie, and son Ryan showed up for the last 5 miles—just what the doctor ordered to get us through that final stage of that late-date run. I felt rejuvenated: I was in better health and better able to cover the miles at nearly half a century than I was in my early forties, when I nearly ended what I'd started all those years ago.

My birthday run is arguably my most challenging event each year, but it's much more than logging miles. It helps me conquer life issues and set goals while I reflect upon the prior year's highlights and heartaches. While I often run in the company of friends and family, there have been hundreds of lonely miles, too; the year I turned 36, for example, I did the entire run alone.

If it was easy, it wouldn't be the challenge it needs to be. The lesson for me is going beyond, digging deep.

Dave, *Cape Cod Times, August 16, 1999*

This "race" gets exponentially more difficult for me, but that's the point. It makes me tougher. I don't ever want to feel old. And at this point in my life, it's more about being mentally ready than physically ready. I choose a day on which to run, and I'm out the door on that date, no matter what the weather.

If I had a personal statistician, I might be able to confirm that at least 75 percent of these celebratory runs have been in the rain. For example, during that 45th birthday day in Falmouth, the rain was sideways in my face and the puddles were so large, I would've been better off wearing waders. Meanwhile, I was plagued by a flare-up of my Achilles tendon.

I don't actually train for the birthday run, though I probably should. I just do my normal stint of a few miles a day, a few times a week, if I'm lucky. About 3 months before my birthday, I head out with just one thing on my mind: How do I feel? How am I going to do this? It happens every year, every time. When a short run of 4 miles seems like a struggle, I wonder how I'm going to do more than 50.

As the date nears, I try to make my running a tad more consistent. I also move some long runs up on the priority list for August, more than I would any other time of year (except maybe March, just before the marathon). I try to get a good night's sleep, and the rest is done on "memory," just as with that other annual run in my life, the Boston Marathon.

The birthday run and the Boston Marathon are powerful forces in my life, each with its own importance and impact on everything else I do. For example, my "first" birthday route became part of the running route for the Bay State Triathlon, the Medford-based Ironman qualifier that I founded more than a decade later.

Just by its repetitive nature, each run becomes more significant every year. The first time out, I simply tried to reach a goal. The second time, particularly with the birthday run, I did it because I had done it the year before. By the third time, it started to feel like a personal obligation, and by the fifth or sixth time, there was no question I would do it. It had become a "thing."

Commitments. Streaks. I'm not sure if there is a word to accurately describe all the "things" that I do annually and without fail. Running Boston every year after my grandfather died, more than 34 years ago, was the only time I actually determined that I would do something "forever." There have also been some smaller, more obscure things—more like "strings" of events—sequences that start and don't finish until they're all played out, like that determination to have perfect attendance at school and to never request a bathroom pass.

My commitments are not limited to physical challenges. For example, there's my annual holiday card: About 12 years ago, I decided to send out Christmas cards. My oldest son, Ryan, was an infant, and new fatherhood didn't leave enough time for me to talk to or see all my friends on a regular basis. I wanted to use my own words rather than send preprinted cards, so I created my own and have done so every year since. I send cards out to nearly 500 people, and the one year I was "late" (I called them New Year's cards), I must have received 40 e-mails from people wondering where their cards were. Apparently, others were making sure I continued my own streak.

Outsiders may perceive these various streaks as showboating or wanting to stand out. I view them as goals set and met. Every time I reach a goal, I gain confidence, and no one can take that great feeling of achievement away from me. That's reason enough to keep up a streak.

> "Pressure is a privilege."
>
> *Billie Jean King, sports pioneer*

The way I feel about my birthday run is similar to how Billie Jean King viewed playing in the Wimbledon finals year after year: Yes, there's pressure, but it's also a privilege. When I was 26, I'd say, "What's the big deal? I run marathons all the time." In my forties: "I averaged 40 miles a day on the cross-country run." Now I'm in my fifties, but I've run 50-plus miles only a handful of times in my life. Now I feel the pressure!

To be even remotely in a position to do this run means I am fortunate. Half of the people I know who are my age have trouble getting out of bed, and I'm planning to run upward of 50 miles. The general thinking is that as you age, you do less. But as I get older, I have to run farther—and this concept thrills me because it goes against all the rules. I have this goal of beating age. I want to attack it.

The birthday run serves as a great reality check. As I set out each year, I face the ultimate test of whether getting older is taking its toll. Of course, there are things I have less control over—say, my eyesight. I have glasses to see at close distances, but I refuse to cave in and wear them, so I squint. It makes me feel as though I'm defying age, even though life would be a lot easier if I'd just rest my ego a bit and put them on.

Once the birthday run has come and gone, I'm able to let it all go for 2 or 3 months, until it's time to start training for my other annual "event." Having the birthday run in the summer and the Boston Marathon in the spring keeps me motivated. I have to get out on the road; those two goals keep me on my toes (and heels) all year long.

That first birthday run, when I wanted to do something really challenging, could've been influenced by Johnny Weissmuller—"Tarzan." I was glued to our black-and-white TV as I watched this incredibly fit and loincloth-clad actor swing through the trees on a rope, and he always got the girl. He was possibly the first superhero that I can recall. My admiration for him was tremendous. His body was chiseled by the hours of training he must have put in each day as an Olympic swimmer, and I wanted to look just like that.

Years later, I was watching the *Tonight Show,* and it was announced that the great Johnny Weissmuller was going to be on with Johnny Carson. I waited with childlike anticipation but was shattered by what I saw. The man whom I had thought extraordinary was weathered and aged. He wasn't Tarzan anymore. It hit me like a ton of bricks. I mean no disrespect to this man who was such an accomplished athlete in his younger days, but I couldn't help but wonder, "How could this happen to someone who had been so fit and so strong?" There may be no rhyme or reason to why some people are dealt life's most debilitating and life-threatening diseases, but seeing him affirmed my desire to work even harder to maintain a certain level of health and fitness throughout my life for as long as possible.

Sports heroes may be awe inspiring during their heydays, but what interests me most is what happens to them when the spotlight has moved on to others, and their numbers hang from the rafters of some arena. To me, a true athlete is someone who tries to maintain physical excellence through all of life's twists and turns—such as Ron Burton, the former star running back for the New England Patriots. As Jimmy Fund Boston Council volunteers, he and I shared the podium several times at fund-raising dinners and worked together for more than 20 years. He was an athlete, philanthropist, motivator, and inspiration to thousands, especially children. Several years ago, Ron passed away from a devastating form of cancer, and his death illustrated that no matter what, aging and illness are two things we can't deny or defy. However, if working out and staying fit better equips me to face the unknown, then that's what I'll do.

I'm also inspired by Bill Riley, another good friend of mine from Cape Cod. Bill just turned 70 and regularly runs races and does triathlons, consistently winning and setting records in his age group. What people like him show me is that being fit is a choice; they are true role models.

Family tops my "what's important" list, of course, but I have to say that the birthday run and Boston Marathon are right up there, too. They represent much more than an athletic challenge. They're both so personal and important to my ego. I must admit that, when the day comes—and it will—that either one of these ends, there is going to be a void in my life too big to fathom. I will have to ask myself, "Well, what have I got left?" It won't be just the run that will disappear. In a way, it will be like mourning the loss of a best friend. It's going to be huge.

If I don't change the rules of the birthday run, it'll be over before the marathon is. The birthday run is already twice as hard and getting harder every year. Perhaps I'll stop when the miles become so great that I have to bring along an extra pair of shoes, a headlamp, and a road atlas—probably all things I could already put to good use.

To me, old age is always 15 years older than I am.

Bernard M. Baruch, US businessman and politician, 1940

When I was running 20 years ago, I felt like Superman. I'd wake up, bang out the birthday run, and move on to the next activity of the day. Now I'm not planning the next thing; the reality of age hits me more than anything because of the fact that the run dominates the day, beginning in the dark of morning and ending in the dark of night.

If you mark your birthday only by eating some cake, maybe having a drink or two, then it doesn't really make that particular day any different from another. My birthday celebration, however, underscores the reality of getting older: I cannot do today what I was able to do yesterday. That's just life. It's a hard lesson that I relearn every year. It's no longer just a long run; it's an *epic*.

I'm a Leo. That's about all I know of my Zodiac sign. However, I did read once about a particular characteristic that Leos share: a desire to make endeavors fun for ourselves and those around us. Indeed, I do try to make work fun, and play even better. So when I turned 50, I threw another party. Having friends to talk and laugh with is far better company than the potential misery I might experience in the last 10 or so miles of a run if I were alone.

Ironically, I was better prepared physically and mentally for 50 than I was at 40, which just shows that it's not how old you are, it's how fit you are. Just 4 months prior, in May 2004, I had once again run across the country, only this time as part of an 11-person relay team called Trek USA. Each of us averaged roughly 15 to 20 miles a day for 25 days. The residual affect, even months later, was that I felt great and ready to run that August.

The final miles of the birthday-party run were done in 1-mile loops so the revelers could do as many or as few as they wanted. The day was capped off with a pool party and barbecue complete with a roast—though unfortunately, it was of me! My siblings got up and uttered a few remembrances of my first half-century of life. It was a personal celebration, not so much about my birthday but of the fact that I got through what I perceived as potentially the last of the birthday-run tradition.

> Once I was looking through the kitchen window at dusk and I saw an old man looking in. Suddenly the light changed and I realized that the old man was myself. You see, it all happens on the outside; inside one doesn't change.
>
> *Molly Keane, Irish novelist*

I set up the dichotomy. It's bittersweet. Look what I did to myself. People who are close to me expect me to do it. As the candles increase each year, so do the miles, but as a present to myself as I get older, I think I'll alter the "rules" just slightly. Maybe I'll start counting backward and begin subtracting miles as I get older, or perhaps I'll use a new formula in which each decade equals 1 mile. Whether I'm riding a bike, pushing a walker, or even pushed in a wheelchair, as long as I cover the miles of whatever goal I choose, that's all that matters.

This whole concept is not easy, and those around me know that I'm not always in the shape I want to be in, but if or when I stray, I always find my way back. I owe that to the birthday run and the Boston Marathon. They both keep me fit in this race against time. Some onlookers may think it interesting or odd that I've done these two runs year after year. In a sense, they're the only constants in my life, and they give me a certain sense of stability and security, especially during times when life is in utter chaos.

The annual run brings new meaning to the phrase "I can hardly wait until next year." What will I do when I'm 90? Who knows? One of these years, I could break my leg the day before, but a physical setback like that is the only thing that will prevent me from at least attempting the run; I know I can overcome the mental battle. Sometimes at the 20- or 30-mile mark, I think I'm not going to be able to do it, but then I talk myself back into it. I know I'll never take the out.

Running all these miles as I hit every chronological milestone of my life has provided a great way for me to monitor my own aging process. The chorus sung at my 7th birthday party is the same one I hope they're still be singing when I'm 70: "How old are you now?" By keeping my birthday suit in excellent working condition, I hope to always keep them guessing about the answer to that one.

CHAPTER 8

Give and Take

The '70s in Boston were very special to the running community, for we were the hub of the marathon boom that would later capture the world's attention. We were fellow members of the North Medford Club, where we shared the typical team competition and camaraderie. What was not typical from this younger-by-14-years friend of mine was his initiative and creativity to use our sport in a very special way: run to raise money for charity.

Ron Kramer, cross-country track and
field coach, relay director, Trek USA

If I depart this world tomorrow, the legacy I hope to leave for my children is that of both a healthy heart and a charitable one. We each measure success in our own way. For me, it is not the miles logged or the awards won. Fulfillment is in knowing that I've created something that directly benefits someone else. This is in some ways a *selfish* notion. At the same time that I raise money or awareness for a cause, I also like the way it makes *me* feel.

When I graduated from college with a degree in math, I never dreamed that I would have the personal tools to effect change in someone's life. I didn't see myself in medicine, social work, or any other vocation in which helping others is an inherent part of the job; to be honest, I didn't put that much thought into it. Now I realize it doesn't matter what you do for a living or what your status is—we can all do a little something each day to help someone else. That is perhaps the most important message that I want to pass down to my children. It seems simple enough, but sometimes focusing their attention on what truly matters is a tremendous challenge amid the competition of computers, video games, and reality TV.

Being smaller than most of the other boys, and nearly every girl, my age proved to be a blessing for me. As I tried to compensate for what I believed was a "handicap," I gained empathy for those with real challenges, like people who live every day from the perspective of a wheelchair or don't have enough money to feed their family. It is these people who inspire me. They remind me how blessed I am for my good health, and that no matter how frustrated I may feel at times about my height, I have an enormous responsibility to maintain my body and mind and not allow either one to go to waste. I also want to ensure that the people close to me in my life, and even those I meet through speaking engagements, road races, and business, know that no matter what the challenge—an athletic aspiration or otherwise—anyone can set goals and achieve success.

Each person has the ability to make a difference in someone else's life. My intent is not to preach about what we should all be doing. I am not perfect by any stretch of the imagination, and what I do for others is very small compared to what is done every day by some exceptional members of the human race. And I don't mean just the people writing the checks—I'm talking about people who have the treasure troves of compassion and a selfless focus to change something for the better.

Help Make a Dream Come True. Support the Jimmy Fund.

Billboard formerly at Fenway Park

Months prior to the run across the country, I had tried to secure the Muscular Dystrophy Association as the benefiting charity for my work, hoping they would allow me to raise money for them as I ran across the United States. "No thanks," they said. That rejection opened the door to something that has been an integral part of my life for more than 25 years. It led me to the Jimmy Fund, the official charity of the Boston Red Sox.

In 1967, the Red Sox finally gave me (and my brother and all of New England) a reason to root for them and put away the Yankees T-shirt I'd been wearing. The "voice of summer," Ken Coleman, brought the dream of a Red Sox championship into our homes every game. He made us true believers in our home-town team. Alan and I, with our renewed faith, were drawn to Fenway Park. Every time we went to a game, I noticed the billboard on the right-field wall.

> Although [former Red Sox owner] Tom Yawkey had banned advertising from Fenway Park in the 1950s, he made an exception for the Jimmy Fund. For more than 50 years, the massive Jimmy Fund sign that was perched on the right-field roof above the club's retired numbers was the only billboard in the stadium.
>
> *JimmyFund.org*

Though I didn't know exactly what it meant, that billboard stuck in my mind, perhaps because it was the only one inside the park. In fact, I could see the back of it poking up from Fenway Park through my office window in the John Hancock Tower. I couldn't see the familiar logo of the little boy wearing the baseball cap, but it was in my mind's eye the afternoon when I called the Jimmy Fund. How could they say no when their bill-board, covered with a thin layer of snow at the time, stated that they needed help making dreams come true? I admit I was very naive when I finally dialed the number the information operator gave me. All I knew was that I had been "rejected" by another charity, and I hoped my second pitch would yield a hit.

The same voice that boomed through my living room via our television and radio answered the phone almost right away. In an instant, I recognized those deep signature tones. I learned that in addition to being the voice of the Red Sox, Ken Coleman had also just taken over as chairman of the Jimmy Fund. After our introductions, I got right down to my reason for calling.

"I see that you guys advertise on a sign in Fenway Park that you help make dreams come true. Will you help make *my* dream come true?" I asked. He laughed, but not in a way that made me feel silly. We then exchanged mission statements. I explained my desire and "dream" to run across the country. Then he thoughtfully explained that the purpose of the Jimmy Fund was to provide funding for the Sidney Farber Cancer Institute in Boston, where researchers and clinicians devote their lives to finding that one break, that one clue to preventing and curing cancer. As Ken explained it, the money raised would help the dream of longevity and health become a reality. These were no ordinary dreams.

Ken invited me to the Jimmy Fund office the very next day. It was the winter of 1978, a very stormy one for New England. There was a ton of snow on the ground and more coming down, but I made my way anyway. I wasn't going to let anything get in the way of actually finding someone who showed interest and support in what I was intending to do.

> Now I'm thinking, "What kind of a kook is this?" But he came in with his whole itinerary—maps, support teams— and went ahead and did it.
>
> *Ken Coleman, Jimmy Fund Archives*

I reviewed every page of my cross-country binder with Ken and detailed how I could accomplish my goal while at the same time educating people west of the Rockies about the work of the Jimmy Fund. We talked for 3 hours. We were both so excited about the marriage of my endeavor and his obvious passion for the Jimmy Fund. Finally, we shook hands. As I left the office and walked into knee-deep snow, I didn't notice if my feet touched the ground or not.

Finally, after all these years, I had found a beneficiary and partner who was willing to take a risk on the unknown. Ken didn't judge me based on my size (in fact, he wasn't so tall, either) or my youth; he liked what I had to say and believed I could help spread the word and raise some money for the charity that meant so much to him.

Weeks later, I made a point of visiting the Jimmy Fund Clinic and did so countless times before the run. I didn't personally know any of the children undergoing treatment—in fact, quite remarkably, no one in my life at that time had cancer—but it was such a compelling place, I just couldn't stay away. Athletes don't usually reveal their training secrets, but I don't mind sharing the fact that the strength I drew from those visits was key to my success. I was inspired by the courageous young children battling the disease at a time when the cure rate for pediatric cancers was abysmal.

I prepared for my journey at the clinic, my mental and emotional "health club." And what a workout! Every time I saw those kids, I was reminded that the challenge that lay ahead of me was in no way as difficult as what they faced.

A sign hanging in the clinic read: "God made only so many perfect heads; the rest have hair on them." That statement had a powerful effect on me. It taught me about turning a negative into a positive and, most of all, being grateful for every day. Once you've visited the Jimmy Fund Clinic, you are left with an indelible memory that is powerful enough to prompt even the most stoic individuals to hug their children a little longer and say "I love you" just one more time before bed.

Nearly 25 years later, in 2004, I coordinated team Trek USA, a group of 11 men who ran across the country relay-style. A few of the members visited the Jimmy Fund Clinic, same as I had done. They were given a tour by Lisa Scherber, the activities coordinator. She showed them treatment rooms and play spaces painted in bright, warm colors and shared stories of incredible courage. By the end of their visit, they had all the motivation they needed to stick to their rigorous training schedule and make sure they did everything they could to succeed. All these years later, the clinic possesses the same life-altering effect.

> Bless you all, especially the Red Sox! Oh, by the way, I'm a Yankee fan—but in time of need, we're all on the same team!
>
> *Note from contributor, Jimmy Fund newsletter, September–October 1978*

I finished my run across the country in Fenway Park in front of 32,000 fans (who coincidentally also happened to be there for a Red Sox game!). As I circled the field, I could not take my eyes off of that darn sign in right field.

By the following day, the Jimmy Fund received 1,500 donations from people who had been at the ballpark or heard about the run on the radio. The gifts totaled $19,607.63, some as large as a $250 check and some small but no less significant, like that $1.26 donated by an 8-year-old boy, and made my accomplishment that much sweeter. All in all, including what was raised on the run as well as donated ticket sales of the game, the endeavor brought in $150,000 for the Jimmy Fund.

To this day, the Jimmy Fund holds a special place in my life. Directly after the run, I joined the Jimmy Fund Advisory Council, a group of volunteers who help to organize fund-raisers and continue to get the message out about the work being done. The Boston Marathon Jimmy Fund Walk, the Swim Across America, Cheers for Children, and several other fund-raising events are all part of my calendar. The people and mission of the Jimmy Fund are intertwined throughout my life.

I assign a high level of importance to "giving back" because, first and foremost, at any time it could be me or someone I love who needs a little help. Life can change on a dime, so while I'm able, I'll do what I can.

I'm not sure if compassion is learned or taught, but I know it was impossible not to be influenced by my mother's actions.

Jacqueline McGillivray quietly made a difference in the world. Twice a week she candy-striped at the local hospital in Medford. When my dad retired and they moved to Florida, she gave her time to the Fawcett Hospital, where patients and other volunteers affectionately called her "Miss Jackie." She was also deeply involved at her church. What made her efforts even more heroic is that all the while she was doing for others, she was battling severe emphysema. In fact, her breathing problems prevented her from walking long distances, so eventually she took a position at the front desk, as close to the entrance as possible. Volunteers had to wheel her out of the hospital after every shift to the parking lot to meet my dad—a volunteer in his own right, as her "ride" several times a week.

No matter her role, be it wife, friend, or (most challenging) mother of five, she wanted everyone to reach and grow toward their full potential. It was never about her; she always made life about others and how she could help, each day providing support and encouragement to everyone in her path. The phenomenal part was that my mother never learned to drive; she often juggled her responsibilities while taking public transportation. All of her kindness came with the price of a bus token.

My own first foray into volunteering was in 1977 to 1978, when I "ran" the United Way campaign for my employer, William Mercer, for which I received an award. I also coordinated charity runs for tuberculosis, cancer, and a health association in Bermuda. In addition, I represented the National Epilepsy Youth Foundation and was the Massachusetts cochairman for the National Run for Life Day. But the time I most truly felt I was helping was when I was running across the country, which marked the beginning of my lifetime commitment to marrying physical endurance with a charitable component.

People give of themselves for all types of reasons. Mine were more practical and logical: I simply had a desire to help others, and, as a dedicated multitasker, I thought I could combine being an athlete, and then a race director, while making my efforts really count. I rarely do only one thing at a time, so if I was going to run coast to coast, why not raise money and help someone else while I'm doing it? And so it began.

> Weighing 35 pounds and standing just 28 inches tall, she was born with a unique form of dwarfism and floppy connective tissue that led to numerous medical problems and life-threatening surgeries, but her life was a series of goals accomplished and hearts lifted. One of her favorite expressions was *parva sed potens,* which is Latin for "small but powerful."

> *Douglas Belkin, the **Boston Globe**, October 25, 2002*

Through my work with the Boston Athletic Association as well as several wonderful charities, I have had the privilege of meeting true heroes. Their actions are not heroic in the sense of rushing into a burning building to save others; these people have been brave in another way. They have had the courage to face their own destinies, perhaps a terminal illness or debilitating condition that makes every day a new obstacle to overcome. One woman possessed intelligence, perseverance, and determination unmatched by any other person I've known. Her name was Katie Lynch.

One day in 2001, as she rolled into my office at the marathon, I could see she was not someone who was "confined" to a wheelchair; that in no way described this incredible woman who had only one question for me: "Dave, I would like to run the Boston Marathon; will you let me?"

I immediately replied, "Now, Katie, do you have any *difficult* questions?" Of course she could run. However, her challenge would be measured in 26.2 *feet,* not miles.

As she left my office, I asked where she was going. She said, "The marathon is only 6 months away—I have to start my training!" I didn't know whether to laugh or cry for her. I immediately fell in love with her positive outlook, vibrancy, and charm.

Katie trained like any other dedicated runner gearing up for the marathon. For her own challenge, Katie needed the same time it takes a healthy person to train for the coveted 26.2 miles of road between Hopkinton and Boston. She would call me at night, leaving messages about her workouts. I was in awe of her determination. She wanted to be an athlete, just as I did. And now, in my eyes and in the eyes of so many, she ranks up there with the greatest athletes of all time.

On race day, we barricaded a 26.2-foot racecourse for her. I sensed everyone would want to witness what I knew would be one of the most memorable moments in Boston Marathon history, but we needed to protect Katie. Her start was at 10 a.m., 2 hours before the official start. There were more cameras, more media, more signs, and more spectators there to see her run than anyone expected—except maybe me. I knew what was about to happen.

When Katie arrived at the starting line, I surprised her by pinning on her bib "2001," representing the year of the race. She was beaming. I counted her down, yelled "*Go!*" and off she went—and she was flying. She had predicted it would take her 15 minutes to finish the course, and she was done in 2½ minutes! In fact, some of us were actually disappointed because we wanted to see her run more, more, and more!

I presented her with a finisher's medal and the victor's laurel wreath. I don't think anyone on this planet could have looked more proud and overwhelmed with joy than Katie did at that moment. We hugged. We cried a bit. She had just finished her first Boston Marathon!

Katie wanted to run again, but the chronic pain she lived with prevented her from doing so. So to keep her involved, we worked out a "scheme" and kept it mostly to ourselves.

Now that Katie had done the start, she wanted to experience the finish. I invited her to speak at the Athletes' Village at the start of the 2002 BAA Boston Marathon, and her words inspired the 17,000 runners who were about to face their own goals. Then we gave her a front-row seat at the start so she could see all her fellow runners from Children's Hospital Boston—where she had been cared for her whole life—take off. From there, she was transported to the finish line with VIP credentials and hung out in her wheelchair, about 200 yards from the finish. Jeff Larson, a mutual friend, was running in the marathon to raise money for Children's Hospital, and he looked for her as he ran down to the finish. A security guard opened the barricades, Katie went out onto the course, and Jeff pushed her across the finish line. It happened like clockwork. Katie had both started the marathon in Hopkinton and finished in Boston. Her biggest challenge was that it took a year to complete!

Then it was my turn. It was the evening of marathon Monday, and I was finishing up my annual night run. As I approached the finish line with my friend Josh, who keeps me awake and motivated out there after the crowds have gone, I could see Katie waiting for me. Turnaround being fair play, she placed a laurel wreath on my head and gave me a medal that she had made. She blurted out, "Ha—I beat you!" I wouldn't have had it any other way.

She presented me with a T-shirt emblazoned with our picture on it and the words "Dave, you are my hero." Well, it takes one to know one—although I'm no hero compared to her. She was an angel then and must surely be one now. One of the greatest honors ever bestowed on me was being invited to speak at her memorial service. Katie died at age 27 in 2003.

So often we are full of self-pity, but in the presence of someone like Katie, we are humbled. She had a way of turning every negative into a positive. She inspired so many. When I think of the Boston Marathon greats, I will remember Kelley, DeMar, Rodgers, Samuelson, and *Lynch*. Every time I cross that finish line, in my mind's eye I will see, feel, and embrace little Katie, my big hero with the huge heart.

I'm struck by how many inspiring people and incredible opportunities I've been given in my life and career. Ken Coleman gave me a *chance,* and I've tried to do the same for others, though often life may just be about good timing, good decisions, and a tiny bit of luck.

There's the case of Jean-Marie Gagnon, someone whom I consider a close friend but have not seen in quite a while. That's partly because he lives in Canada but largely because federal law prohibits him from entering the United States, a fact that has proven to be a huge deterrent to the two of us getting together for coffee. Prior to living in Canada, Jean-Marie's status was as an inmate at Walpole State Prison, now called Cedar Junction, for driving a getaway car in a bank robbery.

Back in 1980, I was contacted by my friend Al Nathan, a member of the West Roxbury Track Club and a social worker for the state of Massachusetts. He worked at many prisons within the commonwealth, and the inmates at Walpole were putting on a 10-K inside the prison and wanted a nonresident to run. Initially, they asked Bill Rodgers, but his schedule would not permit it. As they went down the "runners" food chain, they eventually came to me, and of course I said yes—though I have to admit I was a bit skeptical. I would be the only "outside" participant—32 inmates, two prison employees, and me.

I can now admit to how nervous I was when I walked through those doors and into the prison yard. Talk about feeling vulnerable. I think anyone would require a change of underwear after experiencing that situation! It's the only race I've ever run that required me to walk through a security system similar to that at an airport. That and the sound of the rock-solid steel door clanging behind me did prompt some second thoughts.

> You smell the disinfectant on the floor, walls, and in the air. You see the chipped white paint falling off the walls, and the broken glass in most of the windows. You feel the despair echoing off the ominous white monster of a wall everywhere around the rectangular yard where our race was to be run.
>
> *Jack Connolly, Somerville Journal, April 16, 1981*

As I approached the prison yard, I noticed the inmates warming up on a newly constructed half-mile dirt-and-gravel track. It had been built by three of the inmates, who worked on it from May until November 1979, using only one shovel, a wheelbarrow, and very little outside assistance.

There was no qualifier for this race. We simply drew race numbers out of a hat. I got number 3; lucky me—front of the pack. Some of the inmates wore typical running clothes; others ran in jeans and basketball sneakers. I was told to look for two French Canadians who were the prison's elite runners: Jean-Marie Gagnon and Louis Bourgeois, two of the three men who'd built the track.

Should I try to win or hold back? My gut told me not to be too competitive. The distance was 13 times around the track along the perimeter of the prison walls. There were about 300 inmates out in the yard during the race, some watching, some paying no attention, and some making themselves known.

A verbal command started the run (no starter's gun here), and I stayed just a few paces behind the leader. All of a sudden, he dropped out, and I reluctantly found myself in the lead. I had a few laps to go, and the inmates started yelling obscenities and things like, "If you win, we'll break your legs!" I was definitely not the local favorite.

Would I be safer winning and, perhaps, earning their respect? Or would it be better to let someone else win, lest I appear to be showboating? I decided to go for it and hurtled through the toilet-paper "break tape." One of the inmates asked if he could have the sweaty Bill Rodgers T-shirt I was wearing. As the other inmates finished, they proudly shook hands and congratulated each other.

The inmate who finished fourth told me that he had recently been transferred to Walpole from another prison, where he was placed in solitary confinement for 6½ years. He exercised by running in his cell from wall to wall for countless hours. I couldn't believe how well he ran with that kind of training.

In a thank-you note to me, Jack Hyson, one of the participants, told me that he, Jean-Marie, and Louis Bourgeois wanted to start a running club inside the prison. They asked if I would support them and help with paperwork and the application for official Amateur Athletic Union (AAU) status. During this process, I got to know them all, especially Jean-Marie.

Once the Walpole Prison Yard Runners' Club was established, Jean-Marie and his fellow inmates believed that outside runners could help motivate other inmates to train for the coming competitions. At first, I served more as the PR guy than anything else, working to create interest. We organized 10-Ks and even a marathon. The events consisted of prisoners and select runners from outside the gated community, but we were limited on how many we were allowed to invite in. Our first 10-K was held on Saturday, April 11, 1981. There were 30 inmates and only 20 invited outside runners—not a very comfortable ratio.

> Some of the events were covered by the media, which helped in showing the public that good things were happening even behind those big ugly walls covered by 440-volt electrical wires. To my recollection, this club was the first of its kind in the nation. We signed up 50 inmates as members who paid their annual fee.
>
> *Jean-Marie Gagnon*

These events at Walpole are emblazoned in my mind as some of my most difficult and most rewarding times as an event director. Cedar Junction is security-level six out of *six* levels. In this business, the safety of my participants is always of primary concern, especially now with the world so unsettled. Security at races since 9/11, especially at the Boston Marathon, has never been tighter. However, this was a time when it was my *own* safety that was in question.

> Level Six: A custody level in which both design/construction as well as inmate classification reflect the need to provide maximum external and internal control and supervision of inmates primarily through the use of high-security parameters and extensive use of internal physical barriers and checkpoints. Inmates accorded this status present

serious escape risks or pose serious threats to themselves, to other inmates, to staff, or to the orderly running of the institution. Supervision of inmates is direct and constant.

Massachusetts Department of Correction
quarterly report, 2005

As race director, I had to adhere to strict guidelines, according to prison regulations. First, those coming in from the outside would not be allowed to run if they did not arrive by 8:30 a.m., a full hour before the 9:30 a.m. race start (that should be a rule for all races!). They had to bring a picture ID and not wear jeans or bring in valuables or potentially dangerous items. And they had to preregister at least 3 weeks in advance so the authorities had ample time for a background check: no felons allowed inside the prison. (Shouldn't that be the opposite?)

For more than 2 years, I brought running shoes to more than 550 inmates, both runners and nonrunners. But even the inmates were crime victims. On at least one occasion, the prison guards who checked the boxes confiscated the sneakers before I could distribute them. On later visits, I would see one or two guards wearing them. But no matter; their job was a difficult one, and they were also a lot bigger than me. Merry Christmas.

During the races, one thing moved me: Dave, with his acquired reputation as a strong runner, was not a show-off who would try to cross the line first. Instead, he would run alongside every runner for a time to give advice about proper posture, pace, position of the arms, and breathing and about drinking water. He always had a good word of encouragement when someone was ready to quit, and he would "fall back" just to help set a good pace for that person.

I saw a man who was so happy to be present to those like me who felt abandoned and without much hope. He brought me so much confidence in myself, inspiration, motivation, and something to look forward to. I can also say that Dave is a brave man, because he came into a place which had one of the worst reputations in the country at that time. He gave his time to be part of our activities and training, putting himself in the middle of a crowded yard, full of people convicted of criminal acts. Despite racial tension at the time in that place, many black, white, and Hispanic inmates got together to make those events a success.

Dave emphasized the need for me to pursue my training as a tool to stay mentally and physically fit while staying out of trouble in that negative and violent environment. In those years, Walpole was a "high-pressure cooker." He regularly wrote me letters and sent photos of him and his family. He always sounded so upbeat, and I realize now how "contagious" it was.

Now as a free man, I am doing very well with my life, and I truly believe that the support I received from people such as Dave was instrumental in getting me to where I am today. In my turn, I have learned to give my time to other people, just like he did, without asking anything in return.

Jean-Marie

From the first day I brought donations, I kept noticing new faces on the track. Prisoners who could afford those shoes in their previous lives were wearing the latest gear as they broke up each day's monotony with a run. This lasted for 3 or 4 years, until the club was disbanded. Truth be told, I believe it was becoming a little too organized and influential among the inmates.

Jean-Marie and Louis were temporarily transferred to another facility in Illinois. But after a short while, they were transported back to Walpole. During their return, the vehicle they were in hit traffic and stopped for a bit, and they escaped. How could inmates feel confident enough to escape in traffic, you may ask? It was a combination of their new running sneakers and lean, well-trained marathon legs, brought to them courtesy of Dave McGillivray—at least according to the US marshals who came to my door that day. Louis was caught, but Jean-Marie was nowhere to be found, and I was definitely viewed as an accessory. I was nervous . . . I had the impression that they truly thought I might have something to do with the escape.

Jean-Marie never made contact with me after that. I always wondered where he was. Then one day, I was watching an *Unsolved Mysteries* episode about inmates who had escaped without a trace. As always, I was multitasking and listening more than watching when I heard, "Next up: Armed and dangerous escaped." It was the story of Louis and Jean-Marie.

About 1,200 miles away, in Georgia, Jean-Marie was watching the same show. Knowing his neighbors would immediately recognize him, he instantly left the home he'd been living in for years. He drove his car toward freedom, but he was caught and returned to Walpole.

Helen, a woman he had met and had been living with, called me once Jean-Marie was back behind bars. I went to visit him in the late 1980s. Helen moved to Massachusetts to try to get Jean-Marie out of jail. He had already served 11 years of his sentence, and she felt it was time for him to live his life again. She fought the system for nearly 6 years, during which the two were married in a ceremony in the prison cafeteria. I even tried to help by contacting those I knew at the Massachusetts State House. Eventually, she got him deported to Canada, and they've been there ever since. This man who came to the United States not speaking a word of English is now *teaching* English.

Jean-Marie and this prison-yard experience truly had a profound effect on me. He inspired me through his dedication to training, despite the poor equipment that was available, the controlled schedule, and the terrible prison diet. It has been years since I've seen him, but we both look forward to the day when we can "burn a few miles" side by side—to commemorate our friendship, relive the memories, and acknowledge the circumstances that brought our two different worlds together.

Running in Walpole was a deeply rewarding experience for me. Each prisoner, no matter what the reason he was incarcerated, deserved credit for doing something positive while there and bettering himself. It was the purest form of running that I have ever witnessed. It proved how running can have rehabilitative advantages as well as physical and mental benefits. There was no awards ceremony, no outside spectators, no postrace party. After witnessing the men's determination and concentration, I felt hopeful that someday we'd compete beyond the barbed wire.

What [Dave] does for us just can't be measured. We have been looking forward to this for months, and it's really great for morale. It relieves tensions and lessens the aggressiveness of this place. There's nobody like him.

Louis Bourgeois, inmate,
the Patriot Ledger, April 13, 1981

What I saw at Walpole illustrated that there is good to be found everywhere, even in the most unexpected places. Jean-Marie was incarcerated, but like so many others, he has a real value to add to society—he just needed a second chance. All these years later, I still get inquiries about this. Recently, I received an e-mail from someone at San Quentin State Prison in California who was researching what it would take to put together a running program for the inmates. It would be interesting to study the effects of a program like that. I'm hoping it would lead to positive outcomes.

Putting myself inside that prison and imagining myself in someone else's shoes—specifically, running shoes—provided a quick way to put life in perspective. It offered the chance to make a difference in someone's life and, as a result, change my own life. Giving is just another way of receiving, isn't it? It makes us feel just a little bit better about ourselves.

That's why I wanted to do all I could when my brother Bob asked me to put on a fund-raiser for a cause close to his own heart: the Carroll Center for the Blind, where he has worked for more than 20 years. He had done so much to support me during my cross-country run, and now I could reciprocate, so I agreed, even though I was initially stuck for ideas. Bob suggested running the Boston Marathon, but in 1982, running for a charity was not the "big business" it is today. I'd have to do something unique to raise significant dollars for the nonprofit. As if the 26.2-mile run from Hopkinton to Boston wasn't challenging enough, I decided to do the route blindfolded—that would raise funds *and* understanding of the blind. Dave Laprise, Kent Hawley, and Bill Young agreed to be my guides and serve as my "sight."

Although none of us who are sighted can truly understand what it's like to be visually impaired, I wanted to get at least a firsthand sense of it. However, I was concerned that some people might view this as more of a stunt than a fund-raiser. I didn't want it to look like a mockery. So Dave and I methodically and in a sensitive way approached the Carroll Center's running club, the Inner Visions Track Club, making it clear that our plan was not for our own exposure, and that we would not carry it out without their full support. At the time, the club even offered a class on how to serve as a marathon guide for sightless people.

> As we ran, it was as if we were one. I didn't have to tell Dave which way to move, as he could tell by the way I was moving where we were going and when we were to hurry up or slow down. This was a wonderful experience for me. I could tell from the fans lining the road that they were inspired by our efforts.
>
> *Dave Laprise, Dave's longtime friend*

Dave has always been there for me. He ran a number of my birthday runs, and I was thrilled when he agreed to take on the all-important role of my "eyes" for 26.2 miles. Two other friends were also willing to help—Marty Gabriella and Billy Young—but Dave ran the entire way with me.

At one point, I accidentally hit someone, who grunted when I said hi. I asked what happened, and Dave said, "You just smacked a police officer." I decided to pick it up and get out of there.

Running in "darkness" forced me to focus on my other senses. Listening became of utmost importance as Dave's voice became my eyes, and I was given verbal commands such as "left turn" or "railroad tracks." As we ran, I held Dave's elbow in close proximity to me. You could say he was in my personal space, and it felt strange not to have the freedom of moving in a certain direction or at a certain speed without discussing it first.

Not being able to see for nearly 3 hours and 14 minutes helped me to see a lot more things more clearly. This Occluded Run for the Blind, as I referred to it, taught me many things that cannot be adequately articulated, but I learned about trust and what it's like to be dependent on another human being. And for however long I have a choice in the matter, I want to remain independent so I can continue to help others.

> I expect to pass through this world but once; any good thing therefore that I can do, or any kindness that I can show to any fellow creature, let me do it now; let me not defer or neglect it, for I shall not pass this way again.
>
> *Stephen Grellet, Quaker missionary*

I had one desire as a boy: I wanted to be an athlete like Ted or Yaz, but I kept getting cut. I was cut so many times I was beginning to think I would need stitches. I wasn't given a chance, and because of that, I am driven even more to make sure others have opportunities to shine. That's the reason I have forged a relationship with Lazarus House, a homeless shelter in Medford.

Before taking over as race director of the Feaster Five Thanksgiving Road Race in North Andover, Massachusetts, I'd never heard of Lazarus House. The road race had always benefited this particular charity, and I guess you could say that Lazarus House and I inherited one another—and it has been an incredible relationship. It's a great example of what a few hardworking people can do to change others' lives.

When I think of Lazarus House, I am reminded of that classic *Wizard of Oz* line, "There's no place like home." Every time I do something for Lazarus House, I try to envision what it would be like to be without a home, especially on those subzero New England nights. My to-do list for life includes sleeping outside on the street, with no money, phone, or blanket—just the clothes on my back—not as some sort of exploit but so I can get some idea of the harsh reality of homelessness, if only for a night. All of us are part of one community, and at any time, it could be any of us sleeping in the cold or searching for our next hot meal.

The Lazarus House is a place for second chances in life. In fact, a more appropriate name would be "Lazarus Home." A house is a building, but a home is where one is made to feel comfortable, warm, and safe—and that's what this place gives its homeless clientele. It is a place for opportunity, a place to receive unconditional support, a place to rebuild self-esteem. It also gives the rest of us a chance: a chance to give back, to give thanks for our blessings, even to feel good about ourselves.

I remember the day I backed my car up to Lazarus House to make a delivery of clothes discarded by runners at the start of that year's BAA Boston Marathon. As I was unloading, an older gentleman, whom I think of as "Buddy"—I didn't know his name—offered to help me.

"Are all these yours?" he asked.

"No, they are from runners in the Boston Marathon," I said.

"Gee," said Buddy, "imagine if someday I could run in the Boston Marathon!"

"Well, why don't you?" I asked.

"'Cause I don't run—but I do walk."

I told him about the Boston Marathon Jimmy Fund Walk, where folks walk the marathon course and raise money for the Jimmy Fund. This led to more questions.

"Who is Jimmy?" he asked.

I told him about the little boy who 50 years ago was treated for cancer and became the inspiration behind the Jimmy Fund. Buddy walked slowly away, and that was that. As I drove home that night, it suddenly hit me. Why not produce a walk for Lazarus House so that my new friend Buddy could raise money for a place that he cared about?

I never did see Buddy again, but just as Jimmy inspired the Jimmy Fund Walk, so "Buddy" inspired the Hike for Hope, which now has more than 2,000 participants and raises more than $250,000 annually. Anything is possible.

As I look down the calendar of events that I help coordinate every year, I'm proud that each has some sort of charitable component. That did not happen by accident; if I'm going to work hard at something, it makes it that much more rewarding if it's not just all about getting sponsor money and moving road cones.

In 2004, I established my own foundation, the DMSE Children's Fitness Foundation. For years, the idea of establishing my own nonprofit foundation had bounced around in my head. To me, there's a big difference between being a caretaker for someone else's event and creating something from scratch. I get a huge sense of accomplishment when I know I'm putting hard work into something I've created. I have control over the outcome, through the good and the bad. Same with the charitable part of events: We work on so many throughout the year—all wonderful causes—but it was time to decide for ourselves who should be the beneficiaries of the funds we raise.

> The DMSE Children's Fitness Foundation supports nonprofit organizations whose efforts are directed at solving the epidemic of childhood obesity. Built upon a legacy of inspiration, generosity, and achievement, the DMSE Foundation believes the power of teamwork can bring physical fitness into the life of every child.
>
> *Mission Statement, DMSE Children's Fitness Foundation*

Even though we are still in the infancy stages, we've raised thousands of dollars under the direction of Billy Sheehan. One colleague suggested that we call it the Full Potential Foundation, and though we chose a different name, I do believe that helping kids reach their full potential is the ultimate mission of the DMSE Children's Fitness Foundation.

We've already established a partnership with Children's Hospital Boston, something for which I'm honored to be part of. David Ludwig, MD, has started an OWL (Optimal Weight for Life) program, designed to help children learn about a healthy lifestyle and eating habits and to help stave off the epidemic of obesity in children.

Helping children is so important, especially those who know where they want to go but don't have the resources to get there. Around 1981, when lack of funds endangered the athletic programs of Randolph (Massachusetts) High School, I created the Randolph 10 Mile Dream Run: me against five students and five teachers on the school track. The race raised $3,000.

Last year, I was invited to speak at a meeting of the Merrimack Valley Striders. One of the running club's agenda items caught my attention: A local track team had qualified for a national track meet but could not afford to go. Their coach wrote the Striders and asked for help raising the $4,000 for the trip. I thought it was a perfect opportunity to give kids a chance, so afterward I said I'd be happy to write a check from the DMSE Foundation for the whole thing. The Striders wanted to help, too, so we decided to fund it 50/50. It was a great feeling to give a boost to some kids who really deserved it, and we did the same for a team in the neighboring town of Peabody. The Striders made me a lifetime member, and it's an honor to be part of an organization that gives so much back to the community.

The mission of the DMSE Foundation was a little blurry when my longtime friend John Mancuso and I began the process and paperwork of creating such an entity. All I knew is what I've always known: I want to help. I've run so far and for so long, and having something to show for it and making a difference means I haven't been going in circles. My direction has always been toward giving back.

I received the following note from Barbara Sicuso, a close friend and BAA/DMSE colleague, after she participated in the 2004 Boston Marathon Jimmy Fund Walk. It's an event she has worked on since its inception, yet this time, she found out what the event was like from the "other" side . . . as a walker. She walked to honor our mutual friend Bill Coulter, who was diagnosed with cancer this year.

> Tonight I know I feel like I finally did something for a real cause.
> Tonight I know that Billy Coulter felt better because of us.
> Tonight I know that I wouldn't have finished if it weren't for friends.
> Tonight I know how much pain reliever a person can consume in a day.
> Tonight I know I feel good.
> Tonight I know that I have a finisher's medal from something.
> Tonight I know my kids are proud of me.
> Tonight I am thankful that my husband ordered Chinese food for dinner.
> Tonight I know as soon as I get under the covers, I will sleep.
> Tonight I know I will try to get to the office tomorrow.

The underlying theme of my life, both professionally and personally, is to continue to help prevent others, especially children, from feeling like the last pick. Promoting physical activity and learning about the physical capabilities of the human body serve as the basis for nearly everything I've done. One of my long-term goals for the foundation is to start a camp staffed by nutritionists, coaches, and counselors. I would like to create a place where kids can immerse themselves in positive, affirmative energy, no matter what their capabilities.

This line of thinking led to the first Mini-Olympic Day at my son's school. The goal: Simply let the kids have fun, get their hearts pumping, and see how much fun athletics can be.

> Little Olympians carried a torch, ran a mini-marathon, and paraded around in gold medals at St. Augustine School last week. More than 150 first-, second-, and third-graders got

a taste of the Olympic spirit during the school's second annual Mini-Olympics Fun and Fitness Festival.

*Emily Gold, **Eagle-Tribune**, North Andover, Massachusetts, September 1998*

What started small has grown into a fairly large annual event that includes a 50-yard dash, broad jump, obstacle course, and lots of other challenges that the kids really look forward to. They all get awards, medals, and, hopefully, a big dose of self-esteem.

Olympic Day is personally rewarding because there is no middleman—one of the reasons I wanted my own company. The school and I created the event, and we make it happen, with the help of several volunteers from my company.

I want to help the little guy, partly because I *am* the *little* guy. Yes, I have done the Ironman, run hundreds of marathons and whatever else, but that doesn't make me exceptional—it just makes me appear a bit crazier than the next guy. It's when I know that what I do will help someone who needs a little boost, either financially or emotionally, that I truly feel I'm capable of anything. As one runner said as he was leaving the prison after the 10-K and was quoted in the *Walpole Times:* "We all had on shorts and shoes; there was no difference from you to the next guy."

We are no different than the next guy, and that's all the more reason to help him when he's in need.

CHAPTER 9

The Triathlon of Pain

It is easier to accept a certain degree of physical and mental discomfort if there exists a strong meaning behind it. A person who never pushes himself or herself to this point is obviously learning very little about their own limits and thresholds.

Dave McGillivray, "Pain Is Good," CoolRunning.com, 1996

Achilles: son of Peleus, the bravest hero in the Trojan War, according to Greek mythology. As the story goes, his mother, Thetis, tried to make the boy immortal by dipping him in the river Styx. As she immersed him, she held him by the back of the foot and forgot to dip him a second time so the part her fingers covered could get wet, too. Therefore, that one heel remained unprotected by the magic water and remained mortal and vulnerable.

At times, I've believed that I was immortal, that I could do anything if I tried hard enough. Some may view this as egotistical, but what could be bad about believing that *anything* is possible? Like Achilles, I have a particularly vulnerable body part—but mine is my calf. (Interestingly, the Achilles tendon is actually the tendon that attaches the calf muscles to the heel bone!) The pain of recurring injury to this muscle, which is probably just from overuse, is a small price to pay, considering I've spent my entire life putting my body through hell and back.

Pain is all part of the process, so much so that I even have my own pain-identification system. Nothing in my life escapes being organized, so why should pain? The math/logic half of my brain deals better with this intangible topic by transforming it into three concrete categories: physical, mental, and, finally—the most difficult to manage—emotional pain. None of us are excused from feeling pain; however, it's a personal decision whether to surrender to it or to experience and manage it.

First, there's the obvious: *physical* pain. I have an injury; it hurts. It's the skin and bones of it, the pulled muscle, the blister, the stomachache—those are real things and most likely messages from my body warning me against further injury. *Mental* pain is when the voice in my head is not in sync with my body. It's the 23rd mile of a marathon when something inside me starts to raise doubts about whether I'll make it. This thought paralysis occurred roughly 1,000 miles into my run across the country.

The only visible signs of my 40-plus miles a day were sun blisters, some muscle soreness, and calluses. What no one saw was the mental strength required to hold back my thoughts of home. I would not allow my mind to wander more than a few footsteps ahead of my body. Thoughts of Medford and the people who were waiting for me, and knowing they were so far away, made me fear I might never make it. I needed to focus on the moment.

Between Nevada and Utah, there was about a 150-mile stretch where we didn't even see a gas station. It's boring to drive on that road—imagine running on it. The rhythm of strides often lulled me into a state of detachment with reality. My imagination would fill with everything in my life, from demons to fantasies. Every once in a while, I would snap out of it, only to see I was still running down a double yellow line with just tumbleweed as company.

To a nonathlete, it might seem that the success of my trip

would be determined solely on the merits of my physical train- ing, but physical preparedness alone does not determine out- come. So much of it is a self-fulfilling prophecy: If you think you can, you *can*. If you have too many doubts, you'll doom yourself to a life of mediocrity, and who wants that?

When my confidence is up, the mental aspect of my being is strong, and I am able to persevere through the adversities in my life. It's my brainpower that helps me continue when the physi- cal pain seems too much to tolerate, especially through things like my 24-hour run or the fatigue of doing laps for 24 hours in the Medford High pool, when I literally had moments of decid- ing whether to sink or swim. Pain and aches are part of the effort, but if I am to succeed, my desire to reach my goal must always be stronger than any pain I'm feeling. If it hurts you, run through it.

> We used to fight all the time. We were both upset that David was the last one cut. I was the second-to-last one cut, right before him.

Alan McGillivray, Dave's brother

My feelings were hurt deeply at an early age as I battled to prove that height didn't matter, mostly by showing my strength. It started with Alan; we fought all the time, especially over who controlled what to watch on television or who got to sit in the best spot in front of the TV. One's backside would barely be off the cushion before the other staked claim on the valuable real estate. What is the protocol regarding how long a seat remains vacant before another can take it? My rules depended on who was doing the leaving and who was doing the sitting.

During the day, while my father was at work, Alan and I would beat each other silly until the issue was settled. But if it was in the evening, after my dad had returned home—look out. At the outset of an altercation, my mother would come in and say, "Cut it out or I'm going to tell your faatha," in an accent as quintessentially Boston as a can of baked beans.

Dave would get home from school and put on *Gilligan's Island*. Then I'd come in and say, "What are you watching?" And when I saw his choice, I'd say, "Well, I want to watch F Troop." Then he'd get up to go in the kitchen to get about 400 chocolate-chip cookies, and I'd change the channel while he was gone. He'd come back and say, "Why'd you change the channel?" And I'd say, "Well, you got up." "Well, I was here first . . . " Then my dad would get involved.

Alan

As we got older, we'd pretend to wrestle. Alan would hold me down and shout, "Keep your mouth shut! Feet straight!" mimicking our gym teacher (and former marine drill sergeant), Mr. Trentini. Whoever was on top shouted the orders. This "game" often turned into a fight, and we terrorized each other, perhaps because we simply got in each other's way in our modest house.

Pretending to be marines was not as bad as when we pretended to be ballplayers; that's when things really got nasty. We'd play catch—a wholesome activity for two brothers to engage in. We'd throw the ball back and forth. Inevitably, after a bit, one of us would get it and throw too hard. That led the catcher to accuse the thrower of trying to hit him with a fastball. The gloves would come off, like in a hockey game, and we'd go at it. Then you'd hear from inside the kitchen window, "Mac, they're fighting again!"

Mom used the intercom system that my dad had rigged up between the house and the garden shed, with a speaker close to where we played ball. As soon as the first punch was thrown, an "alert" sounded from somewhere between the potting soil and the shovels. We knew we were in for it.

I remember David always being fierce for a little kid. I think the older kids set him up one day to fight another kid. David was always competitive. I remember the fight. . . . Of course, David won. Everyone in the neighborhood was there.

Alan

I want to be clear on one point: I never *wanted* to fight, and I don't think I ever picked a fight (other than with Alan). If I was "fierce," it was in retaliation—for self-preservation, more than anything else. It was all about making sure kids at school or on the playground who teased, ridiculed, or toyed with me knew that I was not going to be pushed around. I felt that even if I ended up with a few bumps and bruises, as long as I got in some good punches, the person hitting me would think twice about provoking me again. I was fierce in defending myself.

One time I was set up to fight another kid, and I gave it everything I had, even if I was hurt. Athletically, anything I achieved would come with a degree of pain because I didn't have the height or strength of most of my opponents. That meant I would have to dig deeper.

I expect that at some point, I will face a situation or predicament that will call for unusual physical or emotional strength. I believe that by putting myself in challenging circumstances now, I'll be prepared for even tougher tests later. That may be why I didn't mind being set up to fight a fellow classmate. I saw it as preparation for a time when I might otherwise not be ready. As I got older, I realized that fighting with my fists would not gain me respect, especially self-respect. I needed to use brainpower and strive to be the best at whatever I set out to do. It was another way of "fighting" against my anger at getting the short end of the gene pool.

> It is not the critic who counts: not the man who points out how the strong man stumbles or where the doer of deeds could have done better. The credit belongs to the man who is actually in the arena, whose face is marred by dust and sweat and blood; who strives valiantly; who errs and comes short again and again, because there is no effort without error or shortcoming, but who knows great enthusiasms, the great devotions; who spends himself in a worthy cause; who, at the best, knows in the end, the triumph of high achievement, and who, at the worst, if he fails, at least he fails while daring greatly, so that his place shall never be

with those cold and timid souls who know neither victory
nor defeat.

Theodore Roosevelt

Until age 25, I'd dealt with the emotional pain of being small,
but physical and mental pain had never been much of an obstacle. Then came the East Coast Run from Winter Haven Florida
to Boston. The entire thing was a true lesson in humility. My
run partner for that trip was Bob Hall, a pioneer in the world of
wheelchair athletics. At the time that we embarked on our more-
than-1,500-mile journey for the Jimmy Fund, Bob held the
wheelchair marathon *world* record. He was in amazing shape.
In fact, he was using the charity run to train for the Boston
Marathon that year. We'd be returning home just a few weeks
before the April race. I too had trained and felt confident, but
then I suffered a knee injury early in the trip.

For our start in Florida on March 1, 1981, I anticipated warm
sunshine and dry roads, but the cold, wet weather was reminis-
cent of the weather in Oregon during the first few days of the
coast-to-coast run. About 10 miles into the journey, the rain
began. A few miles after that, Bob and I proceeded to run the
wrong way for quite a while before we realized our mistake and
backtracked to the right route, all the while getting soaked. In
fact, it rained *12* days out of the first *18* of the trip, and it was
raw. My spirits were dampened right from the get-go.

Then my mental strength was challenged as it had never been
before. Just outside Orlando, I developed discomfort in my left
knee, and it quickly became a problem I couldn't ignore. I began
staggering and at times had to catch myself from falling down.
The puddles were deep, and every so often I felt myself starting
to falter. By the Georgia state line, I was in all-out excruciating
pain. One morning, I went out for my first split of the day, and
by the time I reached the support vehicle, I knew I couldn't ask
any more of my knee. This was *warning* pain, the kind that
says, "Hey, fella, run anymore and you're really gonna hurt
yourself," like chest pains before a heart attack—as opposed to

challenging pain, like fatigue or blisters, which I could have continued to grind through.

Panic set in, and though I tried not to show it to my companions, I'm sure they knew. There was that voice again: "What if I can't finish? What will the Jimmy Fund say? Will people back home be disappointed in me?" The injury took me by surprise— I had run more than 3,400 miles 2 years before and hadn't experienced anything like that. The realization that I could not continue was as excruciating as the pain itself. It was only a day or two into the trip.

We had brought a bike along so a support crew member could ride next to us. I quickly considered cycling as a way to rest my knee from the unforgiving, daily pounding of running on asphalt. It seemed like a good short-term solution, but at that point, it was the most difficult personal judgment call I'd ever made. I had planned and promised to *run* up the East Coast, not ride. For Bob, the Jimmy Fund, and everyone who had invested in this endeavor, I wanted the trip to be a success. I always profess that the best way to run is to run intelligently—if you have tremendous pain, stop so you don't permanently injure your body. Getting on the bike would help rest the knee and allow us to cover the miles and still meet our timeline.

I got on the bike the next day, knowing that for days, months, even years afterward, I would feel guilty about doing what I perceived as the "easy" way out. Up to that point, I had never "failed" at anything I tried.

That bike decision was a defining moment; it actually brought water to my eyes—a rare occurrence. Out of view of Bob and the others, I cried as I admitted to myself that I needed to stop running for a while, maybe even a few days or weeks. I had to settle down a bit and admit that my body would not always do what I expected of it, a fact we all must face at some point. Even thinking about it today makes me feel uncomfortable. I guess we all have to grow up sometime.

So I rode the bike. Between splashing through the enormous puddles, riding the bike, and running when I could, I had turned my part in the endeavor into the East Coast *Triathlon*.

The shooting pains in my leg became secondary to the reality that I was covering a portion of each day's miles on two wheels instead of on two feet. In Savannah, I consulted a doctor who was referred to me by a friend, but he didn't do much other than prescribe a drug that might help. It didn't.

We were all trying to decide how to "announce" the fact that I was now using a bicycle. I decided to call a local Boston radio personality, Glenn Ordway at WITS, who was at that time in Winter Haven for Red Sox spring training. On air, I made public the fact that I was on the bike and had been for at least a week. I didn't want to hide it or downplay it anymore than I already had. I wondered if others would feel that I was less of a person for not running the entire way. These concerns may sound trivial now, but it was a tremendous blow to my self-esteem.

> I thought riding the bike or walking or crawling, just to get the job done, was fine. To me, it wasn't about running; it was about two guys having to finish a goal they'd set for themselves.
>
> *Bob Hall, Boston Marathon*
> *Wheelchair Division Champion*

Considering the real-life challenges facing others every day, it may seem petty that I thought so much of the fact that I was riding a bike instead of running. However, this was all within the parameters of my world. I made a commitment. I wanted to be, and was supposed to be, running. Bottom line was, the run was a lot bigger than I was. A lot of sponsors, money, time, and Bob's effort were in the balance. So I just kept saying to myself, "I have to continue, and I have to make it."

The knee just wasn't getting better. As a result of favoring my other leg, I severely strained my right quad, so I began to quietly worry about that, too. To make matters a bit more uncomfortable, the big toenail on my left foot was falling off! It sounds as though I was falling apart, but it was just a lot of things happening at once. I remember thinking, "Work through it, Dave; it'll be better on the other side." After all, right next to me was Bob Hall in a wheelchair, with a permanent disability, and he never said a word about it. He was an inspiration to me.

As the injury progressed, the medical advice I received made me feel like a human Ping-Pong ball. An orthopedic surgeon back home said it was important that I continue and not rest too much, lest my muscles atrophy; a doctor in Georgia told me to rest. I received two cortisone shots to the knee from an emergency-room doctor; another doctor told me not to get the shots. I was so frustrated, I thought about flying home to see a doctor if the pain didn't subside by North Carolina.

Finally, on the first day that the weather cooperated and the thermometer had more red than blue, we arrived in Raleigh. A sign at the hotel read, "Welcome Dave McGillivray and Bob Hall." It really boosted my spirits. It was also one of our designated mail stops. We received cards, letters, and cartoons from schoolchildren in the Boston area who wished us well. It was a great mental antidote for the injury in my knee.

That same day, an AP reporter and photographer caught up to us to get some shots of us running. For 4 or 5 days, I hadn't run more than 10 or 20 yards, but the photographer waited down the road a bit so he could snap our picture as we passed by. My ego had silenced me from saying I couldn't run or that I hadn't been running. I grimaced until I finally got into a groove, but I ran about 2 miles. I hopped back on the bike after the shutter clicked on the camera, but the photographer continued shooting. Folks back home (who already knew I was riding) would now have their first visual of me on a two-wheeler.

I abandoned the idea of flying home for medical care. My next short-term goal was to be riding less and running more by the time we got to Washington, DC. I forced myself to be on my feet whenever possible, even if it meant walking. The upside of riding the bike was that Bob and I were both able to "outrun" any dogs that chased us—and there were many.

Around day 33 of the trip, or 1,362.1 miles into it, I started to feel good, and I ran a great distance of 53 miles. Ironically, or maybe not so, it was also the day that my parents showed up and drove by us with signs on their car that said, "Welcome to New England East Coast Runners." Finally, my body was doing what my mind had hoped for all along: I was running and feeling great.

As we entered Connecticut, we were met by a few newspapers and reporters, including Amby Burfoot, the 1968 Boston Marathon winner, who was writing an article for *Front Runner* magazine. Throughout the interviews, I waited with bated breath for the bike question. Even though my rides were common knowledge, I carefully phrased my answers so I didn't specifically mention the bike.

> **WBZ radio's** *Sports Final*: You seem to have zipped up the East Coast pretty quickly. This trip must have been sort of candy for you, as compared to the other one [the cross-country run].
>
> **Dave:** I guess you could probably assume that, but a trip of that distance is difficult. In fact, this one physically was a lot more difficult for me personally than the run across America. I suffered a slight knee problem coming out of Florida, going into Georgia, that I had to deal with the rest of the way up the coast. I did make it. I was fortunate enough that it wasn't so serious that I had to pull out of the thing. . . .

When I was living this experience, I perceived it as failure—one reason I don't talk about this particular endeavor very much. However, a friend of mine recently pointed out that I had been successful in one way. I had two options when my knee went out: I could apologize to everyone involved, then hop a plane back to Boston and call it a day; or I could compromise and cover the miles. I was still powered by my own body but in a way that saved me from doing any long-term harm. Though my ego never fully recovered, my body did indeed heal.

That run was a lesson in dealing with physical pain, along with a lot of emotion thrown in. My deep disappointment hit me like a freight train. For most of my life, I treated such feelings the same way I dealt with a sprained ankle. I kept them to myself, maintained my independence, and didn't ask for help because I didn't want to burden anyone. It was 14 years after the East Coast Run that I learned how to deal a bit better with my emotions. I had to, because I was beginning a personal journey that nearly killed me. It was 1995, the year of the 99th running of the Boston Marathon, the biggest race of the year—the same year that my first marriage started to unravel, the biggest crisis of my entire life.

It was just like the perfect storm; the chances of all those elements coming together at that one time seemed slim. I remained focused, perhaps even more than usual. I worked just as hard, if not harder. But in between the moments when I was called upon to help orchestrate the race, there were quiet times. Those moments were the most painful: I had time to reflect on what was happening in my life and that of my family. For the most part, I was able to still crank ahead, but at the same time, I was so shaken that I would stop dead in my tracks and lose myself in self-pity, which went against my nature.

The most valuable thing I had during that time was people who would listen. My best friends were those who would let me talk. Now when I have friends in the same situation, I fear saying too much. I don't want to say the wrong thing and then feel accountable. Support is one thing, but we have to find solutions for ourselves.

The marathon came and went. My night run of 26.2 came and went. I don't remember a lot from that time. My memories all drowned in my sadness.

Preparation is the cornerstone of my life, but I was not prepared for what was to come for the next few years, all the more reason that it took a toll on me. The sadness of the breakup was overwhelming. I felt guilt and pain, mostly for the innocent victims of the divorce—our children who were so young at the time, too young to be subjected to such emotions.

One year later, I found myself on the heels of the biggest career challenge of my life, the 100th running of the Boston

Marathon. The field size had jumped from about 16,000 the year before to an unprecedented 40,000 runners who wanted to be part of that historic year—the largest field in the marathon's history. Though numerous people add their expertise and countless hours to the event, it was my responsibility to make sure that the BAA and its constituents had as flawless a race as possible. My mind was filled with race timelines and details yet to be confirmed.

Mother Nature reflected what was happening in my personal life. Just a little less than a week before the race, she dumped a freak April snowstorm on the Hopkinton, Massachusetts, area. Snow covered the ground where 40,000 people wearing skimpy clothes would wait for hours on race day; with some melting and more seasonal temperatures, they'd be knee deep in mud. It was the ultimate in crisis management for me as a race director, yet a much easier fix than my personal issues.

It was, without question, the most devastating emotional pain I've ever endured. I didn't know emotion until then. I had been like Superman, just going through life overcoming whatever got in my way. In one fell swoop, I learned that depression, anxiety, and anger were the "kryptonite" that brought me to my knees. I knew that if I was exposed to those emotions long enough, they would kill me. It was my responsibility to get through it, but I couldn't get across that bridge without asking others for help. In fact, one night I called my sister Susan and told her I thought it might be best if I just ended it all. I was drowning in my own grief. It was her lifeline that saved me.

I also found strength. Ultimately, the experience was a learning process. I developed coping skills. I didn't have those before. I also learned to make the most of the limited time I had with my two sons.

With all of that behind me now, I just take one day at a time. Now I have Katie, my best friend and partner, to spend my life with, along with the joy of a new baby. Elle was born when I was 49 years old, and she represents a fresh start to my life. And at age 51, I'm expecting another baby with my wife. We all deserve the chance to begin again.

I miss you David and love you so much. We are so proud of you. Take care of yourself until I can. Love, Mom

Jacqueline McGillivray, diary entry, July 17, 1978

I wish my mom was around to see her newest granddaughter, but she's not. My mother smoked *cigarettes*—to this day, I hate that word—from the time she was a teenager until about 15 years before her death. As we got old enough to voice our opinion about her habit, she hid her cigarettes but fooled no one. We would find them and draw a red circle partway down each one, hoping that she would smoke only until the red line, and then toss it. Eventually, she got the message and quit, but it was too late. She suffered horribly from emphysema and was always short of breath. And then she was diagnosed with cancer.

She and my dad had moved to Florida shortly before her diagnosis. Immediately, I insisted that she come north and be treated at the Dana-Farber Cancer Institute. I'd devoted so much of my time to the place, and I hoped they'd have something to give in return. She did come, and surgery was scheduled to remove the disease. We were all at her bedside the night before. I was vocal that she have the surgery; I just wanted her to be well. But it was not effective, and I've often wondered if the procedure was worth the stress and recovery.

To get rid of the cancer, the doctors would've had to remove part of her lung, where the tumor was attached to both her lung and her back. She would be put on a respirator for the rest of her life, so the doctors decided instead to close her up without doing anything at all. After she recovered, she began a treatment of chemo and radiation. The tumor shrank a bit but only for a short while; when it came back, it was with a vengeance and grew so big that it exasperated the breathing problems she already endured.

During her final years, her quality of life was diminished. She couldn't lie down in bed due to the compression of her lungs, and she also suffered from osteoporosis. She slept in a reclining chair, but she constantly coughed and wheezed. My siblings and

I took turns going to Florida to visit with her, care for her, and help my dad however we could.

During one of her frequent hospital stays, she had a respiratory attack but was "saved." After that episode was 6 weeks of agony for her and my family as we watched her body betray her. There were no miracles, no turning back. It was a matter of any day . . . today, tomorrow, a week, or 5 weeks . . . but it was inevitable.

During one of my sister Susan's visits, she accompanied Dad to his own checkup. He'd spent so much time looking after his wife, and now it was his turn to be taken care of. It turned out that he required immediate surgery—a quadruple bypass, plus a followup operation. For a brief time, Mom and Macadoo were both in the hospital but she in Port Charlotte and he in Punta Gorda.

Throughout that time, I went out for tremendously long and arduous bike rides and ran long distances that pushed me beyond my ordinary threshold. Experiencing some degree of pain at the same time that my mom was suffering somehow made me feel closer to her. I felt that it put us in the same "place." I suppose it was my way of taking empathy to the next level. I felt completely helpless, and that was how I dealt with it.

When she died on October 29, 1991, I was at my DMSE office on Salem Street in Medford. The phone rang; it was *the* phone call, the one that comes only once in a lifetime. My friend Rich, who was with me at the time, recalls that I just put the phone down and said, "She's gone." My body readied its battle stations. Emotional walls were fortified, and almost instantly I went into robot mode, going through the rhythm of the work in front of me, desperate not to let the sadness take over. For hours, I could not get up from my desk. The lump in my throat acted like a cork to keep down the scream and the tears developing within me.

Unfortunately, my family and I were painfully prepared for the end; in fact, we had prayed that her pain would stop. Her death was so protracted that I sometimes think it was worse than had she gone suddenly. We'd watched her deteriorate for 10 years. Though I was as prepared as I could be for her to go to a better place, the finality of it was devastating. She was only 64 years old.

I worried about things I could have done for her or said to her. I kept second-guessing myself: Had I said enough to her? Had I wasted any of the time we had together? I was as proud of her as she was of me, a sentiment that I don't think I ever could have shared enough with her.

My thoughts immediately turned toward my father. Given that he is now 85 and shows no signs of slowing down, I would say he has some amazing inner strength. He's a survivor. My whole family is; though the pain of death is unbearable at times, you get beyond it because you have to. Memories form within the cavity of the deepest aches and help soothe the wound.

No matter how strong the body is, it takes a truly strong mind to carry us through our lives. We all have moments when we don't know whether to give up or make sweeping changes. In some ways, I'm grateful for what I've gone through because of where it has brought me today. I consider myself a spiritual person, albeit perhaps not a "religious" person. I not only believe in God, I talk to him every day. My mom was devoutly religious; she converted from her own Protestant upbringing to that of my father's Catholicism. We went to church every week, even in the New England winters when snow might have kept others at home. My sister Susan has an especially strong faith, a gift passed down from my mother. Susan's strength seemed to light the darkest hours of my toughest times. I knew her schedule better than her husband and kids did. I called her several times a day and well into the night.

As I got older, I felt I didn't always need to go to church to pray—I pray every day, wherever and whenever I need to. Each day, I take a little time out to communicate with God. When I was living alone in a rental apartment and seeing my boys only a few times a week, I prayed, sometimes hour by hour, that I could get through every day. Now I might pray about something that's on my mind or just say a few words of thanks for the health and happiness of those around me. Personal happiness was that brass ring that I thought was no longer possible after what I had been through.

> As rational people, we believe that man is an animal who seeks pleasure and avoids pain. To seek pain is illogical, and to thrive on it is insane. It would appear that the perfect life is pain free, and I don't believe that there's any such thing. So why fight it or fear it? I'd rather just deal with it.
>
> *Dave, "Pain Is Good," CoolRunning.com*

I have been told that I have masochistic tendencies. Why would I voluntarily subject myself to pain and suffering? In a twist on what Michael Douglas's character said in the movie *Wall Street*—that "greed is good"—I believe *pain* is good.

Some may think I'm a little over the edge: "He likes pain?" The answer is, of course, no, I don't *like* pain, but I've spent my life doing everything I can to extend the threshold at which I give in to it. I'll jump into a pool and hold my breath for as long as I can. I do it as a test: Maybe someday I will find myself trapped underwater and need to hold my breath. It's all a learning process for me.

When I'm out running and I feel really, really bad—say, at 4 miles of a 5-mile run—I'll pretend I'm at the 25-mile mark of a marathon and I need to cross the finish line. I simulate the whole thing in my brain. I put myself in these types of situations all the time. It's all part of being prepared.

I do sometimes push my workouts to the point of discomfort but not injury. Call it pain with a purpose: It helps me advance, improve, get stronger. For me, working out to the point of nearly breaking myself and then going through the healing process is cathartic. I believe my body comes out stronger on the other side of the experience. In fact, the more pain I endure, the better prepared I feel for the time when I'm called upon to face it in a real-life situation.

You've got to break down before you can build. It's like scar tissue. After an injury, the subsequent scar is usually thicker and stronger than the skin that was there before. The only really noticeable scar I have on my body is where my appendix was taken out.

The night before I had my surgery, I went bowling. I didn't know I had appendicitis, but I knew my stomach hurt very badly. As I continued the game, the pain grew worse and worse, but I didn't want to stop playing. I had started, and I had to finish it. Call it stubbornness or call it something else, but nothing was getting me off the lane. I had to deny and defy the pain, or it would win.

My mom called Dr. Whelan, the man who delivered all five of us. In those days, there were truly house calls, and thank goodness. He gave me a quick once-over and diagnosed appendicitis. I was rushed to the hospital, where I was pronounced lucky to be alive. The operation was immediate. If I had waited even 1 more day, my appendix most likely would've burst.

My parents came the next morning to check on me, and when they walked into the room, the first thing I said was, "Whatever you do, *don't* make me laugh!" My stomach hurt only if I moved the muscles around it. My dad said, "Well, I brought you something," and handed me a brown paper bag, from which I pulled out a box of caramel popcorn. I don't know what I was expecting, but it certainly wasn't . . . Fiddle Faddle. I burst out laughing, which made my parents start laughing, and none of us could stop. I had to ask my dad to leave the room. The pain was blinding, but I couldn't stop laughing. I said, "Dad, you're killing me," as he closed the door behind him. I laughed and cried at the same time. I could still hear him in the hallway.

The scar from the stitches is a reminder of what I went through. It's kind of like a small, thin, and unattractively bumpy badge of courage.

It's a shallow life that doesn't give a person a few scars.

Garrison Keillor, writer and radio host,
A Prairie Home Companion

Emotional scars cannot be seen, and the healing process is not outwardly visible, but eventually, going through a painful experience will give you a stronger footing with which to deal with subsequent challenges. When I was small and got cut from teams where the other players were bigger than I was, I knew the only way I could advance or achieve was to increase my pain threshold, physically and mentally. I knew that when I did find myself playing a sport against these stronger, vertically gifted boys, I would need to be tough and dig deep to create a pain threshold bigger than that of the guy next to me. I perceive it as acclimating, much like flying out to Colorado to train for a marathon at a high altitude. I want to ready my body and mind in case I am someday called upon to face a challenge beyond my ordinary comfort zone. I want to be prepared for just about anything.

Even when everything seems in order on the surface, there are still days when I wake up and I'm sad, but I always work through it. The death of my mother and grandfather, the breakup of my first marriage, and the toll my body has taken while logging more than 100,000 miles on the road in 51 years are just a few examples of pain I've endured. Others have faced much greater challenges.

Over the course of a lifetime, I suppose all of us pay our dues. None of us escape life's pains. For me, it was always helpful to get out for a run, ride my bike—do anything physical. The combination of healing my mind and my body helped me through the most challenging times of my life. From this perspective, I am able to truly appreciate days of happiness and my own personal peace. Completing a goal of any type leads to conquering the fear of pain. Whether brought on by destiny or by design, pain can teach, shape, and strengthen us and help us continually develop throughout our lives.

CHAPTER 10

Ego Is Not a Four-Letter Word

Our ego ideal is precious to us because it repairs a loss of our earlier childhood, the loss of our image of self as perfect and whole, the loss of a major portion of our infantile, limitless, ain't-I-wonderful narcissism which we had to give up in the face of compelling reality. Modified and reshaped into ethical goals and moral standards and a vision of what at our finest we might be, our dream of perfection lives on—our lost narcissism lives on—in our ego ideal.

Judith Viorst, author, **Necessary Losses**

There are a few conversational-topic taboos in this life. Death is one of them, and another is admitting you have an ego. It seems a little ridiculous that these two things, which occupy so much importance in our lives, should not be talked about—or if they are, that discussing them makes even the most at-ease person want to crawl under a rug or leave the room. However, to me, "ego" is simply my belief in my own abilities; it's my level of confidence. Certainly Freud had a definition of ego— the id—but since I'm not a psychologist, I'll just talk about my own perception of this topic. I almost feel like I should *whisper*.

Ego saved me. Feelings of inadequacy due to my height often haunted me when I was younger. I would be lying if I said that I didn't revisit them from time to time, even as an adult. My accomplishments help me overcome these moments. I am sustained by my ability to do my job well and the support I derive from strong, lasting relationships with friends and family.

> The worst part of success is trying to find someone who is happy for you.
>
> *Bette Midler, actress*

In modern language, the word is synonymous with self-aggrandizing behavior. When I refer to the "ego," I'm referring to the part of the brain that can be nurtured to produce a sense of positive self-worth and ability. I have a *healthy* ego, and I have no regrets in saying so, though I realize that makes me vulnerable to those who will misinterpret my character as being "full of myself." Each of us must have confidence in his or her own abilities in order to succeed. I won't apologize for that.

Had I not believed that I could actually run across the United States, I would still be sitting at my desk as an actuary, a job that was definitely not for me (no offense to any members of this esteemed profession). It was the team of me, myself, and I, along with exhaustive preparation, that provided the jolt I needed to accomplish the unlikely goal of running more than 3,000 miles in 80 days.

The ego can also work against you, if you allow it to. I was so much smaller than the other kids at school. That "sticks and stones" saying is not true, in my opinion. Name-calling stinks. I'd rather be struck by sticks. After constantly hearing "shorty" and every other name that goes with it, there were two paths I could take: Either allow the kids' remarks to sink in and hurt me at my very core, or believe in myself and figure out ways to prove to them (and myself) that I was no different—and in some ways, maybe even better—than they were. That's the road I tried to take more often, especially as I got older.

Education was always of the utmost importance to me. After my first year at Merrimack, I decided to transfer in search of scholarship opportunities. It bothered me that many of the student athletes got a free ride. It went back to the fact that I wasn't a candidate for an athletic scholarship. The other guys were—the ones who were the *first* pick.

I went on a fishing expedition for scholarship money to see if I could improve my financial situation. In my sophomore year, I applied to transfer to Tufts, where I was accepted for the second time. I also threw Harvard into the application mix; why not? I was accepted, but the sophomore class was full, so I'd have to transfer in as a freshman. That was out of the question, even if it meant an ivy-covered degree. Knowing it was an option did give me great satisfaction, however.

My next step, which maybe should've been my first, was to meet with the president of Merrimack, Father John Aherne, one of the first people to give me the chance I needed to succeed. He listened patiently as I told him, in so many words, that I "deserved" personal assistance because of what I would be able to give back to the college in the future. Without realizing it, I was in the midst of giving my first DMSE sponsor pitch. I needed a sponsor to fund my education, and I got it. My approach to raising funds worked; in fact, it worked *too well.*

A week or two after that meeting, I was given a job as a resident assistant in the men's dormitory. I also applied for a presidential grant and one other scholarship. After the checks began to arrive, I realized that I actually had a surplus of cash—the scholarship money coming in was more than the cost of tuition! I was getting a great education *and* earning an income. I felt a tad uncomfortable with this, so I let the administration know what was happening. The woman I spoke with in the financial aid office said, "We're going to have to look into this." And I thought, "Well, don't look too deep!"

Give a man a fish and you feed him for a day. Teach a man
to fish and you feed him for a lifetime.

Chinese proverb

The scholarships and the resident position allowed me to stay at
school without being a financial burden to my family. Thank
goodness I asked questions and didn't just go with the status
quo. I ask *a lot* of questions; if you don't ask, you don't *learn*.
With a newfound sense of financial security, I decided to really
dig in and make the most of my experience at school.

Each of us has potential for personal achievement. I could've
said the heck with college—who needs it? Or the expense
could've prevented me from continuing. But I believed in myself,
and that made the difference.

My next challenge was joining the Merrimack cross-country
team. The problem was, there was no cross-country team that
year. I "signed up" anyway and became a team of one. I credit
Father Tom Walsh, who became the coach of the cross-country
"team." He'd drive me to meets so I could represent the school,
even though as a school we weren't in a position to win. I always
appreciated what he did for me.

Seeking financial opportunities wasn't new to me—our family of seven was middle-class at best. Even when I was younger,
I delivered papers so that I wouldn't have to ask my folks for
spending money. My friend and I shared the route. He'd collect
the money, then sometimes go buy candy, pop, cigarettes—you
name it. Then he'd divide what was left over between us. It was
not the way I handled my part of the "partnership." We used to
fight about this all the time! In fact, his mother usually had to
come down in the basement, where we dealt with financial matters, and break us apart.

Sometimes I would be short a few papers for the route, so I'd
ride my bike to the store and buy copies with my own money.
That was just what I thought was right.

My freshman year of high school, I worked at the Malden
Hospital in their main kitchen. From 7 to 11 a.m. Monday

through Friday, I washed dishes and helped the cooks. I was free in the morning because half of my high school had burned. There wasn't enough room for all grades to go at the same time that year, so freshmen attended classes in the afternoon while juniors, sophomores, and seniors went in the morning. School was within walking distance of my job, but even better was when I got out of work in time to catch the bus that stopped right in front of school.

After college, I held a few jobs, searching for the one that fit me best. None seemed right, so that's when I planned the run. Being away for nearly 3 months did not endear me to my boss, and I was fired. But destiny was calling, even if I followed a rather circuitous route. I don't think it's mere coincidence that my job at Mercer was in the John Hancock Tower on Clarendon Street in Boston, diagonally across the street from the BAA office, or that the view on the other side was of the marathon's finish line. It was all just a process of connecting the dots.

It took only a few weeks before Pro Specs hired me. What a great place it was—no suit required. It gave me the freedom to continue to do endurance events and charity runs, but I still wanted to do more.

In 1982, while working at Pro Specs, I decided to get my feet wet in the event-management arena. My good friend Jack Dempsey and I opened an athletic footwear and apparel store in Medford Square, the Dave McGillivray Running and Sports Center. I had recently returned from the Ironman and was pumped up about it, so I decided to produce my own triathlon to bring the sport to New England and help promote the store. Rather than start out with an ultradistance, I settled on a shorter distance and called it the Bay State Triathlon: a 1-mile swim, 40-mile bike ride, and 10-mile run.

The Bay State Triathlon attracted some great athletes but perhaps none with more guts and sheer strength than Dick Hoyt. I met Dick at the Falmouth Road Race, where we were both competing in the early '80s. My first glimpse of him was of his back as he passed me while pushing a boy in a wheelchair—his son, Rick, who was born as a spastic quadriplegic and has cerebral palsy. I could see Dick was tough, and I asked him if he'd ever thought about a doing a swim-bike-run event.

We exchanged numbers, and later I got a call from Dick saying he'd try the Tri, but "I just need to figure out how I'm going to compete with Rick." I hadn't expected a two-in-one competitor, but Dick made it work by pulling his son in a rubber dingy during the swim. That 1985 event marked the first triathlon for Team Hoyt, a father-son duo now well known in the world of endurance sports.

If McGillivray is involved, you don't need a second opinion.

Hal Gabriel

After a few years of successful triathlons at this long-course distance, I decided to try the Ironman distance event and created the Cape Cod Endurance Triathlon. It was a full Ironman, with the official 2.4-mile swim, 112-mile bike, and 26.2-mile run. We held the event on the Cape for 5 years, until logistics made it nearly impossible to continue there. The weekend we held it was close to Labor Day, which was becoming busier on the Cape each year. Officials in the towns we went through said they would require that each cyclist stop for red lights and obey the rules of the road. That wouldn't bode well for people wanting to finish in under 24 hours! We changed the name to the Endurance and moved the event to New Hampshire, where the roads and traffic patterns lent themselves more to such an event. Though it no longer exists, the Endurance was my favorite event of those early years in the business.

The McGillivray Mile was also one of the store promotions. It was a 1-mile point-to-point race that started at the top of a steep hill and went down to my store, along a road called Fellsway West. I invited a lot of local celebs to come up and run it. Steve Grogan of the New England Patriots and TV personalities Robin Young and Paula Zahn took part.

Meanwhile, on the recommendation of my friend Bob Drapeau, I took a full-time job as national director of promotions at Saucony and left the store under Jack's management. I helped develop Saucony's racing and triathlon teams, handled their race sponsorships, and worked with many of the professional athletes they sponsored, including Carl Yastrzemski, George Scott, George Brett, and OJ Simpson. It was great experience, but it took me about 2 minutes to realize I wanted something to call my own again, and something more than a storefront. It took a little longer to get it all planned out. At one point, I was juggling the store, working full-time at Saucony, and producing events.

Throughout all this, an up-and-coming triathlete and college student, Harold Robinson, wanted to know if I'd be interested in representing him as his sports agent. I'd never given this area of the business much thought. It entails handling an athlete's sponsorship and corporate portfolio, helping to strategize the race schedule, and, sometimes, cutting deals with event directors to waive registration fees and arrange for transportation and accommodations. Because of my involvement in directing races, I already knew potential sponsors, so I thought, sure, why not? There weren't many agents for triathletes at that time—I saw my role as offering friendly advice as opposed to what I would deem a hard-core agent. As I would learn, the trick was to balance it all with no perceived conflict of interest.

Soon after I agreed to represent Harold, another young athlete named Mike Pigg stopped by my office the day after he had competed, and came in second, in the Bay State Triathlon. Mike was one of a handful of top athletes whom I had personally invited to Medford for the event. He wanted to know if I would consider representing him, too. I agreed. Mike went on to become a four-time National Champion and Triathlete of the Year, staying with me for most of his career.

I represented 12 athletes in all, 11 simultaneously, while also producing races. These top triathletes included Dave Scott, six-time Ironman World Champion; and Karen Smyers, a three-time World Champion, including the Ironman in Hawaii; as well as Scott Molina, Erin Bakker, Jan Ripple, and Ken Glah. As the sport evolved, the athletes began to demand most of my time. Financially, it didn't make sense for me to continue in this role. I needed to focus more on the events I was directing and producing.

I enjoyed the agent aspect because, unlike an event, which is inanimate, an athlete could give me feedback. There was a lot of emotion associated with it because I was affecting the livelihood of these athletes. It was about trusting and believing in one another. I was selling them and making them look good, and, in turn, when they did well, I felt good about my role in their success. The experience gave me a taste for another part of the business, and I did it just long enough: about 10 to 15 years.

Being an agent allowed me to enhance my DMSE races by viewing an event from both the athlete side and the director/sponsorship side. But it was balancing act: A sponsor might call me about a particular athlete, when in fact, I represented many. Whose name should I throw out and whose should I hold back? One athlete might hear of another's sponsorship and say, "Well, what about me?" I tried to deal sensitively with the delicate situation and different personalities, a skill I've had to refine and hone throughout my entire career.

The balance sheet for being an agent ultimately did not work out in my favor, nor did the one at the Running Center. Eventually, we sold the store for $2. Jack got one dollar, and I got the other. I never even received a cancelled check from the venture. A few years later, the store went out of business. That was that.

> I did the Endurance Triathlon in '83 and '84. In '84, the water was so cold that I came out and was shaking like a leaf. A local TV news magazine, *Chronicle,* filmed the whole thing. They were there to do a profile of the event. They kept the camera on me all day, so I decided to have fun with it. I found this perfectly shaped banana, and I taped it to the top of my helmet. I became known as Banana Man that day, and I did quite well.
>
> *Rich Havens, president, Time Out! Productions*

I plunged full-time into the world of event management and opened an office with my partner Bob Donohoe just five doors down from the storefront. There were just a few people managing races back then. In 1985, I scheduled a meeting of local race directors, believing there might be strength in numbers, and we could help each other out.

Shortly before the scheduled meeting, I got a call from someone interested in being part of the Saucony Running Team. Before we hung up, he said, "By the way, I competed in your triathlon last year. I was the one with the banana helmet."

This guy had made an impression on me, so I invited him to join the other race directors and me that Sunday. Just 2 days before, he got fed up with his office job as director of purchasing for a New Hampshire hotel and gave notice, dreaming of a job where he could wear shorts and a T-shirt to work every day and actually have some fun.

"What I need is a director of the New England Triathlon Series," I said to all who were in the room. "And I think I have one." I gestured toward Rich Havens, whose first response was "Who, me?" After the meeting, he and I went to the Salem Street Deli and ate and talked. I asked Rich to get me a résumé. He obliged, and Friday I called and welcomed him to DMSE: Dave McGillivray Sports Enterprises, Inc.

Quite a long name for a business and, I admit, not very catchy—but I pinned my reputation on it. I was more than a little apprehensive about a company named after myself, but I'd been advised that it was the way to go. At the time, I was in the news a lot, doing physical challenges and raising money for charity. My name was becoming recognizable in the community.

I even made Norma Nathan's list of "Boston's Most Eligible Bachelors." Nathan was a celebrity columnist for the *Boston Herald* and wrote a book about 100 of the city's most eligible guys. I was listed among names like Ted Kennedy, Walt Dropo of the Red Sox, Tommy Gilligan of Marathon Tours, and Congressman Ed Markey. Though I know I should've been flattered, I felt that being labeled a bachelor meant that no one had yet "caught" me, perhaps because no one thought I was worthy. I took it to mean the exact opposite of the way it was intended. I didn't tout the title a lot, and the mention didn't get me a lot of dates, but it did put my name out there at about the time I left my job at Saucony to focus on producing events. I think I stayed a bachelor for a while because I was truly married to creating my own business.

Medford seemed the logical place for home base. My hometown had rallied around me and made me feel like a king during my '78 run; they even made me grand marshal of that year's Columbus Day Parade. The *Medford Mercury* had an article about me every day for 80 days. I was so grateful for all of the support I received, and I wanted to keep my roots there.

The food at DePasquales in Medford helped replenish my carbs after races, and I brought in triathletes and friends like Scott Tinley and Julie Moss after they participated in the Bay State Triathlon. Being born and bred in "Meffa" and being a local quasi-celebrity qualified me to have my photo displayed in the restaurant. I think that picture is now in the broom closet, but as long as it's my photo collecting dust and not my body, I'm okay with that.

"McGillivray" is on the DMSE letterhead (and the checkbook), but the heart of the company is the team of people I've assembled over the years, the first being Georgie Marino. I've surrounded myself with great friends who also turned out to be great colleagues. Back then DMSE had eight full-time employees plus a number of part-timers on the payroll.

DMSE's first "warehouse" was in Dave's store, next to his apartment on Lambert Street in Medford. Basically, all of our equipment was shoved down the cellar; it was a real hassle.

Tim Barry, DMSE consultant

At our busiest, we did 30 to 40 events a year, starting with the Boston Marathon in April and going through October. We'd work 3 weeks at a time without a weekend off. After 15 years, it got to be a bit much, and I decided to downsize the operation. Rich took the triathlons and spun them off into his own company, Time Out! Productions. It worked out great for both of us.

Today, more than 70 consultants make up the team, and the beauty of it is that I'm the only full-time employee. The consultants all have full-time jobs and *choose* to work together on events because of their passion for the business, the charities we benefit, and the pure enjoyment of that race-day "high." We also now have a large warehouse with a loading dock, which may not sound glamorous—but in the world of generators and road barricades, it's pretty luxurious.

In addition to the warehouse, I have a secret key to the executive washroom—ah, the glamour continues. Porta-Johns are on the race director's radar screen. No matter how many elite-runner meetings or press briefings you attend, or celebrity runners you have your photo taken with, the bottom line is that the number of portable toilets can make or break a race.

Near the start of the Boston Marathon, there's always a locked Porta-John reserved for me and some of the public-safety officers. A few years ago, I unlocked it just before the start of the race—after all, I didn't want to be on a motorcycle for 2 hours, going down course with the leaders of the race, and suddenly have to pull off. After I had entered, some security person, doing his job to the letter, noticed that the lock was undone, so he relocked the door. I finally got out after yelling and screaming and banging on the door—I almost knocked the thing over. I doubt I would've been allowed anywhere near the start of the race if that had happened.

Truth be told, even if I had been locked in the darn thing for the race, I know my team could've carried on without me. My goal has always been to create an environment where everyone understands their importance to the big picture and works hard, whether putting up road cones or planning a postevent awards ceremony. In fact, when I revamped the company 20 years after I founded it, I began referring to it as "Team" DMSE.

Leading a team, to me, means providing the overall plan as well as being ready to dig in whenever and wherever help is needed. In my case, this often means picking up roadkill at 3 a.m. the morning of a race or cleaning up banana peels until 9 p.m. that night. In between, I may say a few words to participants or do media interviews. It's all part of the territory, and I do what it takes to get the job done. That's what it's all about.

DMSE's reputation is all I have to keep the phone ringing on the desk in my office, and I was thrilled when I answered a call one day and was told I'd been selected to be the competition manager of the Goodwill Games Triathlon in New York City in 1998. To direct 80 of the world's finest triathletes in one of the most important triathlons just prior to the opening of the Olympic Triathlon in Sydney, Australia, was truly an honor. With the job came the reality that successful businesspeople should not only be confident in their area of expertise, but perhaps even more important, they must not be afraid to take responsibility when something doesn't go as planned.

In a lot of ways, the triathlon was more logistically challenging than the 100th running of the marathon. Imagine trying to have people swim (in the Hudson!), run, and bike through the streets of Manhattan. At first, I thought that to keep participants' teeth from rattling as they traveled over potholes, we should include mouth guards in the goody bags. But the city rose to the occasion, and the course was smooth, although far from flawless.

I worked very closely with the New York City Marathon start coordinator, Vic Navarra. He and many others on the Goodwill staff spent nearly 2 years charting no less than 10 different race courses before we finally came up with one that satisfied both the city and the game organizers. I thought the hardest part would be the water-quality issues; it took more than 20 tests to finally prove that the Hudson River was safe. We collected permits from city and state agencies, and we had to change the bike course 2 days before the race because of a scaffolding collapse in Times Square that, tragically, killed one person.

The whole event was intense: Hot weather had attracted jellyfish to the river for the first time in years. Near the start was a steam-pipe break covered by a steel plate, which during the race heated up to about 500 degrees. The Department of Public Works responded to make sure there were no potholes that could injure an athlete. We couldn't set up the start until 8 p.m. the night before, or the finish until 10 p.m., so no one on my crew slept until the race was over and wrapped up the next day.

Despite all those extreme conditions, we handled the event well. The swim and bike courses were definitely challenges, and I was relieved once the athletes got out of the water and entered Central Park. I thought the run would be seamless, but it wasn't. The participants were to do an 0.8-mile out-and-back loop before completing three full laps of the lower section of the park. An informed volunteer and road cones were placed at the turn-around. However, as the runners approached the turnaround, a park official who was unaware of the course thought the cones were in the runners' way and removed them. As a result, athletes continued past the cones instead of turning.

I had just arrived on the scene as I made my way back from the start (getting in an automobile accident along the way!). I immediately recognized the problem and met with a number of my staff. We decided to add the out-and-back loop onto the finish once the runners completed the three laps, thus "recovering completely" from the mistake. Unfortunately, the volunteer at the turnaround became even more confused and misdirected three of the 25 athletes. They happened to be the men in fourth, fifth, and sixth places, and I knew I would have to face the music. There would be people wanting answers, including athletes, coaches, and the media.

My immediate reaction was to avoid the finish line. I found a big oak tree and hid there for at least 10 minutes. I was so overwhelmed; I couldn't imagine a bigger blunder in an event than what was unfolding—and being televised. I felt my business and reputation unraveling along with the event. At that moment, I was scared.

All of a sudden, I felt a tap on my shoulder. It was Katie. She comforted me but also pointed out an obvious fact: "You obviously can't stay here," she said.

I just needed some space and time to regroup before going into the lion's den. This event was so important: It involved Turner Sports and Goodwill; it was in downtown New York City; it included the best athletes in the world. And it was all coming apart—on my watch.

I unglued myself from the tree and went to the press conference, explained the situation, and took the blame. I received so much positive support. In a very classy move, Turner stepped up to the plate and came up with money for the actual fourth-, fifth-, and sixth-place winners as well as those who hadn't officially run the route and were disqualified.

I had done everything I could to ensure a perfect race, but unless I could clone myself to be everywhere at all times, I had to trust the systems my staff and I had created. But my name was on the event, and I took full responsibility for what happened. I immediately sent a letter of apology to the triathlon community. All involved were so gracious, including the winner, Simon Lessing of Great Britain, who at a press conference stated that the problems were due to the complexity of the sport.

Even with all the support and kind words from those who had hired me and the athletes themselves, I lost sleep over this one for weeks. One cone. One moved cone and one person in the wrong place at the wrong time. It underscored the fact that just one small thing or moment can change the course of your life forever, for the better or for the worst. Eventually, I let it go and learned to be happy with what we had accomplished. Don't worry too much when you stumble. Just learn from it, and move on.

Dave is known throughout the running world as a technical wizard when it comes to road races. He is much more than technician. He is also teacher, motivator, leader, and mentor. He enthusiastically and unselfishly shares his in-depth knowledge and expertise with staff and volunteers, while instilling a sense of pride and accomplishment within each and every person with whom he interacts.

Joan Samuelson, founder,
TD Banknorth Beach to Beacon 10-K

I've received many awards over the years, but those that mean the most to me are the ones presented by others in the industry. *Running Times* magazine and Road Race Management present an annual Race Director of the Year award, and I was nominated for my role in the TD Banknorth Beach to Beacon 10-K Road Race in Cape Elizabeth, Maine, a race founded by Joan Benoit Samuelson, 1984 Olympic marathon runner. Although I didn't win the award the first time I was nominated, I did receive the honor in 2002 for my direction of the Beach to Beacon.

I have my hands in so many races that it doesn't seem fair to compare them, but I believe the TD Banknorth Beach to Beacon 10-K is the finest race that DMSE puts on all year. It's always been special to me because Joan herself called me one day and asked if I'd consider helping her with her desire to put on a world-class event in her hometown. We met at a Dunkin' Donuts in Maine to chat, and I was flattered that she thought enough of me to ask. I decided to give it a try, but creating a race that would measure up to the reputation of this Olympic great was a challenge. This race had to be spectacular, and I had only 5 months between when I accepted the role and August 1, 1998, when the starter's gun would go off.

As a race director, I believe that I am not needed on race day if I've done my job well. By race day, my mind is clear to think about the unthinkable and ready to take action. Case in point was the night before that first "B2B." I was lying in bed—not sleeping, of course—and thinking about the balloon arches over the road at each of the water stations along the course. It suddenly "popped" into my head that the balloons might not be high enough for the press truck to clear, and no one had informed the driver about the arch's height. At 3:30 a.m., I ran out onto the course to take a look. Much to my dismay, I was right. I got on the phone with the balloon company and by 4:30 the arches were higher. I was able to anticipate the problem because all else was done, and my mind had the luxury of concentrating on these details.

We had 2,817 runners that first year. By year 3, to the credit of Joan, the sponsors, and everyone who helps organize it, the event had already gained an international following in the running world; how could it not, with Joan's name on it?

That first year, Johnny Kelley came to the event and spoke at the finish. "Dave is a genius," he said in his remarks to the crowd at the awards ceremony. A comment like that out of the mouth of a legend was truly humbling. I also knew that what he experienced that weekend was a combination of Joannie's influence and vision, along with the beauty of Cape Elizabeth and the Maine coast, complete with a lighthouse finish. There's not much more a runner could want, except maybe one more helping of chowder at the postevent clambake.

With all my events, I try to be the first one there and the last to leave. An hour or two after that first race, Joan radioed me and said, "Dave, I'm on the lower field; can you send the cleanup crew down? There's still a lot of trash here." I radioed back as I was picking up trash on the upper field: "Joan, we are the cleanup crew." Welcome to the world of event management.

> **Pioneer:** One who ventures into unknown or unclaimed territory to settle
>
> *The American Heritage Dictionary:*
> *Fourth Edition*

When I first started out in the event business, there were not too many people directing races, especially triathlons, as a career. It was a "make it up as you go along" type of job. With each event, I learned more about the sport and what to expect, but most important, I've learned to expect the unexpected.

My standard business contract now includes provisions for

even the most bizarre circumstances. Several years ago, there was an issue with Porta-Johns for the Jimmy Fund Walk (yes, another Porta-John story, but I'll stop at two). Per usual, they were delivered to Copley Square Park in Boston. The night before the walk, someone with a bit too much time on their hands decided to set one on fire, and all 10 went up in flames. It caused a bit of damage to the park, and who would pay for it became an issue. Who could even anticipate this sort of thing? Well, I do now; nothing surprises me anymore.

In this business, anything can happen. One of the greatest lessons my mother taught me was to never assume anything, and I don't. I am obsessed with follow-up. Sometimes those working with me get annoyed that I question them incessantly, perturbed that I call them numerous times to make sure they are doing what is expected of them and that critical steps are being completed.

There's no such thing as checking and rechecking too much. Consider what I refer to as the 700 Club fiasco. DMSE was putting on the 1984 United States Triathlete Series (USTS) race in Boston, and we had a whopping 2,200 competitors and perhaps the most complex and ridiculous race course I've ever laid out. The night before, we had to collect 2,200 pairs of shoes, transport them to the transition area, and lay out each pair next to its owner's bike rack.

Unbeknownst to us, a box of 50 pairs had been stolen from the service elevator as we were transporting them out to the truck. It wasn't pretty at racks 700 to 750 when those triathletes came bombing in after biking 25 miles, only to find blades of grass beneath their bikes. Spectators began taking their own sneakers off and throwing them to the irate competitors. Surprisingly, none were thrown at me.

Then, in 1986, Rich Havens and I were putting on a triathlon in Connecticut as part of the six-state New England Triathlon Series. Everything was all set—or so we thought. That's probably why I know better when I hear someone who responds with "all set" after I ask if they've done everything they need to prior to a race, especially a triathlon, which is probably the most logistically challenging of all sporting events.

We had our course permits. Entries were pouring in. Things were going well. What could go wrong? The answer truly *drained* our enthusiasm for the entire event.

Two weeks before the race, Rich and I drove down to Connecticut to check things out and confirm final arrangements. As we approached the swim venue, I remember telling Rich that I thought this was one of the best race venues in the entire series; it was definitely going to be our finest race—I just knew it.

What did my mother teach me again? Never assume *anything*. As in, never assume that a body of water that has been there forever will still be there after you've just invited hundreds of athletes to pay for the privilege of competing and swimming in it.

I couldn't believe my eyes. The lake was empty. It was almost like a mirage. Someone had actually drained the bloody lake. Not a bit of condensation was left. No water. Nothing. Rich and I went from event mode to crisis mode in the time it took for us to regain our breath.

Later, we found out that the town had drained the lake to do some work on it and intended to fill it back up—but that would take *months*! They'd be skating on it by the time it was done. No one had thought to let us know. In 2 weeks, we had 500 triathletes coming to swim 1 mile in a dirt pit. Maybe we'd change the name to the Lake Bottom Duathlon . . . a run, bike, run on the floor of the lake?

Seeing as Rich, a garden hose, and I were not going to get the lake filled up in time, we headed back home. As we crossed the Connecticut River, I turned to him and said, "We have no choice. We've got to use the river. We just don't have time to find an entirely new bike and run course."

At the time, no one had ever done a swim in the Connecticut River, at least not close to Hartford. We were desperate. So a few days later, I returned to Connecticut to beg for permission to use the river for the race. I also jumped in the water to test it out for myself and was pleasantly surprised. It turned out to be much cleaner and calmer than its reputation, which was not that good back then. My pleading worked.

The race was a week later. As I got to the swim start on race morning, I looked down at the edge of the river and noticed a dead fish. Taped to its side was "Dave McGillivray Sports Enterprises." To date, no one has ever admitted to the prank. Hey, sometimes you just have to do what you have to do. That fish was the only one in the river who had a problem that morning. It had all worked out.

The unexpected at races can come in all shapes and sizes. The year I was directing the Triathlon World Championships at Disney World was the year my son Ryan was born. One week before the race, my (then) wife, Sue, called me in Orlando at 2 a.m. She was in labor. Actually, she called my sister Susan first. Susan was a midwife and was with Sue through the whole labor. In between plane changes en route to Boston, I checked in by telephone to see how close I was to being a dad. After I arrived at Logan, I frantically waved down a cabbie. I jumped in and said, "Drive like you stole it!" He looked at me in the rearview mirror as if to say, "I did."

I just made it into the labor room; less than 30 minutes later, my sister wrapped Ryan up and gave him to me. My first thought was, "What? No Operations Manual?" The only thing I knew for sure was which end was up. Being a parent is the most important job in the world, so how come you don't have to qualify for it? I spent a few days with Sue and the baby and then had to return to Florida to direct the event.

My second surprise while directing that race was the bill I received months after it was over—for $350,000! How would I pay for Ryan's college tuition? They charged me for labor (not Sue's), equipment, supplies—even replacing the sand on the beach that spectators took away. I had to go through the bill in detail to challenge each line item one by one. I sent back a 30-page document indicating that none of this had been agreed to up front. Of the $350,000, they said I was ultimately responsible for about $22,000—and they ended up eating the whole thing.

Then there was the Olympics. I finally made it to the Olympics, but not as an athlete. I was hired as part of the Venue

Management Team for all eight road events at Atlanta in 1996. The final event was the men's marathon. We were told that the tunnel leading into the stadium would be closed 2½ hours after the start of the race to allow time to set up for the closing ceremonies and that if any runners were still out on the course after that time, we were to direct them to a high school grass field to finish. One runner from Afghanistan was having a lot of difficulty and did not make the cutoff time. In fact, he was on a 3½-hour pace, great for a local marathon but not the Olympics. However, I just didn't think it was in the true spirit of the Games to redirect this poor guy away from the Olympic Stadium and onto a grass field where about 10 people and three pigeons would be waiting for him. He was, after all, an Olympian representing his country.

I got on the two-way radio and instructed my team to ignore the order from above. We were going to send this guy into the stadium no matter what. I ran down the track and begged the band practicing for closing ceremonies to instead play a tune for this last lonely runner. They were happy to do it. Laborers were covering the track with tarp, and we asked them to rip up a section so the runner could go down one lane. I immediately looked around for a break tape and ripped up some white duct tape that was holding down TV cables. I asked a medical person for a black marker and hurriedly wrote "Atanta '96" on the tape. (Yes, I misspelled "Atlanta" in my rush.) Live television broke in from other programming when they heard about the commotion at the stadium. With not even the slightest hesitancy, we moved the Olympic road cones and redirected the last runner right past security and into the tunnel. He completed one lap and crossed the finish, breaking the tape I was holding. He collapsed in tears, as did all of us.

That Afghan runner gave all of us an opportunity to experience a true test of courage and athletic spirit. He finished, and I hope he felt a sense of accomplishment, no matter what the time clock said.

In 2004, I was honored to direct the Olympic Team Trials–Women's Marathon in April in St. Louis. It was especially great because there happened to be six female Olympic hopefuls from the Merrimack Valley Striders, a running club of which I am a member. That was a high point of my career; there's something uniquely special about helping to qualify the best US team.

> [Dave] was great . . . always enthusiastic. Very organized; we had a schedule, but there was also time built in for us to just play. He was a great role model for all of us young kids.

> *Mark Smith, director of parks and recreation, Medford*

I hoped to bring a spirit of friendly competition to the kids in the Medford Parks Department summer program, where I worked as a park instructor beginning in the summer of 1973. The next year, I suggested a road race to Frank Sollito, my boss, the director of the parks and recreation program. With his go-ahead, I went out and measured a 2.6-mile course to coordinate with the marathon distance. The Medford Recreation Mini-Marathon began in West Medford and ended at Playstead Park. More than 300 kids covered the route lined with instructors.

After I ran across the country, the parks department decided to rename the race the McGillivray Mini-Marathon as well as make me a member of the board. It meant so much to me to be recognized like this by my hometown, especially within the park system, which had such a strong influence on me as I was growing up. In anticipation of an annual invitation to the race, I would save items left behind at my events: water bottles, hats, fanny packs, and the like. The kids were pumped to get a "gift" like that along with a certificate once they crossed the finish line.

When I didn't get a call about the race from the parks department in the summer of 2001, I didn't think much about it, but by the next year, I realized that perhaps the race had ended. Sure enough, in 2002, road construction along the route prevented the event from taking place. The year after that, staff cuts made it nearly impossible to carry it off. And most kids simply didn't want to run 2 miles anymore.

Still, that race lasted more than 20 years, and it was so great because it was all about the pure joy of youth and running and competition. I'm sad that Mini-Marathon is no more but glad to know that its impact was felt for years afterward. Being a park instructor gave me the opportunity to mentor some of those kids. I hope that I instilled the love of athletics in even one child.

Even today, the races I'm most proud of are community-based events, traditions that families can look forward to. With 7,000 participants, the 5-K and 5-mile Feaster Five Road Race is the largest annual race I direct, after the Boston Marathon. This race is one of my favorites: Where else do you walk away with a free apple pie, a long-sleeve T-shirt, and the daily newspaper (courtesy of the *Eagle-Tribune*) after your run? This Thanksgiving Day race draws people from all over the North Shore— we even had actor Matt Damon, his brother Kyle, and their dad run in it a few years back.

Nearly 6 years ago, I received an e-mail from a woman whose family has made the Feaster Five part of their Thanksgiving tradition; she and her mother usually place high among the winners. Her message confirmed why I do what I do.

> This summer, my mother found a lump in her breast and was diagnosed with breast cancer. She began chemotherapy in September and has begun the long journey of managing and surviving her disease. My mother is making small, personal successes by living through every day and each treatment, and she continues her commitment to her exercise regimen. She registered and walked in this year's Feaster Five because she views her participation as another small, albeit important, victory in her battle with cancer. Although her results were disappointing for her this year, my family and I see her commitment as a personal victory in her struggle with cancer.
>
> Thanks—for managing a great race, helping us get our day off to a great start, and providing motivation for my mother to keep up the good fight.

That woman is a real-life hero for getting out there and getting it done. In fact, so many of the people who really influenced me were what I call "blue collar" heroes—real people who did real things, such as Paul McKeon, a gym teacher I had in grade school. Once a week, he taught phys ed. He was a bit older and very athletic. I remember looking at him and wishing I could do all the things that he did.

One day when we were playing softball, I took a hit right on the mouth. My lip split open and was bleeding, and Mr. McKeon gave me his handkerchief to hold on the wound as I rode to the hospital. My mom was going to toss the handkerchief, but I said, "*No*—I want to keep it." I washed it and put it in my drawer. That handkerchief was something real and tangible from someone I admired. I suppose it was in the same genre as having his autograph, but this was a piece of himself that he had given to comfort me.

Autographs have both intrigued and puzzled me. My first experience with autograph signing was very disenchanting; it was when I saw Celtic great Bill Russell and I asked him for his. He said no, and I never forgot it. I was 15, and I felt so bad that he refused me. After that, I decided getting autographs wasn't worth the chance of rejection. I stuck by that rule for years— until I came face-to-face with perhaps my one true hero.

When I was in the Rocky Mountains en route across the United States, a young boy came up to me, looked me right in the eye, and then took in the motor home covered in Jimmy Fund banners. "Hey, who's this Jimmy guy?" he asked. I had no answer. I really didn't know just who this Jimmy guy was, and at that time, no one at the Jimmy Fund knew him, either.

For a long time "Jimmy" was just a legend, a memory of a patient who was treated by Dr. Sidney Farber. The debate of whether or not he was alive went on for years. Only a few people thought he was alive; after all, back then, the prognosis for cancer was almost always death. Then one letter ended the mystery. After years of silence, Jimmy's sister wrote the Jimmy Fund to let them know he was still alive. Reluctantly, Einar Gustafson, alias Jimmy, came forward to confirm that he was the little boy treated by Dr. Farber so long ago. Many at the Jimmy Fund could not believe it. I'll never forget the moment that I actually met him at a 1998 reception for top fund-raisers of the Boston Marathon Jimmy Fund Walk.

A hero is defined as a person who is noted for feats of courage or nobility of purpose. I can't imagine a braver person than one who faces his own mortality and then has the strength to carry on. He was the hero who was by my side each step of the way, protecting and encouraging me as I ran thousands of miles across the country to raise money for other "Jimmies." But until the moment I met him, I never had a face to connect to the name that had been (and continues to be) a major part of my life and motivation for nearly 20 years. It was overwhelming. I asked this man who towered over me, "Will you kindly sign my program for my two sons, Ryan and Max, Mr. Gustafson?" I wanted my children to know who he was. I shook uncontrollably and nearly cried when he was signing it. In that moment, I realized that "Jimmy" was my hero.

After that meeting, I decided to plan a trip to Einar's hometown in Maine so I could show him the slide show of my cross-country run. I wanted to share the experience with him and personally thank him for being with me all those days and nights, even if he had no idea at the time. I regret that I never did this, but something held me back. I was afraid of looking as if I was showing off. Then, after only a few years of being "back," Einar "Jimmy" Gustafson was gone again. He died in January 2001.

Back to the Bill Russell story. . . . Many years after I'd been denied his autograph, I was putting on a road race at a place called Healthpoint in Waltham, Massachusetts. This was also the training facility of the Boston Celtics. As part of the weekend events, a celebrity sports clinic was scheduled for the next day. I read the list of who would be there and saw Bill Russell's name. I immediately called my brother Alan.

Later that day, Alan showed up with the program from the Celtics game we had gone to 30 years earlier—and inside the program was the blank scrap of paper I had given Bill Russell to sign. I remembered the exchange like it was yesterday.

We went up to one of the Healthpoint general managers and told him the story. He said, "Let me get you closure on this." And off he went to find Bill Russell.

Less than 10 minutes later, he was back with the same blank slip of paper.

Years later, I saw an interview with Tommy Heinsohn, TV analyst for the Celtics and a former player, and he was asked why Bill Russell doesn't give autographs. The response: Bill doesn't place a lot of value on an autograph; he believes a firm handshake is more valuable. That 30-second response provided some resolution to the disappointment I'd felt since age 15, when I had approached Russell in the Boston Garden. I also learned a little something about rushing to judgment. Without knowing the facts, I'd decided he was just being mean, when in fact, he and I actually see eye to eye (sort of) on the value of someone's signature.

When I was at the height of doing endurance events, I was asked for my own autograph thousands of times. I signed everything from photos to sneakers. To this day, however, I question what's behind it. Maybe an autograph from someone like Bill Russell is framed and displayed for life. However, I feel asking for my autograph is simply an impulse; at that moment, you want to feel connected to someone. What's the big deal? It's only ink.

Now, it's a rare occasion when someone asks for my autograph. And the next time it happens, I just probably will sign it, look that person in the eye, and shake their hand, too.

> Dave was self-promoting, but not of himself. He was promoting what he stood for and what he was about.
>
> *Rob Roy McGregor, DPM*

My parents never stood in the way of their children's larger-than-life ideas. They always encouraged us, as have the majority of friends and family in my life. Nonetheless, at the end of the day, the person that I count on most to get me through is the one looking back at me from the mirror. When you tell yourself every day that you can do something, chances are you will eventually attain your goals. Most times, I don't even have past experience to help affirm my thoughts; I just state the desired result as if it's a fact, and, eventually, the idea turns into reality. Ask any marathon runner or triathlete what the "magic bullet" is that gets them to the finish, and though they may not admit it or even be able to articulate it, it's all about the ego. If you don't believe in you, who will?

CHAPTER 11

Changing the Rules

And as you travel the path you have chosen, I feel experience will teach you that life is not a book with old age as a last chapter, but rather a series of short stories, each with its own unfolding.

Senator Denis L. McKenna, letter to Dave following his valedictory speech at Merrimack College in June 1976

When I was very young, I lived at 53 Billings Avenue in South Medford. Recently, I went back; it had been at least 20 years since I had driven down the street. Ours was a two-family house, right across the street from my friend John Alexander. My 7-year-old eyes thought we lived in a mansion, but in reality, it was pretty small for our family of seven; perspective certainly changes with age. Our neighbor, Mr. Penny, never even had electricity. Life was so different back then, and in many ways, I think it was better because we had less of just about everything.

No one had electronic games or instant messaging. The center of our world was not the mall—it was a street corner. Everyone from the neighborhood would hang out in the street; playing ball against the stairs or just yelling and screaming with the sheer enjoyment of being a kid. I can't remember a single one of us being overweight, which is not surprising since we were *always* moving. TV was a privilege, not a perceived "necessity."

That neighborhood was a huge part of my upbringing, and everyone in my family was very attached to it. Our houses were all close to one another, and we were close as a family. My aunts lived on nearby streets. And no matter what the Sunday weather, we always made it to St. Clement Church, a few blocks away.

When we moved only 4 miles across town to North Medford, it seemed like another world. I didn't see any of those kids again until high school, and by then, they had all grown *up*, and I hadn't—at least not in any quantifiable way.

> What grew was his burning desire to achieve. He just needed the right forum, a place where there would not be a coach to tell him to go home because he wasn't good enough or big enough. He found his place in running, a sport that was all substance, no style. Go out and get results. Put your shoes on, and go until you can't go anymore. That was Dave McGillivray's kind of sport. But he wanted to do something in running that would make a statement. Running a marathon was nice, but lots of people were running marathons. So he decided he would run the country. Yup, the entire US of A.
>
> *Don Allison, "Dave McGillivray Is Thinking Big,"*
> *CoolRunning.com, 1998*

I'm not a kid anymore, and I'm not the 23-year-old "runner" anymore, either. But as the 25th anniversary of my run approached, I thought a lot—again—about what it would be like to do it again.

The idea to repeat the run began to form while I was at a Jimmy Fund advisory council meeting sometime in the mid '90s. Having the idea was one thing; assessing the reality of where I was in my life, job, personal commitments, age, and physical conditioning all needed to come into play. I had to take a dose of my own medicine and not set any "reckless" goals. A solo run was not realistic for many reasons, but a relay format, with each person doing 15 to 20 miles a day, just might work.

Years came and went, and so did the thought. As I approached my 50th birthday, the idea lingered a while instead of being replaced with something else on my to-do list. Then one day, it stuck.

I was running along the Virginia Beach boardwalk with my friend Josh—the two of us were there to produce a new marathon—and I just said, "How'd you like to run across the country?" Asking Josh that question was like asking a kid if he'd like a piece of candy. His answer was immediate and affirmative.

> Many, many times people told me I was crazy, I was a luna-
> tic. . . . Never, and I emphasize this, never underestimate
> yourself. Everyone has ability, no matter what it is. It's up to
> you to draw it out. You have to set goals for yourself and
> they become something to strive for, to dedicate yourself to.

Dave, Lawrence-Eagle Tribune, Friday, October 6, 1978

We talked it all out and decided to give it 2 years. We believed it could work if we gave ourselves enough time to plan. We agreed that a relay format would allow us to cross the country much faster and with less risk of injury than any other method. With families, careers, and all else, we couldn't just check out for a few months to go running across the United States.

We assembled a few close friends, and they brought a few close friends, and before we knew it, there was a team of us planning the Trek USA Charity Relay for Kids. I handed the director's clipboard to Ron Kramer, the Captain, to handle the details. I was just along for the ride this time as part of a team with Mike Barry, Fernando Braz, Harrison "Hap" Farber, Bill Lapsley, Tom Licciardello, Bob Lussier, Paul McGovern, Josh Nemzer, Mike Thompson, and Bob Whirty. Our support crew included Zoë Alexi, Bob Ell, Dave Leonard, and Lyn Licciardello.

We planned the route—3,555 miles, to be covered from May 1 through 25—from SBC Park in San Francisco to Fenway. The Giants and the Red Sox were both on board to help with the start and finish. This time there were two motor homes, and two teams of five leapfrogged each other across the United States to benefit the Jimmy Fund as well as the Red Auerbach Youth Foundation, the Doug Flutie Jr. Foundation for Autism, the Cam Neely Foundation for Cancer Care, and the DMSE Children's Fitness Foundation.

The two runs were different in many ways, and to compare them would be unfair. However, in the big picture, I think that technological advancements created the most significant contrast between the two. Wireless cards, cellular phones, and laptops were in constant use in the RV between California and Massachusetts. My wife was able to e-mail me photos of our brand-new baby girl, who was born just 1 week before I left. One team member, Hap, a physician, even wrote a grant proposal en route. We were apart from our homes but very much connected. Our biggest frustration was not the lack of payphones but, rather, the presence of holes in the cellular service area.

With Trek, I changed my rules of what it meant to run across the country. It was not an attempt to relive the past but rather a search for creative ways to reinvent the future. One day soon, I'm going to have to look at my night run of the Boston Marathon and decide if or when I want to change that format, too. It's always good to have options.

The same holds true for the birthday run. Not long ago, I turned 51. In the months leading up to my birthday, I spent endless hours debating if I wanted to continue my tradition in its original state and run 1 mile for each year. By the time I turned 50, that run had become a certifiable monster! Sooner or later, I would have to figure out how to make the challenge more reasonable, and I already had a solution: Instead of continuing to add 1 mile for every year of my age, I would subtract 1 mile and run "only" 49 miles when I turned 51. This new equation would gradually decrease the miles year after year and potentially make my 99th birthday run a bit more doable!

Finally, August 21, 2005, arrived; it was the day before my birthday and the day I decided to get it over with. With the decision still plaguing me, I wasn't all that excited about the run. It was 3 a.m. when Josh and I set out from my driveway, accompanied by Captain Ron on a bike. As Josh and I ran loop after loop after loop around my neighborhood, my thoughts were spinning in similar fashion. By noontime, we had covered approximately 40 miles. The August heat soared into the high 80s, and I decided to hold off until the sun sank a little lower.

I was feeling pretty lousy from dehydration; I found out later that I had lost 8 pounds, just 1 pound shy of what I lost for the entire run from Medford to Medford. Josh and Ron went home, and when I continued with my twisted idea of a birthday celebration, I was joined for the next 7 miles by Mike Thompson, my friend and coworker. After that, I was alone with the 4 most challenging miles.

At mile 49, I stopped dead in my tracks. For at least a year, I had struggled with my decision to change something that had been a mainstay in my life for 39 years. I've always said the "intersection" is suicide: You either hit the brake or hit the accelerator. These runs are not going to get any easier, and eventually they are going to have to either end or morph into something else—but would 2005 be the year? I stood directly in front of my house with a big question mark looming over my head. Then something inside me said, "Don't change the rules yet— keep going." And that's exactly what I did. I just about crawled for those last 2 miles but was happy that this streak would continue in its original form, at least for a while.

> Often, the media will capture a person's achievements in a way that makes them seem possible only by someone with superhuman genetic endowment. Dave McGillivray, Patti Lyons, and Bill Rodgers have all achieved personal success that could seem out of reach of the average person.
>
> I respect and congratulate each of them for their achievements, and even more, for the inspiration of the stories behind their success. Rather than seeming distant, they

each become very real as they candidly shared the stories of their accomplishments. There appears to be a common theme of how each had to find a way through the many discouraging barriers to their goals.

As you read our three feature articles, I hope you are inspired, as I have been, by the understanding that, while you may not want to run across the country or win a marathon, your individual goals are important and worth pursuing.

Jean A. DuVoisin, publisher,
New England Running magazine

I was on the cover of the October 1978 issue of *New England Running* magazine. The photo depicts me in all my "glory." I had a thick black mustache, my hair was a bit long, and I was wearing a Pro Specs T-shirt. Boston's Long Wharf buildings provided the backdrop (this was before the price of a condo started at six figures). I was deeply humbled both then and now to see my name in ink in the company of Patti Lyons, one of New England's best female runners at the time, and Bill Rodgers, who to this day remains a running icon.

I still receive e-mails, letters, and phone calls from enthusiastic men and women who want to run, bike, unicycle, or in-line skate across the country. They are all looking for a bit of the magic formula of success, and, of course, there is no magic to it at all. No matter if the goal is a cross-country run or finally getting an MBA; it takes preparation, support, and a belief in yourself that no one should ever try to take away from you.

These days, I run fewer events but produce more of them. The annual DMSE calendar is action-packed with everything from a 1,000-person race to the marathon, which has 20,000. In between, I devote a lot of time to speaking to people young and old about how to achieve their dreams. My first official speaking gig was probably my valedictory address at Medford High School and then again at Merrimack; since then, I've spoken to about 1,800 audiences.

From the moment I returned from the cross-country run, I

had become a sort of homegrown "celebrity"—and I use that term loosely. People knew my name and often asked me to speak at a Rotary Club meeting or be grand marshal of a local 10-K.

As executive director for the Massachusetts Special Olympics, Ken Hodge, a former Boston Bruin, learned of my desire to bring attention and funding to people in need. He asked me to represent Massachusetts at the sixth International Special Olympics Summer Games, which would be held at Louisiana State University in Baton Rouge in 1983. Of course I said yes, and next thing I knew, I was on a plane to Tiger Stadium to escort my state's delegation of the Special Olympics. There were to be 60,000 people in attendance and 4,000 athletes. We rehearsed the day before, with every country and state represented led by a celebrity.

When I arrived at the stadium the next morning, I was approached by someone from Special Olympics. "Dave, we need to talk to you," he said. "Senator Ted Kennedy arrived here unannounced, and we really need to have *him* escort the delegation into the stadium." How could I argue, when I knew that the Special Olympics had been founded by Eunice Kennedy Shriver? I was disappointed but understood the situation.

However, they still wanted me to escort a delegation, so I was reassigned. A little while later, a national anthem (unrecognizable to most in the stadium, including me) resounded as I led the delegation from the country of Barbados into their place in the processional. Suffice it to say I looked like a fish out of water. If memory serves, I believe Arnold Schwarzenegger led a delegation behind me, and Susan St. James was in front of me—and there I was, leading the charge of about five smiling kids. I was happy to be part of it, no matter how awkward I felt.

Experiences are never more meaningful than when you share them with others. It's always an honor to be asked to speak in front of an audience about challenges I've faced, but a few times, it was the speaking engagement itself that was the challenge. When I spoke at the Rochester Institute of Technology for the Deaf, I was flanked by an interpreter on both sides. It was just me and 300 hearing-impaired people in the room.

Every once in a while, I'd say something I truly thought was funny, but there was absolutely no reaction, which tripped me up a bit. Then a good 3 or 4 seconds later, the audience would burst out laughing at a time when I wasn't making any jokes. It took a while to get used to the fact that I was getting audience feedback in a kind of lag time instead of real time. Mostly, though, there was total silence. When I looked out at the audience, people were signing to each other. It was definitely a learning experience, and an interesting one at that.

Anyone who does public speaking on a regular basis has stories of faux pas and blunders. I have one such memory that still makes me cringe. It was when I insulted the group of people who have been the cornerstone of nearly every fund-raising endeavor I've ever accomplished.

It was the day of the Boston Marathon Jimmy Fund Walk, and I was one of the speakers at the start of the 3-mile patient walk from Dana-Farber to Copley Square. Every time I speak to audiences, I refer to the young cancer patients from the Jimmy Fund, and now I had the honor of addressing that very audience. I knew exactly what to say because it's the most important point of every speaking engagement I do: No matter how difficult running more than 4.5 million footsteps across the country was—or anything else I've done, for that matter—*nothing* could be as difficult as what those kids face every day of their illness. I try to put my life and all that I do in perspective and hope that my audiences will do the same.

Walk day began at 3 a.m. for me as director of the event, and perhaps I was just a bit too tired by 3 p.m., when I got up on the podium to address the thousands of patients and their families looking up at me. I wished them well and said, "The battle that you're going through is *in no way* as difficult as my 80 days running across the United States."

As I said it, I heard it, and I stopped mid-sentence. I don't even know how I ended it; I was so flustered. I had never made that mistake the other 1,200 times I had said it. I went off on some horrible tangent and then gave myself the hook as quickly as possible. I had my young son Max with me, and he was sitting on the stage eating cotton candy. I grabbed him and said, "Max, let's get the heck out of here fast." I jumped into the car to head down to the finish of the walk in Copley Square, and all the while I tried to get hold of Jack Leduc, a colleague who does the announcing for most DMSE events. I knew he'd been there and could confirm what he heard or didn't hear. I finally reached him.

"Jack, did I say what I thought I said? Did I just insult the kids?" I worriedly inquired.

"Yes, you did," he said. "Seriously though, I don't think anyone really got it."

For the next 3 months, I worried that I was going to get phone calls from angry parents. I never heard from anyone, but it remains one of the most awful moments of my speaking career.

I've spoken to Harvard Business School, New York Life, IBM, and most Rotary Clubs and running clubs along the eastern seaboard. Once, I even spoke at a Junior Catholic Daughters of America Association meeting. It was just me and 300 women in the room, and I still drove home alone!

I enjoy getting up in front of an audience—most of the time. In fact, ever since I had the lead in the play *Adaptation* in college, I've had the bug. Actors can be whomever they want to be. Maybe someday I'll give community theater a try, but for now, acting out my own life experience as a one-man show will have to do.

> He taught me that you don't always have to be the first one to cross the finish line to be a winner!
>
> *Adam Potts, Dave's nephew and US marine;*
> *served two tours of duty in Iraq*

I've logged thousands of miles and witnessed so many strange and wonderful things. I'm especially grateful to a friend and mentor of mine, Joe Kelley, who opened my eyes to other parts of the world. He asked me if I'd like to travel with him to Poland over Christmas break during my senior year of college. We went to visit a woman he was seeing, Alina, who has been his wife now for many years. That trip had a profound and lasting effect on me for several reasons.

Before our plane touched down in Poland, I would say that Worcester, Massachusetts, was the farthest I'd traveled from home. Joe refers to our trip as the Education of Dave McGillivray. I was taken aback from the moment we got off the plane. Everyone was wearing gray, dark wool, and it was dreary and cold. I wasn't expecting Disney World, but I also didn't know what it meant to visit or live in a communist nation.

We ended up staying with Alina's family. It was big-time culture shock, and it would've been difficult for me to make a trip like that alone. No one spoke English. Everything we did, we did together. The only thing I did alone was go for a run—in a Bill Rodgers running suit, which was basically contradictory to the palette (or lack of one) of everything else outside. The vivid colors of my clothes shouted, "Stare at me! Stare at me! I'm an American!"

There was an army barracks near the apartment where we stayed, and I remember running by the soldiers stationed all around it. I was scared. But I had been cooped up in the little apartment for days, and I just had to get some air—though it was hardly "fresh." The air was black. When I came back, I could taste the soot in my mouth. It wasn't healthy to breathe it, but I did only 3 to 5 miles around the block. I was thrilled when I made it back without incident.

Another memorable (but perhaps best forgotten) run took place a few years ago. I went to the New York City Marathon to observe the race at the invitation of my friend, Vic Navarra, the start director. I brought Mike Thompson along with me. Vic made sure we had a great vantage point at the start, and we were having a great time and got caught up in the excitement. We decided to run, right then and there! How could we not—it was the New York City Marathon!

Only one problem: The only appropriate running attire we had on was our shoes, and it was a particularly cold day. But as the runners got ready, they discarded most of their outer clothes. As those 40,000 "disrobed," Mike and I started trying stuff on as if we were in a sporting-goods store. A few women's items fit me, so that's what I wore: a jacket, hat, gloves, pants (nothing pink). . . . I hope to this day no one noticed the race director of the Boston Marathon running the NYC Marathon in women's clothes!

It is not the size of a man but the size of his heart that matters.

Evander Holyfield,
four-time world heavyweight champion

We all have our own idea of happiness. What makes me happy may not make the next person happy. The trick is to find that "something" early and go after it with all your might.

As a child, I had aspirations of someday making it into the *Guinness Book of World Records.* I thought it would be for situps, and then pushups, then for running across the country or for my 24-hour run. For 40 years, I wanted to set a record, any record. And I got my wish on July 14, 2004. My son Ryan and I were part of the largest-ever game of Duck, Duck, Goose. It didn't sound like much until I had to run around the circle of 500 people and select someone to be the next goose!

This game was played after a baseball game at the LaLecheur Park, home of the Lowell Spinners, a Class A affiliate of the Boston Red Sox. We all went onto the field for our game. A record is a record, and, ironically, if I hadn't played, my own world's record would've consisted of one big goose egg.

A goal without a plan is just a wish.

Antoine de Saint-Exupéry, poet and aviator

I've spent the last few years laying groundwork for the next 50 years of my personal and professional life. It all came together in 2002, when I designed the course that would lead me into the future. I asked my girlfriend, Katie Breen, to marry me. I'd already asked her mom for permission, and, with her approval, I planned to ask Katie on Thanksgiving morning at the 2002 Feaster Five race. I got to work, treating it as an event within a DMSE event. It needed to be well orchestrated and creative.

I started by phoning a friend, Bob Rottenberg, of Long's Jewelers in Burlington, Massachusetts. I had no clue what I was looking for. I know as much about diamond rings as I know how to speak Chinese, but I looked at a few samples and he made suggestions. I thought about it overnight and e-mailed him with my decision in the morning. I needed the ring on Thanksgiving, and snow was forecast for the day before. Bob personally delivered the package to my house on Tuesday so the weather would not hinder this event as it does so many of my others. All systems go.

I had permission and the ring. Now, how to give it to her—in a book? Katie loves books. That didn't seem to work. Time was running out; it was Wednesday morning, the snow was really coming down, and I had to get over to Brickstone Square in North Andover to start setting up for the race. It takes place no matter what the weather—rain, snow, or wind. I was really getting nervous.

I had a 7,000-person race in 24 hours; the same 24 hours in which I intended to propose to Katie, yet I still didn't know exactly how. While I was running around the site of the race, I looked up at the Brickstone Tree, the tallest Christmas tree in America: 100 feet tall, 10 stories up. It also happens to be right next to the finish line. That was it: I would wrap the ring over the star at the top of the tree.

I hunted down Mark Donahoe, the owner of Riverside Landscaping, who each year finds and decorates the tree. I said, "Mark, I need a favor"—a really tall favor. First, I needed him to put the ring in something that could fit on the top of the tree, and then I needed him to take Katie and me up in the bucket truck to retrieve it at the finish of the race. We shook hands. Now there was just one more deal to close.

I awoke at 3 a.m. on Thanksgiving Day. I found Mark's associate, Dan, at about 6:30 and gave him the package. Despite cold weather—it was 16 degrees—I broke out in a sweat from nerves, hoping that all would work out and Katie would say yes.

The runners took off and so did I, in search of Mark. He gave me the thumbs up—way up! I fixed my eyes on the top of the tree, knowing that the ring was up there and I would retrieve it with Katie in tow. I contacted her on my walkie-talkie and asked her to meet me at the finish. Katie worked for DMSE at the time and had taken over for me as race director that year.

Then Mark—and the moment of truth—approached. What if she didn't want to go in the bucket truck? Mark asked us if we wanted to check out the finish from above. Katie didn't hesitate. "Sure," she said. At about 50 feet, she said, "Okay, I think this is high enough."

Mark insisted, "Hey, we are almost at the top; it's good luck to touch the top of the tree and to touch the star. Let's do that!" Katie was turning pale. I suddenly realized she was not fond of heights. No turning back.

We reached the top. It was clear and beautiful and *cold*. There were nearly 10,000 people below us, racers and spectators alike, and not one had a clue what was going on. I wanted this to be private. I guess 100 feet in the air is private enough! It was fitting: the end of a long event season and, hopefully, the start of a long life together.

Mark had placed the ring in a decorated basket looped around the star. Katie and I touched the star together for "good luck." Then I reached into the basket. I kept reaching . . . I couldn't feel the ring beneath my fingers . . . where was it? Mark!?! Finally, after what was only seconds but felt like minutes, I lifted it out of the basket. Next challenge: to not drop the ring!

I reached into the jewelry pouch and took out a note that read, "Katie, I just asked your mother if I could become a member of your family. Now I am asking you if you will become a member of mine. Will you?"

Thumbs up. The kiss. The hug. And, yes, the ring did fit. Katie has helped me to change all the rules. At age 51, I will be the father of four kids, ages 15, 12, 2, and newborn, confirming that, yes, eventually I will find myself a good rocking chair to use as I get older—but only for the purpose of cradling my newest addition.

> Sometimes I think our age difference *is* a problem. . . . I'm just not young enough to keep his pace.
>
> *Katie Breen McGillivray, Dave's wife*

My wife has youth on her side, but since I'm a little bit ahead of her—16 years and 10 months, to be exact—I have to do all I can to keep on my toes. In 2002, I did that by helping create a race called the Run for All Ages, hosted by the New England 65-Plus Runners Club. The members are all 65 and over, and they don't sit around all day, talking about the old days. They train and train *hard*. Where do I sign up?

Along with race director Jerry Panarese, my team and I donate our time to coordinating the race logistics. The club helps keep these people young as they participate in races of all distances; several members are triathletes and marathoners. I was truly touched last year when they presented the race proceeds to the DMSE Children's Fitness Foundation. My long-term goal is to become a member of that club.

NE 65-Plus encourages race directors to include age categories up to at least 80 years in their events. Selfishly, I'm happy that the BAA decided to relax its own qualifying standards for the older division of the Boston Marathon. Before I know it, the entire division will be made up of my contemporaries.

As I get older, my tolerance for the cold diminishes. That may be one of the main reasons that I've established DMSE "South." It began with the Boca Town Classic in Boca Raton, Florida, which my team and I directed for a few years. I also now direct the Marathon of the Palm Beaches, and there are a few other races in the works. The more warm-weather gigs I get, the happier I'll be. New England holds my heart, but the rest of my body prefers the warmth of a 70-plus-degree day, especially in winter.

Be not afraid to grow slowly. Be only afraid of standing still.

Chinese proverb

When I least expect it, those old feelings about not being tall enough for society's cruel standards come rushing back to me. I remember being a college freshman and walking down the street with my girlfriend at the time. She was only an inch or two taller than I was, but that day she was wearing high heels. I saw the reflection of the two of us in a store window. It was just for an instant, but I couldn't stomach our height difference. It didn't seem fair.

In a twist of fate, that unspeakable feeling of being small was the catalyst for happiness in my life. Running led me to races, and races led me to a career I'm passionate about—and to my wife. It also gave me a tool I could use to help others.

It seems that I could either slow down now or really kick it into gear—and since the former is never an option with me, I'm going to hit the accelerator.

The first period is won by the best technician. The second period is won by the kid in the best shape. The third period is won by the kid with the biggest heart.

Dan Gable, wrestler; winner of Olympic gold
and three-time NCAA Coach of the Year

When all is said and done, there's not much that has happened in my life that I would "rewrite." Even when things seemed not to be going my way, they had a purpose. The tough times strengthened me, and the good times energized me.

Sports and athleticism, the biggest parts of my life, were not meant to be, in the way that I had initially hoped. As coach of the Greater Boston Track Club, Bill Squires worked with runners of the highest caliber, such as Alberto Salazar and Bill Rodgers. In 1979, Coach Squires had a number of us, including friend Fred Doyle, run the Oregon Track Club (OTC) Marathon for the sole purpose of, hopefully, qualifying for the Olympic Trials. I was in the best shape of my life; I'd run my fastest time at Boston that same year and was standing at the threshold of either becoming an elite athlete, or going in a different direction. Within that first mile, I knew the former wasn't going to happen. I ran well, but not well enough to run a qualifying time for the trials. However, in the "long run"—Coach Squires's nickname for me—everything worked out just fine for me.

Most people who achieve a personal dream don't do it alone. Coach Squires gave me a chance. Ken Coleman gave *the* chance. He died suddenly several years ago, and I wish I'd had the opportunity to thank him for his unwavering confidence in me. He never questioned my ability or my motives. His influence on the outcome of my life cannot be underestimated. It's something I think about when I am contacted by others with a vision to do something unconventional or seemingly impossible.

I've run up mountains. I've run in the desert. I've run in the rain (more than anything else!). I've run in the dark. I've run in the brightest of sunlight. I've run blindfolded. I've run for 24 hours. I've run alone. I've run with thousands. I've run from dogs. I've run toward home. I've tried to do everything I possibly could for others, my family, my friends, and myself. I will keep going until some higher power decides it's time for me to stop. Just as with running a marathon, you don't want to say at the end that you had a lot left to give.

If you run a race correctly, then you planned wisely and gave it everything, so that by the time you finish, you've given your all. At the end of my life, I'd like to think I gave everything I had and then some, right up until I simply run out of time.

MOM'S CHOCOLATE-CHIP COOKIES

From the kitchen of Jackie McGillivray (aka Mom to Dave, Bob, Alan, Susan, and Denise)

A recipe for the very cookies that both sustained me during and after a long run and rewarded me (immediate gratification) for each effort. Mom's "CCCs" were my "energy bars" back in the '70s and '80s. Mom was known by many far and wide for her chocolate-chip cookies. No matter how many journeys I took, the smell of the brown sugar and the melted chocolate always meant home was not very far away.

1 cup shortening

2 eggs

½ teaspoon vanilla extract

¾ cup granulated sugar

¾ cup brown sugar

2¼ cups flour

1 teaspoon baking soda

1 teaspoon salt

1 bag (12 ounces) semi-sweet chocolate chips

Cream together the shortening, eggs, vanilla, and sugars. Add the flour, baking soda, and salt. Stir in the chocolate chips.

Form into balls and place on a cookie sheet. Flatten with the palm of your hand. If batter is sticky, add more flour.

Bake at 350°F for about 9 minutes, or until golden brown.

PARTIAL LIST OF ACCOMPLISHMENTS

(Chronological order)

1966   Began streak of running same number of miles as age on 12th birthday

1970   Won high school physical fitness contest

1972   Won Richard J. Phelan Award

1972   Valedictorian, class of 1972, Medford High School

1974   Created McGillivray Mini-Marathon in Medford, Massachusetts, parks department

1976   Valedictorian, class of 1976, Merrimack College

1977   Solo Trial Run—Medford, Massachusetts, to Albany, New York

1978   Ran 3,452 miles from Medford, Oregon, to Medford, Massachusetts, for the Jimmy Fund

1980   Competed in the third annual Ironman Triathlon, Hawaii—14th place

1980   Opened Dave McGillivray Running and Sports Center, Medford, Massachusetts

1980   Completed a 24-hour, 120-mile run for Wrentham (Massachusetts) State School

1980   Completed the 1,520-mile East Coast Run for the Jimmy Fund, Florida to Massachusetts

1981   Completed the 1,522-mile New England Run (swim, bike, run) for the Jimmy Fund

1982   Incorporated Dave McGillivray Sports Enterprises (DMSE)

1982   Completed the Martha's Vineyard Swim (7 miles) for the Jimmy Fund

1982   Ran the Boston Marathon blindfolded in 3:14 to raise money for the Carroll Center for the Blind, Newton, Massachusetts

1983   Completed 24-hour, 26.2-mile swim in Medford High School pool for the Jimmy Fund

1983   Biked 1,000 miles around New England to raise money for Merrimack College

1986   Completed 24-hour, 385-mile bike ride in Medford, Massachusetts, for the Jimmy Fund

1988   Named technical director of the BAA Boston Marathon

1990   Directed the 1990 ITU Triathlon World Championship, Walt Disney World, Orlando, Florida

2000   Named Race Director of the Year by Road Race Management and *Running Times* magazine

2000   Received Lifetime Achievement Award from *Competitor* magazine

2001   Named race director of the BAA Boston Marathon

2003   Created the DMSE Children's Fitness Foundation

2004   Ran across the country in relay style as part of Trek USA, helping to raise $300,000 for five children's charities

2005   Inducted into the Running USA Hall of Champions

ADDITIONAL ACCOMPLISHMENTS AND AWARDS

Competed in 118 marathons, including the Boston Marathon for the past 34 consecutive years; personal best 2:29:58

Eight-time competitor in the Ironman Triathlon World Championship; personal best 10:36:42

Logged more than 120,000 miles (to date)

Directed or consulted on more than 700 events

Gave more than 1,400 motivational speeches throughout the United States and the world

Raised more than $50 million for charity through both personal efforts and DMSE-managed events

Race director, 2004 US Women's Olympic Marathon Trials

Race consultant, 1996 Atlanta Olympic Games

Voted Outstanding Young Man of America

Chosen as one of Boston's "10 Most Outstanding Young Leaders"

Medford (Massachusetts) Citizen of the Year

Honorary coach, Massachusetts Special Olympics Team

Past member, Governor's Committee of Physical Fitness and Sports

Past member, Board of Advisors of the Sports Museum of New England

Past president, Board of Directors of Massachusetts Bay State Games

Past vice president, Jimmy Fund Council of Greater Boston

Honorary chairman, annual McGillivray Mini-Marathon